Election Administration and the Politics of Voter Access

Democratic countries vary widely in the extent to which the administration of the electoral process facilitates voter participation, showing a great deal of variation in everything from voter registration to the casting of ballots.

This book is the first systematic study to investigate why it is easier to vote in some democracies than in others. It develops the concept of election administration inclusiveness, which considers all of the administrative requirements and procedures that a citizen confronts in exercising his or her right to vote. It then draws on in-depth case studies from Central America and data from Latin America more broadly to address how political parties and other actors interact in constructing election administration rules and procedures. Using a theoretical framework centered on electoral threat, party capacity, and electoral management body composition, the author identifies multiple pathways to inclusive and restrictive election administration.

This book will be of key interest to students and scholars of elections, democracy studies, Latin American politics and, more broadly, comparative politics and law.

Kevin Pallister is Assistant Professor of Political Science at Bridgewater College, USA. He has worked as an international election observer in Guatemala for the Organization of American States and his work has been published in the journal *Latin American Politics and Society* and the *Routledge Handbook of Comparative Political Institutions* (2015).

Routledge Studies in Elections, Democracy and Autocracy

Series editors:

Pippa Norris

Harvard University, USA, and the University of Sydney, Australia

and

Carolien van Ham

The University of New South Wales, Australia

This series addresses the quality of elections, how and why electoral contests fall short of international standards, and the implications of flawed elections for democracy and autocracy. The series is published in association with the Electoral Integrity Project.

1 **Election Administration and the Politics of Voter Access**
Kevin Pallister

2 **Electoral Rights in Europe**
Advances and Challenges
Edited by Helen Hardman and Brice Dickson

3 **Electoral Integrity and Political Regimes**
Actors, Strategies and Consequences
Edited by Holly Ann Garnett and Margarita Zavadskaya

Election Administration and the Politics of Voter Access

Kevin Pallister

Routledge
Taylor & Francis Group
LONDON AND NEW YORK

First published 2017 by Routledge

2 Park Square, Milton Park, Abingdon, Oxfordshire OX14 4RN
52 Vanderbilt Avenue, New York, NY 10017

Routledge is an imprint of the Taylor & Francis Group, an informa business

First issued in paperback 2018

British Library Cataloguing in Publication Data
A catalogue record for this book is available from the British Library

Library of Congress Cataloging in Publication Data
Names: Pallister, Kevin, author.
Title: Election administration and the politics of voter access / Kevin Pallister.
Description: Abingdon, Oxon ; New York, NY : Routledge, 2017. | Series: Routledge studies in elections, democracy and autocracy ; 1 | Includes bibliographical references and index.
Identifiers: LCCN 2016056815 | ISBN 9780415793179 (hardback) | ISBN 9781315211244 (ebook)
Subjects: LCSH: Elections–Central America–Management. | Election law–Central America. | Suffrage–Central America. | Voting–Central America. | Political participation–Central America. | Representative government and representation–Central America. | Central America–Politics and government–1979-
Classification: LCC JL1418 .P35 2017 | DDC 324.6/509728–dc23
LC record available at https://lccn.loc.gov/2016056815

ISBN: 978-0-415-79317-9 (hbk)
ISBN: 978-0-367-22166-9 (pbk)

Typeset in Times New Roman
by Wearset Ltd, Boldon, Tyne and Wear

Contents

Illustrations

Figure

Tables

Acknowledgments

Many people helped make the completion of this project possible. I would like to thank Fred Schaffer for his thoughtful guidance throughout the process of writing the doctoral dissertation on which this book is based. I also thank Susan Hyde, Ray La Raja, James Boyce, and two anonymous reviewers for helpful comments.

I also wish to express my appreciation to the staff at the Congressional Library and at the documentation centers at the Supreme Electoral Tribunal and ASIES in Guatemala, the staff at the National Assembly library in Nicaragua, and the staff at the Legislative Assembly in El Salvador. Special thanks go to Eduardo Fernandez at the Universidad Francisco Marroquín in Guatemala City for his hospitality. Finally, my heartfelt gratitude goes to all of the people who generously offered their time in taking part in interviews for this project. I wish to offer special thanks to Julieta Sandoval, Alberto Dávila, and Juan José Martel for going out of their way to help me during the research process.

1 Introduction

Elections are complex affairs, requiring an administrative apparatus that can undertake a wide range of activities prior to, during, and after election day. Election administration involves appointing and training election officials, registering voters and candidates, distributing voter identification documents, carrying out voter-information campaigns, installing polling places and delivering election materials prior to election day, administering the voting process, and counting the ballots and transmitting the results, among other tasks. Given the administrative complexity of conducting elections, the potential exists for electoral fraud, voter exclusion, or general mismanagement at numerous steps in the process.

The administration of elections bears directly on election quality through a number of avenues, such as by making fraudulent practices more or less likely and influencing the fairness of electoral competition. Many of the administrative procedures involved in conducting an election also bear directly on another aspect of its democratic quality: the ease or difficulty with which citizens can exercise the right to vote. Indeed, election administration practices, and the institutions that govern them, vary dramatically across countries in the extent to which they make the voting process accessible to all citizens. In some countries, citizens are required to register to vote on their own initiative months in advance of an election, while other countries automatically register voters up until election day. In some areas, voters must travel long distances to reach their polling place to cast their votes, while elsewhere polling stations are located in even the most remote villages. From voter registration requirements and the location of polling stations to the identification documents that voters are required to show and the means by which voters cast their ballots, there is a great deal of diversity in the extent to which countries holding competitive elections make voting accessible to all citizens.

Why do some democracies adopt election administration practices that facilitate voter participation, while others adopt rules that raise prohibitive obstacles to the participation of at least some citizens? More simply, why is it easier to vote in some democracies than in others? Despite growing interest in election administration since 2000, scholars have not systematically studied the origins of different election administration practices and institutions, especially as they bear on voter access to the ballot box. Through a comparative study of Central American countries that have differed widely in their election administration practices, I offer an explanation of why some countries lower barriers to the ballot box while others impose administrative obstacles to voter participation. My account shows how political parties, election administrators, civic groups, and international actors interact – both cooperatively and contentiously – to shape the administrative rules of voter participation, and why efforts to reduce or raise administrative barriers to voting are successful in some times and places and unsuccessful in others.

The study of election administration speaks to enduring normative concerns of equality and democracy. Because elections serve as a central means for citizens to hold their representatives accountable, administrative obstacles that impede voter participation – particularly among marginal groups least able to overcome such obstacles – may diminish the quality and legitimacy of representative democracy. In some cases, procedural barriers to voting that effectively keep some voters from participating affect election outcomes. Even where election outcomes are not clearly swayed by barriers to voting, by turning some voters away, onerous procedural hurdles may disengage some citizens from politics more generally. Administrative problems, including those that impede voting (such as missing names on the voter rolls and long lines at polling places), can foster mistrust in the electoral process and, in some cases, lead to election-related violence between competing parties. Conversely, rules that facilitate voting may increase the legitimacy of winning candidates and, by increasing participation among people otherwise unlikely to participate, make elected officials responsive to a broader electorate.

Of course, the ease of voting is only one element of ensuring citizens their right to freely cast a ballot. Where meaningful electoral competition is circumscribed, or where a voter's choice is coerced or effectively ignored through the manipulation of election results, the ease with which one may vote means little. In the context of relatively fair competitive elections, however, administrative barriers to voting carry significant practical and normative implications.

Election administration inclusiveness

A central concern of scholars studying election administration has been the effect of election administration variables on voter turnout (see Chapter 2). The underlying premise of much of this research is that rules and procedures that raise the cost of voting (in terms of money, time, or effort) will lead some potential voters to weigh the costs greater than the benefits and decide to abstain (Alvarez, Bailey, and Katz 2007, 5–6). Of course, the administrative procedures surrounding voting are not the only, or even the most important, determinants of voter participation. Both individual-level demographic and socioeconomic variables (such as education, age, and residential mobility) and institutional and contextual variables (such as political mobilization, electoral systems, and compulsory voting laws) affect turnout levels (see, e.g., Blais 2006; Geys 2006). But administrative measures that make voting more or less accessible to citizens may affect turnout and other political outcomes of interest.

The administrative rules and procedures that shape voters' access to the ballot are wide-ranging. The difficulty of voter registration requirements, whether elections are held on weekends or holidays, the number and location of polling sites, the ways in which voters cast a ballot, the ability of poll workers to turn away voters, and many other factors can all contribute to voter inclusion or exclusion. Table 1.1 provides a list of the factors affecting voter access, divided into four broad categories (voter registration, getting to the ballot box, casting a ballot, and voter education), as well as descriptions of the types of rules and practices that make up high, medium, and low levels of inclusiveness for each factor.

Collectively, these electoral procedures determine the level of what I call *election administration inclusiveness*, or the degree to which the administration of the electoral process facilitates or hinders the ability of eligible citizens to vote. The concept of election administration inclusiveness is related to, yet distinct from, other concepts in the scholarly literature and policy debates about election administration. One such concept, *voter suppression*, tends to assume a partisan intent to manipulate electoral outcomes by raising the costs of voting for certain groups of citizens (see, e.g., Wang 2012). Similarly, the concept of *administrative disenfranchisement* has been used to denote situations in which "a citizen formally and legally has the right to vote and to register to vote, but is prevented from exercising that right because the costs of doing so are too high" (ACE Project n.d.[a]). While useful, this definition only treats a limited range of the inclusiveness spectrum – namely, the end of the spectrum in which administrative restrictions effectively prevent a voter from participating. Finally, the concept of *convenience voting* has been employed in much research on election administration in the United States and refers to the variety of modes of casting a ballot that have become common since the 1990s – such as early in-person voting and vote by mail – that offer voters more accessible means of casting a ballot (see Stein and Vonnahme 2011, 307). Like administrative disenfranchisement, however, convenience voting treats a narrow range of variation in inclusiveness and does not address the inclusiveness of traditional electoral procedures such as voter registration.

I propose election administration inclusiveness as a broader conceptualization of the administrative and procedural steps that a prospective voter must negotiate in order to cast a vote. The concept does not assume partisan intent in making voting easier or more difficult, nor is it limited to instances in which the costs of voting effectively prevent the participation of some voters.[1] Rather, the concept considers election administration from the voter's perspective, incorporating all of the administrative measures – both formal rules and procedures and informal practices[2] – that bear on the ease or difficulty of voting, and ranges from high inclusiveness (where registration and voting are highly accessible and convenient for all eligible voters) to low inclusiveness (where registration and voting procedures pose significant barriers to large numbers of voters).

While election administration inclusiveness is a broader concept than voter suppression or convenience voting, it is also narrower than measurements of overall election quality. Elections are often marked by a wide range of problems

Table 1.1 Factors affecting levels of election administration inclusiveness

	High	*Medium*	*Low*
Voter registration			
1 Extent of state responsibility for registering voters	The state registers voters through automatic registration (drawing voter rolls from a national civil registry or other data-sharing arrangements between government agencies) or door-to-door registration by election officials.	Registration is voter-initiated, but the state makes efforts to facilitate registration (such as registration drives targeted at certain populations or mobile registration units in remote areas).	Registration is voter-initiated, and the state makes little or no targeted efforts to facilitate registration.
2 Difficulty of registration process (for voter-initiated registration systems)	Simple registration process. Registration sites are accessible and have ample hours of operation; mail and/or online registration is allowed; and voters can complete the registration process (including obtaining voter ID, where applicable) in one step.	Moderately complex registration process involving at least one barrier, such as difficult-to-reach registration sites with limited hours of operation or a process requiring multiple trips to a registration office.	Complex registration process marked by some combination of barriers, such as difficult-to-reach registration sites with limited hours of operation and a process requiring multiple trips to a registration office.
3 Ease of access to ID documents required for registration	ID documents are accessible with minimal effort and are free of charge.	Obtaining ID documents is difficult for at least some voters and/or entails a modest financial cost.	Obtaining ID documents is difficult for many voters and/or entails a significant financial cost.
4 Registration closing date*	Registration closes within 1–2 weeks of election day.	Registration closes between two weeks and three months before election day.	Registration closes more than three months before election day.
5 Residency requirements	There is no residency requirement to register in a new precinct, and registration automatically transfers when voters change residence.	There is a modest residency requirement (3 months or less) to register in a new precinct, and/or re-registration is required when voters change residence.	There is a lengthy residency requirement (more than 3 months) to register in a new precinct, and re-registration is required when voters change residence.

6 Provisional registration	Citizens may pre-register in the year or two before coming of voting age.	Citizens coming of voting age may pre-register under limited conditions (e.g., only during a registration drive of limited duration).	Citizens may not pre-register prior to reaching voting age.
7 Registry consultation	Provisional voter rolls are distributed to parties and posted publicly in accessible locations and formats (including online) for voters to review and correct errors.	Provisional voter rolls are available for review but are not easily accessible (e.g., posted in a limited number of places, not searchable online) and/or do not contain all relevant information (e.g., the polling places to which voters are assigned).	Provisional voter rolls are generally not available for review by parties or voters.
8 Purging of voter rolls	Voters are not purged from the rolls for failure to vote.	Voters may be purged from the rolls for failure to vote in three consecutive elections.	Voters may be purged from the voter rolls for failure to vote in one or two elections.
Getting to the ballot box			
9 Accessibility of polling places	Polling places are generally a short distance from voters' residences; public transportation is available on election day, where needed; mobile voting units are used for remote areas, where applicable.	Polling places are generally a short distance from voters' residences, but some polling places are distant, and public transportation on election day is limited.	Polling places are highly centralized or otherwise distant from many voters' residences, and public transportation on election day is limited.
10 Assignment of voters to polling places	Voters are assigned to the polling place closest to their residence.	Some voters are assigned to polling places based on residence, while others are assigned by non-residence criteria (e.g., alphabetically).	Voters are assigned to polling places by non-residence criteria (e.g., alphabetically).

continued

Table 1.1 Continued

	High	*Medium*	*Low*
11 Convenience voting measures	Several convenience voting measures are widely available, such as early voting, absentee voting, and voting by mail.	Some convenience voting measures are available, but their accessibility is limited (e.g., available for only a short period or for small segments of the electorate).	No convenience voting measures are available.
12 Electoral calendar**	Voting is held on a weekend or holiday during a time of year when travel to the polls is not unduly burdensome.	Either the day or the season when voting is held presents a modest barrier to participation for some voters.	Voting is held on a day or during a season that presents significant barriers to participation for a large number of voters.
Casting a ballot			
13 Voter identification requirements	No identification is required to vote, or witnesses or various types of identification are accepted as proof of identity.	Identification is required to vote, and only a limited number of ID forms are accepted.	Identification is required to vote, and only a limited number of forms of ID are accepted. Obtaining the requisite ID is costly and/or time consuming.
14 Wait time at the polling place	Waiting time for most voters is minimal (less than 30 minutes) and most polling places open on time.	Long lines and/or late opening of polling places result in modest waiting times (30–60 minutes) for many voters.	Long lines and/or late opening of polling places result in long waiting times (exceeding one hour) for many voters.
15 Provisional or tendered ballots	Provisional or tendered ballots are available for all or most voters whose information on the voter rolls appears to contain errors.	Provisional or tendered ballots are available only for a limited segment of voters whose information on the voter rolls appears to contain errors.	Provisional and tendered ballots are not allowed.

16 Assistance for disabled, illiterate, or other voters at the polls	Ballots are available in all major local languages and include party symbols or pictures of candidates, and voting mechanics include measures to assist disabled voters in casting a ballot.	Ballots and/or voting mechanics pose difficulties for relatively small segments of voters (e.g., blind, illiterate, or language minority voters).	Ballots and/or voting mechanics pose significant difficulties for substantial segments of voters (e.g., blind, illiterate, or language minority voters).
Voter education			
17 State efforts to inform voters of where and how to register and vote	The EMB or other state agency makes extensive efforts to inform voters of electoral procedures; voter education campaigns have extensive territorial reach, are conducted in all major languages and through diverse media, and are carried out for a significant period of time before key deadlines (e.g., registration closing date).	The EMB or other state agency makes efforts to inform voters of electoral procedures, but voter education campaigns are limited in territorial reach, linguistic coverage, diversity of media usage, or duration.	There are no efforts to disseminate information to voters, or efforts are severely limited in reach and duration.

Notes

* The significance of the voter registration closing date for inclusiveness depends on whether registration is automatic or voter-initiated. Where registration is automatic, the closing date is less relevant.

** The barriers posed by holding voting on a weekday or during a particular season depend on local conditions, including labor migration patterns, prevailing work schedules, and the availability of convenience voting measures such as early voting and absentee balloting.

that undermine effective democratic choice, and only some of these problems relate to inclusiveness. Competition between candidates and parties may be skewed by unequal access to the media, the abuse of state resources for campaigning, inequities in campaign financing, and vote buying, while the will of voters may be undermined by alteration of the final vote tally. Thus, the quality of an election depends upon a myriad of factors in addition to voter access, such as equitable access to campaign finance and the media, the fairness and efficiency of voting procedures, the accuracy and transparency of the vote count, and so on (Elklit and Reynolds 2005; Norris, Frank, and Martínez i Coma 2013).

The importance of so many electoral features in ensuring effective democratic contestation and participation has led scholars to develop several broad measures of the quality of elections. These include cross-national measures of election quality (Kelley and Kolev 2010), "electoral malpractice" (Birch 2011), "electoral misconduct" (Donno 2013), and "electoral integrity" (Norris 2014; Norris, Frank, and Martínez i Coma 2013), while in the US context scholars and policy practitioners have developed measures of election administration quality (Gerken 2009; Pew Charitable Trusts 2014). Such measures attempt to capture the overall quality of electoral processes, and they include some (but not all) elements related to voter access to the ballot box. Yet previous research has not focused on systematically measuring – let alone explaining – variations in election administration rules bearing on voter access. It is on this dimension of election quality that I focus.

Voter registration

A principal election administration measure that may pose an obstacle to voting is voter registration. As Wolfinger and Rosenstone (1980, 61) explain:

> Registration raises the costs of voting. Citizens must first perform a separate task that lacks the immediate gratification characterizing other forms of political expression (such as voting). Registration is usually more difficult than voting, often involving more obscure information and a longer journey at a less convenient time, to complete a more complicated procedure. Moreover, it must usually be done before interest in the campaign has reached its peak.

A range of details may make the voter registration process more or less accessible. These include: whether the responsibility for registration falls primarily on the citizen or the state; the complexity of the registration process, including the accessibility of registration offices, their hours of operation, and the number of visits required to complete the process; the documentation required to register; the registration deadline; how a change of residence affects one's registration status; the ability of underage citizens to provisionally register; the measures in place for voters to consult the registry and correct inaccuracies; and whether those who do not vote are purged from the voter rolls (see ACE Project n.d.[a];

Carbó and Wright 2008, 66; Rosenstone and Wolfinger 1978, 24). On top of these formal aspects of voter registration, incumbents may manipulate the process to make it more difficult for likely opposition supporters to register.[3]

The types of obstacles voter registration imposes depend on the particular voter registration system used by a given country. A basic distinction is between ad hoc voter registries that are compiled before each election, either through door-to-door visits by enumerators or the use of registration centers, and a permanent voter registry, which is maintained from one election to the next and updated to incorporate new voters and changes of residence. Ad hoc registration tends to be inclusive, as the burden is placed on election administrators to register voters, but it is expensive (Robert 2009, 3–4). Permanent registries are much more common.

Of central importance is the extent to which the state takes the initiative in two related aspects of voter registration: distributing the identification documents that citizens need to register and actually registering voters. Registering to vote often requires that a citizen provide documentation to prove his or her identity, which in turn necessitates obtaining the required identification. Countries vary widely in the documentation accepted for registration, with some countries accepting only one or a small number of forms of ID and other countries accepting many ID forms or witnesses that attest to a voter's identity (Carter Center 2013; Schaffer and Wang 2009). The most inclusive systems make obtaining the necessary identification documents simple and automatically register documented citizens to vote through various methods of data-sharing between government agencies (commonly by adding data from the civil registry directly to the voter registry). Such automatic registration eliminates the need for citizens to carry out the additional step of registering to vote and is common in Western Europe and Latin America, where many countries use a single national ID card which citizens are required to possess (Robert 2009; Rosenberg 2009). Not surprisingly, countries with automatic registration typically have very high voter registration rates (Robert 2009, 2; Rosenberg 2009, 3). Yet while automatic registration eliminates steps in the registration process, the first step of obtaining an ID card or other necessary documents (such as a birth certificate) remains; the difficulty of obtaining such documentation varies greatly across countries (Carter Center 2013).

While some states take responsibility for registering citizens through automatic registration, in other countries the responsibility to register is placed on the citizen. When, where, and how a citizen must register in these systems vary greatly, and different methods can present greater or lesser difficulty.

In some countries the voter registration period may be limited, and the voter rolls may be closed months prior to election day – before the election campaign and media coverage reach their peak. In other cases, registration is allowed up to and including election day – such as in a number of American states that allow election day registration (EDR). Where EDR occurs at the polling place, it also spares the voter the time and potential expense needed to travel to a separate registration site. EDR is of particular use to young voters and the residentially mobile who may be inclined to leave registering til the last moment before an election. An additional measure related to the timeframe of registration is provisional registration, whereby young people can be added to the voter registry within one or two years of turning voting age and are then automatically added to the active voter roll upon coming of age. Provisional registration is used in a number of countries, including Argentina, Australia, New Zealand, and Portugal, as well as a number of American states (Robert 2009, 15; Rosenberg 2009, 3).

Aside from the registration deadline, the location and operating hours of voter registration sites affect the ease with which citizens may register. Distant registration offices and limited hours (for instance, offering registration services only during weekdays) can present barriers to registration. These obstacles can be minimized where election administrators complement their ordinary voter registration procedures with targeted door-to-door registration of certain populations, such as remote rural communities (Robert 2009, 4; Rosenberg 2009, 13–14, 21). This is the case, for instance, in Mexico, where "the government deploys mobile units to register voters in rural areas and other places with historically low registration rates" (Rosenberg 2009, 5). The obstacles posed by distant locations and limited hours are also eliminated through mail or online registration, both of which are becoming more common, at least among high-income countries (Robert 2009, 6–7). When in-person registration is required, a further impediment can be the need to make multiple visits to a registry office; for instance, one visit to fill out registration paperwork and a later visit to retrieve a voter registration card.

Once a voter is registered, a change of residence may affect one's registration status. In some countries, a change of residence (especially to a different election precinct) requires re-registering to update one's residence on the voter rolls. Like first-time registrations, such changes of residence on the voter rolls may be prohibited many months before election day in order to prevent fraud, and a voter may be required to live in a jurisdiction for a specified period before being eligible to register. In other countries where the state more actively registers voters, election authorities share data with other agencies (such as the postal service) "to learn of address changes without having to rely on voters to remember to submit the necessary paperwork to election authorities every time they change residences" (Rosenberg 2009, 16).

Even after having registered, the voter registry may contain inaccuracies that prevent qualified citizens from voting. Many countries try to minimize this risk of disenfranchisement by publicizing the provisional voter rolls before election day – such as by posting them in local public spaces, mailing personalized registration information to voters, and providing search tools online – and allowing voters the opportunity to correct any errors (Rosenberg 2009, 20). Finally, provisions for purging voters from the rolls for not voting vary by country. Purging voters for failing to turn out for two or three consecutive national elections has the benefit of eliminating "deadwood" (deceased or emigrated voters) from the voter rolls but also entails the risk that citizens who vote irregularly will face the burden of re-registering.

Getting to the ballot box

Another component of election administration inclusiveness is the accessibility of polling places. Where polling places are remote, voters are burdened with time and travel costs. This obstacle is more severe where public transportation is not available or is relatively costly. Polling stations may also be relocated at the last minute to confuse voters, a trick used historically in the United States (Campbell 2005, 7). Countries vary in the lengths they go to make polling places accessible. An example at the inclusive end of the spectrum is India, where polling stations must be located within 2 km of every community, and election officials trek through jungles, swamps, and mountains to bring voting machines to settlements consisting of as few as two people (Mukherji and Anand 2014).

The burden of reaching a polling station can be reduced by the availability of absentee voting, especially for those who are not in their normal precinct on election day. Absentee voting can be conducted in a variety of ways, including by mail, in person at a restricted number of polling stations, or in person at any polling station. Some countries make absentee voting available for all voters, for some subset of voters (such as those hospitalized or serving in the military), or not at all (see ACE Project n.d.[b]).

Polling-place accessibility is determined not only by where polling places are located but also by when voting is held. The hours that the polls are open affect accessibility, as does the day(s) on which voting is held. Convenience is increased when voting is held on the weekend or election day is a holiday, and when election day falls during a time of year when travel is convenient (Katz 1997, 116). Early voting allows voters to cast a ballot, either in person or by mail, before the official election day and thus reduces potential time constraints for voters. Where it is used, the early voting period may range from several days to several weeks and, like absentee balloting, may be available to all voters or only certain types of eligible voters (ACE Project n.d.[b]).

Casting a ballot

Once at the polling place, voters may be impeded from casting a ballot by several factors. Overcrowded polling places may generate long waits and confusion, and some voters may give up without voting. A potentially greater obstacle is that voters may be required to prove their identity by showing ID at the polls. Countries vary in the conditions under which voters must show ID, the types of identification papers accepted to vote, the ease with which citizens can obtain the necessary documents, and the provisions in place for voters who lack identification documents (Schaffer and Wang 2009). Identification requirements pose little burden on voters where the government or election officials make significant efforts to ensure eligible voters obtain ID (as in many European countries) and where witnesses can vouch for the identity of voters lacking ID (as in Canada, Italy, and Portugal, for example) (Schaffer and Wang 2009, 401–3). Where obtaining the requisite identification is onerous and where there are few provisions for voters lacking identification, however, voter ID requirements may impede participation.

In Latin America, most countries require a national ID card to vote, although the difficulty of obtaining the ID varies, in part due to differences in formal regulations and state capacity. Partisan manipulation of the distribution of ID cards has also posed obstacles for some voters in several Latin American and African countries (Carter Center 2013, 10, 18).

Even duly registered and documented voters may find that their name does not appear on the voters list when trying to cast a ballot. Erroneous omissions from the voters list can result from technical problems and administrative inefficiencies, as occurs even in advanced industrial democracies like the United States, where paper-based registration in many jurisdictions results in some registered voters not appearing on the rolls (Pew Center on the States 2010; Ponoroff 2010). Omissions from the voter rolls can also be an intentional strategy of electoral manipulation, as partisan election officials may "remove, misspell, or leave off names of voters who are members of certain demographic groups, such as first-time voters or those concentrated in geographic areas where support for opposition candidates is strongest" (Calingaert 2006, 140). Such manipulation of the voter rolls is thought to be a common (and difficult to verify) practice; for instance, the 1999 presidential election in the Dominican Republic is thought to have been stolen by the incumbent through the deletion of 100–200,000 names from the voter registry (Birch 2011, 36).

A partial remedy for such situations is provisional balloting, which allows a voter to cast a ballot (which may or may not be counted, depending on the circumstances), even if there is a discrepancy between their identity document and the information on the voters list, or their name does not appear on the voters list. In these circumstances, or where poll workers erroneously mark someone on the voter list as having voted, provisional balloting can prevent disenfranchisement. Yet, the availability and ease of provisional balloting varies by country, and its use requires safeguards against multiple voting.

Voter education

Aside from (and intersecting with) the procedures for registering, obtaining identification, arriving at the polling place, and casting a ballot is the issue of voter education. In order to meet the requirements of voter registration and identification, and to reach one's polling place at the appropriate day and time equipped with some familiarity with the voting act, citizens must be informed of the administrative procedures to follow. Voter education involves publicizing information about when and how to register, how to find the appropriate polling place and check one's status on the registry, what documents to bring to the polling place, how to mark one's ballot, and so on.[4] Modes of voter education range from printed fliers and posters in public spaces to telephone hotlines, newspaper advertisements, mobile brigades and kiosks, radio and television ads, websites, direct mailings, and text messaging (ACE Project n.d.[b]; Ellis et al.

2006, 20–21). Such voter education activities are typically considered the responsibility of electoral management bodies, although civil society organizations also often carry out similar activities.

Even in long-standing democracies, voters may lack information about registration and voting procedures;[5] in newer democracies and countries with low levels of literacy or access to information technology, the problems are often more severe. Thus the extent of voter education – including its geographic coverage and duration, its provision in all major languages within a country, and the fit between the informational content and delivery and wider cultural norms – can be a significant factor in the ease or difficulty of voting.

Measuring election administration inclusiveness

Because prior research has focused largely on isolating the effects of individual administrative measures on voter turnout (see Chapter 2), we know little about how different administrative rules are combined in practice to produce more or less inclusive election administration regimes. There are no existing datasets that document – much less quantify – the inclusiveness of election administration practices across countries, and even information clearinghouses such as International Institute for Democracy and Electoral Assistance (International IDEA)[6] and the ACE Electoral Knowledge Network (or ACE Project)[7] do not compile systematic data on most election administration practices.

Compounding the problem of the lack of cross-national data are challenges of measurement and aggregation. As Table 1.1 suggests, a large number of administrative practices affect inclusiveness and, while measuring some of these practices (such as whether or not early voting is used) is fairly straightforward, measurement of other practices (such as the quality of voter education) is much more difficult. Even more challenging is the issue of aggregation, as it is not readily apparent how the components of election administration inclusiveness might be aggregated into a quantitative index in a theoretically meaningful way.[8] The challenge of aggregating and weighting different features of an electoral process – and whether it is "possible to develop a uniform weighting scheme that is meaningful and applicable cross-nationally to countries all around the world" (Carroll and Davis-Roberts 2013, 93) – is noted by scholars and election observers with regard to determining the overall quality of elections more generally (see Kelley 2012, 13). The problem of aggregation is particularly important because many (perhaps most) cases will likely exhibit complex combinations of scores on individual components – low barriers to access on some measures, and more restrictive practices on others.

Given the complexity of election administration inclusiveness and lack of existing measures, it is difficult to determine the range of values that inclusiveness takes across countries that hold competitive elections.[9] The most readily available measure, voter turnout, cannot be used as a direct indicator of election administration inclusiveness, since many other factors affect voter turnout. Voter registration rates might be a useful indicator of the restrictiveness of registration laws, but reliable comparative data on registration rates is lacking.[10] Even fewer comparative data are readily available for such factors as the accessibility of polling places.

In the absence of systematic comparative data or even reliable indirect measures of election administration inclusiveness, I rely on coding the inclusiveness of election administration practices based on the close examination of cases. Drawing on each country's election laws, documents from electoral management bodies, election observer reports, and secondary literature, I gathered data on as many indicators listed in Table 1.1 as possible and, given the problems of aggregation noted above, used qualitative assessment to place cases on an ordinal scale of inclusiveness (high, medium, and low). While factors shown in the existing literature to pose high barriers to participation, such as registration requirements and polling locations, are given particular consideration, coding through qualitative assessment allowed for consideration of the totality of circumstances surrounding a country's election administration, rather than assigning scoring weights to each component of the inclusiveness variable *a priori*.[11]

Why Central America?

Because the causes of variation in election administration practices have not been the focus of systematic study, we lack not only measures of election administration inclusiveness but also theories that offer explanations of variation in inclusiveness.[12] Lacking well-developed extant theories, I undertake an inductive approach to theory development, seeking to identify the causal factors and mechanisms that explain variation in election administration inclusiveness through the careful examination of cases.

I do this through in-depth examination and comparison of election administration in three Central American countries – Guatemala, Nicaragua, and El Salvador – as well as briefer analyses of Honduras and the United States. The selection of the Central American cases is guided by several criteria. First, these cases exhibit significant variation in the inclusiveness of election administration practices across countries. Examining cases with wide variation on the dependent variable facilitates theory generation by allowing the researcher to identify causal factors associated with different outcomes across cases (Seawright and Gerring 2008, 300).

Second, these cases are similar on several potentially relevant variables, such as the level of economic development, the political culture, and a shared history of political violence. Thus, this study employs the most similar systems method of controlled comparison, which entails comparing cases that vary on the dependent variable but are similar on a number of other dimensions. This allows the isolation of different conditions across cases that account for differences in outcomes, while controlling for other conditions that are constant across cases.

Finally, given the limitations of small-n controlled comparison for causal inference, within-case analysis is a necessary complement to controlled comparison, and this is facilitated by studying cases that vary on the dependent variable over time. Not only has there been significant variation in election administration practices across Central American countries but each country also shows significant variation in inclusiveness over time. This over-time variation allows for congruence tests to determine whether independent and dependent variables co-vary in expected directions within a case over time (George and Bennett 2005).

Thus, the cases exhibit wide variation in inclusiveness, vary over time in their election administration practices and share a number of background similarities. All of these countries transitioned to a democratic regime with free elections between the early 1980s and mid-1990s, but they have differed widely in the extent to which the administration of elections has posed obstacles to voter participation, with Guatemala, El Salvador, and Honduras initially having low levels of inclusiveness and Nicaragua having a high level of inclusiveness. Over time, however, the former countries became more inclusive, while Nicaragua's election administration became less so after the mid-2000s.

In Guatemala, administrative features of the electoral process – particularly difficult voter registration procedures, highly centralized polling locations, insufficient voter education efforts, and the holding of elections during the rural labor migration season – posed significant obstacles to participation for many citizens. Yet, over time, electoral reforms increased the inclusiveness of the country's election administration practices, most notably by decentralizing polling sites to reduce travel time for rural voters.

In El Salvador, administrative barriers to voter participation were initially similar to those in Guatemala, including onerous voter registration and identification requirements, and centralized and inaccessible polling places. Yet, like Guatemala, El Salvador's electoral administration practices have become more inclusive over time, though in a different sequence: voter registration processes became simplified by automatically adding citizens to the voter rolls once they obtain a national identity card, while the decentralization of polling places was implemented gradually after repeated delays.

In contrast to Guatemala and El Salvador, Nicaragua established fairly inclusive election administration practices in its early democratic period. The voter registration process was easy to negotiate, with the state making significant efforts to register voters and distribute identification documents. Additionally, polling locations tended to be highly decentralized, so that travel to the polls was minimized. The accessibility of voter registration and convenient polling locations was re-inforced by other measures related to voter education and casting a ballot. Yet beginning in the mid-2000s, obtaining an identity card needed to vote became more difficult for those not tied to the governing party, while voter education efforts diminished.

Thus, emerging from similar processes of democratic transition, Nicaragua adopted election administration practices that kept barriers to voter participation low, while El Salvador and Guatemala adopted measures that made voting a costly and time-consuming activity for many would-be voters. Over time, this pattern began to reverse. The empirical focus of this book is to explain this initial variation and subsequent dynamics in an effort to shed light on the broader question of why democratic countries vary in the extent to which voting is accessible to all citizens.

To do so, I not only make comparisons across the three cases but also make use of process tracing to evaluate the causal mechanisms underlying the relationship between causal variables and outcomes within each case. Such process tracing involves fine-grained analysis of the causal chain leading from cause to effect (George and Bennett 2005) – in this case, the process by which hypothesized causal variables led to the adoption of particular laws and administrative practices bearing on voter access.[13] To carry out such within-case analysis, I draw on a wide array of data sources, including electoral laws, election observer reports, news sources, archival sources (particularly legislative records and documents from electoral management bodies), and the secondary literature. I also draw on over 60 interviews with current and former election officials, legislators and political party leaders, civil society leaders, academics, journalists, and international experts.[14]

A limitation of this type of small-n research design involves generalizing from a small number of cases to a wider population. In particular, the Central American cases are post-conflict countries, and the dynamics of institutional development in these cases may be unique to such settings. In particular, the destruction of physical infrastructure and the problems of enfranchising voters who have been displaced by violence and often lack identification documents pose particularly severe logistical and political challenges for election administration (Lyons 2004, 46; Prather and Herron 2007, 354).

Additionally, the Central American cases are developing countries, and the findings of this project may not generalize to developed democracies that face different sets of election administration challenges. The ability of election administrators to reduce barriers to voting is likely affected by the availability of financial resources and technical capacity. After all, state efforts to register voters, conduct voter-information campaigns and employ a large number of polling places on election day can be costly. The availability of resources and technical capacity is, in turn, partly a product of a country's level of economic development.[15]

Nevertheless, it is reasonable to take as a starting point for theory development that all democracies – whether rich or poor, post-conflict or not – face similar tasks of voter registration, polling location, voter identification, voter education, and so on. Additionally, the identification of cases that exhibit significant variation in election administration inclusiveness, despite similarly being post-conflict developing countries, suggests that differences among cases within these categories may result from general causal factors at work in other contexts. There are thus no strong *a priori* grounds for assuming that the findings in these cases will not have broader applicability, and Chapter 3 includes a brief analysis of the United States to test the applicability of the main argument to a case outside of Latin America. At the same time, the challenges of generalizability and the importance of clarifying scope conditions must be kept in mind.

The argument

The argument developed through the case studies in the following chapters focuses on several key explanatory factors that shaped election administration inclusiveness in the countries studied. This section briefly lays out the general argument; I elaborate on it in Chapter 2 and the conclusion.

I argue that historical antecedents powerfully shaped the initial choice of election administration rules in these new democracies. In particular, where major episodes of election fraud had occurred under authoritarian or semi-authoritarian regimes, democratizing regimes adopted election administration rules that sought to ensure the rectitude of electoral processes at all costs, resulting in election procedures that impeded voter participation. As memories of these fraudulent practices faded, less restrictive election administration measures became politically possible. However, institutional inertia and path dependence caused some election procedures that were instituted under authoritarian or early democratic regimes to persist long after the initial conditions that gave rise to those procedures had faded.

Partisan interests also affect election administration practices, although only under certain conditions. I find that only where incumbent political parties face a competitive electoral environment and are able to identify opposition supporters in the electorate do they attempt to suppress the vote of those who are not their own partisans, for instance through manipulating the delivery of voter ID cards. Partisan calculations can also delay the introduction of inclusive election administration measures if the major parties are uncertain of the electoral consequences of reform. Parties that lack knowledge of voter loyalties (typically catch-all or weakly institutionalized parties) are less likely to attempt exclusion through election administration measures and are less reluctant to make voting easier.

I also argue that the composition of a country's electoral management body (the agency charged with administering elections) is an important variable affecting election administration inclusiveness. I find that a non-partisan electoral management body (EMB) can be an independent and authoritative force for inclusive electoral reform (for instance, by drafting legislation and lobbying for reform in the legislature) and is also more likely to develop the bureaucratic capacity that is often necessary to reduce procedural barriers facing voters. Yet, non-partisanship is neither a necessary nor sufficient condition for inclusive electoral procedures: rather, EMBs staffed by partisan appointees can also carry out inclusive practices under some conditions, such as when the dominant party on the EMB expects electoral victory in a fair contest or when there is intense pressure to legitimize elections to an international audience.

Finally, I consider the effects of international influences, particularly international election observation and technical and financial assistance for elections, as well as the effects of domestic advocacy for electoral reform from civil society groups. I argue that international financial and technical assistance are often necessary for less developed countries to institute inclusive election administration practices, but such assistance is not sufficient to ensure inclusiveness.

Recommendations from election observers have less impact: while they overwhelmingly tend to advocate for inclusive practices, they ultimately have little impact on domestic election reform processes. I find that domestic civil society groups, including election observers, have minimal influence on election administration practices, despite their persistent efforts in advocating electoral reforms. Civic groups and public opinion exercise little influence in shaping the rules of the electoral game; in fact, election administration is an elite game dominated by legislators, party officials, and election administrators.

Thus, key influences on election administration practices in the cases under study include historical experiences with election fraud, partisan interests and the nature of the party system, EMB institutional design, international political pressures, and international electoral assistance. The argument presented here is thus, to be sure, far from parsimonious. Yet, this is consistent with other work on election-related phenomena that identifies a wide range of causal variables, such as research on electoral system reform (Renwick 2010) and on vote buying (Schaffer 2007, 194). Like these other areas, the case studies in the following chapters strongly suggest that election administration rules and practices are subject to multiple historical, institutional, and instrumental influences.

The remainder of the book proceeds as follows. Chapter 2 surveys the literature on election administration, draws hypotheses from prior work regarding the influences on election administration inclusiveness and presents the book's theory of the determinants of inclusiveness. Chapter 3 presents descriptive data on election administration practices in Latin America, offers a preliminary quantitative test of the effects of electoral management body composition on inclusiveness and presents brief case studies of Honduras and the United States to illustrate the plausibility of the theory. Chapters 4 through 8 present in-depth case studies. Chapter 4 analyzes Guatemala's restrictive election administration rules from its democratic transition in the 1980s up until the early 2000s. Guatemala's electoral reform process that significantly lowered barriers to voting is the subject of Chapter 5. Chapter 6 discusses Nicaragua's election administration during the 1984–1996 period, during which administrative practices were largely inclusive. The erosion of its election administration inclusiveness after the mid-2000s is taken up in Chapter 7. Chapter 8 analyzes the case of El Salvador, covering both the country's early period of highly restrictive election administration and the long period of electoral reform that gradually lowered obstacles to participation. The conclusion in Chapter 9 offers a summary of findings and a discussion of their implications.

Notes

1 The effects of administrative inclusiveness on turnout may depend on a variety of motivational and contextual factors. It is possible that even under highly burdensome election administration procedures that raise the costs of voting, most voters may be highly motivated and undeterred by administrative barriers; conversely, in some contexts, even mild administrative burdens may be sufficient to deter the participation of many voters.

2 I include measures that are specified in electoral laws and administrative regulations, as well as practices that are not legally mandated. In part, this is because elements of election administration vary in their extent of legal institutionalization across countries – such that one aspect of election administration may be regulated by the electoral law in one country and left entirely to the discretion of election administrators in another. For instance, the location of polling places is regulated by the electoral law in Guatemala, left to the discretion of election administrators in Nicaragua, and jointly regulated by legislation and administrative discretion in El Salvador.

3 This has happened, for instance, before Cambodia's 2003 elections (Calingaert 2006, 140) and arguably before El Salvador's 1994 elections.

4 Ellis et al. (2006, 20) label these types of activities "information campaigns" and distinguish them from "advertising campaigns," which "address the motivational issue as to why electors should participate in the electoral event." Information campaigns focus on the "how" of voting, while advertising campaigns emphasize the "why." Sometimes electoral management bodies conduct both types of campaign, although the motivational messages are sometimes the domain of civic groups (21). This study is more concerned with information campaigns that lower barriers to voting, rather than advertising campaigns intended to motivate citizens to vote.

5 In the United States, for instance, a large post-election survey in 2008 found that many people lacked knowledge about how residence changes affect voter registration and how to update one's registration (Pew Center on the States 2010, 7).

6 www.idea.int.

7 aceproject.org.

8 For instance, it is not clear how each component should be weighted – e.g., whether convenient polling-site location should be weighted equally with election day registration. Some work has developed measures of voter registration restrictiveness; for example, Bowler and Donovan (2008) construct an index based on ten factors, each one measured dichotomously, which are then aggregated. While useful for their purposes, such aggregation assumes that each factor – such as whether one must register to vote prior to election day, or whether there is a cutoff date for receiving an absentee ballot – poses an equal barrier to participation. Similar aggregation problems plague measurements of other concepts, such as indices of democracy (see Munck and Verkuilen 2002).

9 Electoral authoritarian regimes in which competition is restricted and election results are determined *a priori* through fraud or other means may mobilize voters in order to generate high turnout to legitimize the regime. In these cases, the inclusiveness of election administration is less relevant than it is for democratic regimes.

10 For instance, International IDEA compiles turnout and registration data on their website for most countries, but in some cases the number of registered voters in a country exceeds estimates of the country's voting-age population. This is often a result of outdated or otherwise inaccurate voter registries or census data. See IDEA's methodology web page at www.idea.int/vt/methodology.cfm.

11 Descriptions of election administration inclusiveness are presented in each case-study chapter. Due to a lack of systematic data, I exclude waiting time at the polling place (row 14 of Table 1.1) and assistance for voters (row 16 of Table 1.1) from the tables in the case-study chapters, although I discuss those issues in the case narratives where the data permits.

12 Though, as discussed in Chapter 2, hypotheses can be gleaned from the existing literature.

13 Thus process tracing – or what Collier, Mahoney, and Seawright (2004) call "causal process observations" – relies not on correlations across cases but careful analysis of evidence that links cause and effect within each case.

14 Most of these interviews were conducted in the three case study countries in 2011 and 2012. For a complete list of interviews, see the references section.

15 Regarding the state's role in voter registration, one source notes that state-initiated registration is more costly and requires greater capacity than voter-initiated registration, and "[t]his capacity is likely to exist in an economically advanced country" (ACE Project n.d.[a]).

References

ACE Project. n.d.[a]. Encyclopaedia – Voter Registration. http://aceproject.org/ace-en/topics/vr.

ACE Project. n.d.[b]. Encyclopaedia – Voting Operations. http://aceproject.org/ace-en/topics/vo/vob/vob04.

Alvarez, R. Michael, Delia Bailey, and Jonathan N. Katz. 2007. "The Effect of Voter Identification Laws on Turnout." California Institute of Technology, Social Science Working Paper 1267.

Birch, Sarah. 2011. *Electoral Malpractice*. New York: Oxford University Press.

Blais, André. 2006. "What Affects Voter Turnout?" *Annual Review of Political Science* 9: 111–25.

Bowler, Shaun, and Todd Donovan. 2008. "Barriers to Participation for Whom? Regulations on Voting and Uncompetitive Elections." In *Designing Democratic Government: Making Institutions Work*, Margaret Levi, James Johnson, Jack Knight, and Susan Stokes, eds. New York: Russell Sage Foundation.

Calingaert, Daniel. 2006. "Election Rigging and How to Fight It." *Journal of Democracy* 17 (3): 138–51.

Campbell, Tracy. 2005. *Deliver the Vote: A History of Election Fraud, an American Political Tradition—1742–2004*. New York: Carroll & Graf Publishers.

Carbó, Steven, and Brenda Wright. 2008. "Promise and Practice of Election Day Registration." In *America Votes! A Guide to Modern Election Law and Voting Rights*, Benjamin E. Griffith, ed. American Bar Association Section of State and Local Government Law.

Carroll, David J., and Avery Davis-Roberts. 2013. "The Carter Center and Election Observation: An Obligations-Based Approach for Assessing Elections." *Election Law Journal* 12 (1): 87–93.

Carter Center. 2013. Voter Identification Requirements and Public International Law: An Examination of Africa and Latin America. www.cartercenter.org/resources/pdfs/peace/democracy/des/voter-identification-requirements.pdf.

Collier, David, James Mahoney, and Jason Seawright. 2004. "Claiming Too Much: Warnings about Selection Bias." In *Rethinking Social Inquiry: Diverse Tools, Shared Standards*, Henry E. Brady and David Collier, eds. Lanham, MD: Rowman & Littlefield Publishers.

Donno, Daniela. 2013. *Defending Democratic Norms: International Actors and the Politics of Electoral Misconduct*. New York: Oxford University Press.

Elklit, Jorgen, and Andrew Reynolds. 2002. "The Impact of Election Administration on the Legitimacy of Emerging Democracies: A New Comparative Politics Research Agenda." *Commonwealth and Comparative Politics* 40 (2): 86–119.

Ellis, Andrew, Maria Gratschew, Jon H. Pammett, and Erin Thiessen, eds. 2006. *Engaging the Electorate: Initiatives to Promote Voter Turnout from around the World*. Stockholm: International Institute for Democracy and Electoral Assistance.

George, Alexander, and Andrew Bennett. 2005. *Case Studies and Theory Development in the Social Sciences*. Cambridge, MA: MIT Press.

Gerken, Heather K. 2009. *The Democracy Index: Why Our Election System Is Failing and How to Fix It*. Princeton: Princeton University Press.

Geys, Benny. 2006. "Explaining Voter Turnout: A Review of Aggregate-Level Research." *Electoral Studies* 25 (4): 637–63.

Katz, Richard S. 1997. *Democracy and Elections*. New York: Oxford University Press.

Kelley, Judith G. 2012. *Monitoring Democracy: When International Election Observation Works, and Why It Often Fails*. Princeton: Princeton University Press.

Kelley, Judith G., and Kiril Kolev. 2010. Election Quality and International Observation 1975–2004: Two New Datasets. http://ssrn.com/abstract=1694654.

Lyons, Terrence. 2004. "Post-conflict Elections and the Process of Demilitarizing Politics: The Role of Electoral Administration." *Democratization* 11 (3): 36–62.

Mukherji, Biman, and Shefali Anand. 2014. "In India, Election Officials Brave Hungry Crocodiles to Reach Voters." *Wall Street Journal*, April 23.

Munck, Gerardo L., and Jay Verkuilen. 2002. "Conceptualizing and Measuring Democracy: Evaluating Alternative Indices." *Comparative Political Studies* 35 (1): 5–34.

Norris, Pippa. 2014. *Why Electoral Integrity Matters*. New York: Cambridge University Press.

Norris, Pippa, Richard W. Frank, and Ferran Martínez i Coma. 2013. "Assessing the Quality of Elections." *Journal of Democracy* 24 (4): 124–35.

Pew Center on the States. 2010. Upgrading Democracy: Improving America's Elections by Modernizing States' Voter Registration Systems. www.pewstates.org/research/reports/upgrading-democracy-85899378733.

Pew Charitable Trusts. 2014. The Elections Performance Index 2012. www.pewtrusts.org/~/media/Assets/2014/04/07/EPI_brief.pdf.

Ponoroff, Christopher. 2010. "Voter Registration in a Digital Age." Brennan Center for Justice. www.brennancenter.org/publication/voter-registration-digital-age.

Prather, Lauren, and Erik S. Herron. 2007. "Enfranchising Displaced Voters: Lessons from Bosnia-Herzegovina." *Election Law Journal* 6 (4): 354–71.

Renwick, Alan. 2010. *The Politics of Electoral Reform: Changing the Rules of Democracy*. New York: Cambridge University Press.

Robert, Eve. 2009. "Voter Registration: An International Perspective." Fairvote.org. http://archive.fairvote.org/rtv/Universal%20Voter%20Registration-4-21-09.pdf.

Rosenberg, Jennifer S., with Margaret Chen. 2009. "Expanding Democracy: Voter Registration around the World." Brennan Center for Justice. www.brennancenter.org/publication/expanding-democracy-voter-registration-around-world.

Rosenstone, Steven J., and Raymond E. Wolfinger. 1978. "The Effects of Registration Laws on Voter Turnout." *American Political Science Review* 72 (1): 22–45.

Schaffer, Frederic Charles. 2007. "Lessons Learned." In *Elections for Sale: The Causes and Consequences of Vote Buying*, Frederic Charles Schaffer, ed. Boulder: Lynne Rienner Publishers.

Schaffer, Frederic Charles, and Tova Andrea Wang. 2009. "Is Everyone Else Doing It? Indiana's Voter Identification Law in International Perspective." *Harvard Law & Policy Review* 3 (2): 397–412.

Seawright, Jason, and John Gerring. 2008. "Case Selection Techniques in Case Study Research." *Political Research Quarterly* 61 (2): 294–308.

Stein, Robert M., and Greg Vonnahme. 2011. "Voting at Non-Precinct Polling Places: A Review and Research Agenda." *Election Law Journal* 10 (3): 307–11.

Wang, Tova Andrea. 2012. *The Politics of Voter Suppression: Defending and Expanding Americans' Right to Vote*. Ithaca: Cornell University Press.

Wolfinger, Raymond E., and Steven J. Rosenstone. 1980. *Who Votes?* New Haven: Yale University Press.

2 Election administration inclusiveness

The comparative study of electoral institutions was long dominated by a focus on rules for translating votes into seats in the legislature. Issues of election administration – the administrative and bureaucratic rules and procedures governing electoral processes – received little attention. Most scholars simply did not "think enough about the nitty-gritty of carrying out elections – about how the registry is prepared, what documents voters must present, how voters cast their ballots, and how ballots are counted" (Schaffer 2008, 5).

Yet, in the wake of the administrative problems surrounding the 2000 US presidential election, as well as similar experiences in democracies in developing countries, scholars have paid more attention to the extensive logistical and technical components of election administration. This has opened up fruitful new lines of research. But the study of election administration has focused overwhelmingly on the effects of election administration variables rather than on the origins of different election administration practices. In this chapter, I briefly summarize what is known about how election administration practices affect voter participation and then draw together several strands of research to identify the factors that influence election administration practices. As I show, previous research suggests that partisan interests, the composition of electoral management bodies, concerns about voter fraud, the activities of civil society, and international democracy-promotion efforts influence how countries administer their elections. I then tie these factors together into a model of how election administration practices are shaped and show how my findings from Central American cases support some of the previous findings in the literature while extending and challenging others.

The consequences of election administration

Election administration practices can have important consequences for voter participation, popular confidence in the electoral process, the outcome of elections, and the potential for violent election-related disputes. Much of the scholarship on election administration has focused on the effects of election measures that make voting more difficult or more convenient, particularly in the United States. This research has studied the effects on voter turnout of voter registration rules, early voting, mail voting, voter ID requirements, and the location of polling places. The results have been mixed, with some administrative measures (such as voter ID rules and early voting) showing no consistent impact on aggregate turnout.[1] But the research does show that some factors that shape the convenience or difficulty of voting – particularly voter registration laws and the accessibility of polling places – have noticeable effects on the number of people that participate, even within the limited range of variation found across the 50 American states.

The burdens imposed by voter registration requirements have long been studied (Merriam and Gosnell 1924), and the role of registration laws involving poll taxes and literacy tests in disenfranchising African-American and poor white voters in the post-Reconstruction South are well known (Kousser 1974). A number of studies find that restrictive voter registration requirements, such as early deadlines for registration and limited registration office hours, lower voter turnout (Mitchell and Wlezien 1995; Rosenstone and Wolfinger 1978) and that the elimination of registration burdens through election-day registration increases turnout (Brians and Grofman 2001; Fenster 1994; Knack 2001).[2]

In addition to voter registration, studies also find that the accessibility of polling places affects voter turnout. Several studies at the municipal or county level in the United States have found that turnout is lowered by greater distances between voters' residences and polling places (Dyck and Gimpel 2005; Gimpel and Schuknecht 2003; Haspel and Knotts 2005) and reducing the number of polling places (Brady and McNulty 2011; McNulty, Dowling, and Ariotti 2009). At the same time, the use of election day vote centers – which allow voters to choose a polling location that may be on the way to work or other daily destinations – may increase turnout (Stein and Vonnahme 2008). Thus, even within a limited range of variation in the location of polling places in America, studies find noticeable (if relatively small) effects on voter turnout of distance to the polls, the convenience of polling locations, and the information costs of finding out where one is assigned to vote. At least one study outside of the United States finds similar effects: Lehoucq and Wall (2004) found that, controlling for other factors, voter turnout in Guatemala was lower in larger municipalities, suggesting that longer distances to polling sites depress voter participation.

Thus, while there are many other factors that affect voter turnout, the literature on participation in the United States shows that some factors that shape the convenience or difficulty of voting – particularly registration laws and the accessibility of polling places – have noticeable effects on the number of people that participate. Less is known about the effects of election administration variables outside of America, though the subject has garnered more attention since the early 2000s. General analyses have emphasized the importance of high-quality election administration for the legitimacy of new democracies (Elklit and Reynolds 2002) and for stability in post-conflict societies (Lyons 2004). It is widely recognized that administratively flawed elections may weaken popular confidence in the electoral process and undermine democratic consolidation.

Moreover, country studies often note the importance of election administration for participation. And although cross-national studies of the effects of election administration practices on voter turnout are scarce,[3] one wide-ranging study (Schaffer 2008) demonstrates that election administration reforms, ostensibly aimed at eliminating fraud and misconduct, can effectively disenfranchise or exclude some voters.

Explaining election administration practices

As the previous section shows, a large body of scholarship on election administration has developed in recent years. This literature shows that several facets of the administration of elections have discernible effects on voter turnout in US elections and that efforts to clean up elections (such as through the introduction of voter identification requirements) can have disenfranchising effects. More generally, the comparative literature suggests the importance of election administration for overall election quality and possibly for larger outcomes such as democratic consolidation.

Yet, despite this extensive literature, very little work has addressed the origins of different election administration practices. In other words, scholars have largely treated election administration as an independent rather than dependent variable. This has important implications for understanding the effects of election administration practices, where unknown factors may be correlated with both the adoption of particular practices and with outcomes such as voter turnout (see Hanmer 2009, 7, 26). It also means that we know little about the origins and evolution of an important subset of electoral institutions that may be pivotal in struggles for political power.

Despite the focus of prior work on the consequences of election administration, however, a number of factors influencing the origins of election administration practices can be gleaned from the broader body of scholarship on electoral systems and suffrage rights. In this section, I draw out these potential causal factors and distill what might be considered the conventional wisdom regarding the origins of election administration practices. In the following section, I develop a model of election administration inclusiveness, situating my argument in the context of previous research.

Partisan interests

Because election administration practices affect voters' access to the ballot and potentially influence election outcomes, partisan interests are thought to play a large role in the adoption of electoral procedures – as they do in the adoption of other electoral rules. Indeed, most studies of electoral system choice adopt an office-seeking approach focused on partisan interests.[4] In this view, "parties prefer electoral rules that maximize their seat share relative to those of other parties" (Benoit 2007, 378), and ruling parties prefer to maintain existing electoral rules unless the competitive environment changes, at which point they will seek electoral reforms to stay in office or minimize their losses (Benoit 2007; Boix 1999, 2010).

Specifically with regard to election administration, ruling parties may craft electoral procedures to facilitate the participation of their supporters and/or impede the participation of opposition voters. This may take the form of requiring voter identification documents that opposition voters are less likely to possess, or adopting voter registration rules that make it more difficult to register in rural areas, among many other possibilities. An example of partisan jockeying over election administration rules comes from Britain, where Labor has sought "to lower the cost of voting and thereby increase participation (particularly among key Labour constituencies)" while Conservatives and Liberal Democrats "have invoked the specter of fraud in pushing for greater controls on access to voting" (Elmendorf 2006, 432).

The literature also suggests the potential for major parties to collude in restricting participation to their mutual benefit (Bowler and Donovan 2008). In this view, incumbent politicians who have been elected under current rules have individual (rather than strictly partisan) interests in maintaining those rules, and the interests of incumbency drive the choice of electoral procedures. In a comparative study of electoral system reform, Bowler, Donovan, and Karp (2006) find that incumbents are less likely to support electoral reforms than are outsider politicians and that "[w]inners from government and opposition parties appear quite similar in their hesitance to endorse electoral system change" (441).

While politicians may have partisan or individual interests in increasing or limiting access to the ballot through administrative measures, little is known about which parties will pursue voter inclusion or exclusion, or under what conditions. I address this question below.

Electoral management body structure

Related to partisan interests is the institutional structure of electoral management bodies (EMBs), the agencies charged with carrying out the administration of electoral processes, and in particular the independence or partisanship of election administrators. While parties can legislate election rules that shape voter access to the ballot, election administrators often have significant discretion in implementing election rules and deciding electoral procedures not specified by law.

Of particular concern has been the independence of EMBs from the government and political party influence, which has received much attention in the election policy community (International IDEA 2006; López-Pintor 2000). A fairly strong consensus holds that EMBs that are independent of the executive branch of government are preferable to government-run EMBs (Birch 2008, 308; López-Pintor 2000), and most countries outside of Western Europe have some form of independent EMB. Yet formal independence from the government does not necessarily mean actual independence from partisan interests. An important distinction is between party-based EMBs, where election officials represent party interests (either by design or de facto), and expert-based EMBs, where election officials are not affiliated with political parties and are selected based on their expertise.[5] Many analysts suggest the importance of non-partisan EMBs for election quality (e.g., Pastor 1999, 18; Reilly 2003, 21), and international election observers often recommend that countries move toward the non-partisan EMB model to improve election quality. Some evidence supports the common-sense notion that elections administered by non-partisan EMBs are of higher quality than elections run by partisan-based EMBs (Hartlyn, McCoy, and Mustillo 2008).

Less is known about the specific effects of various EMB institutional arrangements on election administration practices. In particular, although non-partisan EMBs may tend to oversee higher-quality elections, it is not known whether they tend to implement more inclusive rules and practices or to be conservative in making voting easier (whether to limit election costs or to safeguard against fraud). Yet, the conventional wisdom suggests that partisan EMBs will tend to make voting more difficult for some voters, as partisan interests infiltrate the administration of elections. Top-level election officials with partisan ties may directly institute measures that facilitate or impede voting, depending on their party's interests. Such measures might include decisions about where to locate polling places, what paperwork to require for voter registration, or how vigorously to conduct voter education campaigns. Non-partisan election administrators, in contrast, will have no partisan motives to institute rules that hinder voter participation. As Schaffer and Wang (2009, 411) note in comparing a partisan election official in the United States to his non-partisan counterpart in Canada, "the Chief Electoral Officer in Canada has a freer hand and clearer mandate to protect the voting rights of *all* citizens, regardless of how they are likely to vote."

At lower levels of the election administration, the discretion of election workers at the local level may result in administrative impediments to voting, a possibility made more likely if local workers are partisan appointees. Poll workers play an important role given their "discretion in deciding who must show identification at the polls, how to handle voters who cannot be readily located in the voter registration rolls, and how to handle problems at the polls" (Alvarez and Hall 2006, 496). Thus, if an EMB's partisan makeup penetrates down to the poll-worker level, the potential for exclusion of voters at the polls increases.

Thus, although some analyses suggest that non-partisan EMBs may be associated with more inclusive election administration practices, previous work has not determined empirically whether, and under what conditions, non-partisan electoral management bodies are more likely to lower barriers to voting than are partisan electoral bodies. The model of election administration inclusiveness presented below addresses this issue.

Access versus integrity: the specter of election fraud

Another prominent theme in the literature and in wider contemporary debates about election administration is the potential trade-off between making voting easier and preventing electoral fraud. As Schaffer (2008) demonstrates, election administration measures aimed at ensuring that only eligible voters cast ballots and that they cast them freely may – either intentionally or not – make it more difficult for eligible citizens to vote. This "access versus integrity" trade-off (Hasen 2012, 163) is evident in debates over voter identification and voter registration in the United States and in discussions of online voting generally. Proponents of voter identification laws and opponents of election day registration cite concerns about voter fraud, while others emphasize the potential for strict rules keeping people from the polls. These debates are not new: in early-twentieth-century Costa Rica, for example, a requirement to show photo ID at the polls was "repeatedly postponed … ostensibly because legitimate voters would be deprived of their suffrage rights because they had not obtained their photographic identification cards" (Lehoucq 2000, 462). While the remedies for fraud have been numerous, so too have the types of election fraud that reformers have sought to curb, including double voting, voting by non-citizens, and the importation of voters from outside jurisdictions – a phenomenon variously named colonizing, pipe-laying (Campbell 2005, 19, 23), and pre-electoral residential registration (Fukumoto and Horiuchi 2011).

Despite the centrality of the "access versus integrity" theme in many election administration debates, there is little comparative analysis of how these trade-offs manifest themselves and how they are resolved in different contexts. There are thus few clear hypotheses offered in the literature regarding how concerns about election fraud shape election administration inclusiveness.

Civil society

Another potential influence on election administration comes from civil society groups. Civil society groups may pressure for more inclusive administrative practices, and several episodes of reform in the United States are suggestive of civil society's influence. Voter registration reform was carried out by several states in the 1980s "thanks in part to the energetic lobbying of a broad coalition of progressive and good-government groups" (Keyssar 2001, 255), while "[i]t could be argued that the quiet activism of the disabilities rights community was responsible for the accessibility requirements that were built into" the Help America Vote Act (Stewart 2011, 372). Comparatively, Birch (2011) finds that the strength of civil society and especially a free media are associated with higher-quality elections, as they make electoral manipulation more costly for political elites.

Yet, little scholarly attention has been given to a form of civil society activity that is particularly likely to influence election administration: domestic election monitoring. Such monitoring groups have been active in at least 66 countries worldwide and engage in a range of activities, including advocating for electoral reform and offering recommendations for improving election administration (Lean 2007). Given their efforts to ensure fair and inclusive elections, the presence and strength of such groups (in terms of size, prestige, mobilizational capacity, and so on) could be an important factor in explaining election administration practices.

I examine the impact of domestic election monitors and other civil society actors and find that although they actively advocate inclusive election administration measures, they exercise relatively little influence on legislative and administrative reform. Contrary to expectations, organized civil society has little effect on election administration inclusiveness. Rather, election administration is a highly elite affair among partisan actors and election administrators, who are only modestly constrained by organized civic groups.

International influences

Lastly, international factors can also affect the administrative conduct of elections. This is particularly true of international election observation. A wide variety of intergovernmental and non-governmental organizations monitor elections,[6] and by the early 2000s about 80 percent of elections in "non-established" democracies were monitored (Beaulieu and Hyde 2009, 406; Kelley 2008, 223). Election observation missions typically monitor all facets of the electoral process, meet regularly with election officials and political parties, issue periodic statements during the electoral process, and issue a final report after each election containing specific recommendations for improvements in future elections.

Observers may improve the quality of elections through several mechanisms: by increasing the costs to incumbents of cheating and raising the benefits of holding clean elections through international verification; by offering recommendations for improvements in the electoral process; and, over the medium or long term, by socializing domestic actors into norms of electoral conduct through repeated interaction (Kelley 2012, 10–11). Recent research has uncovered some evidence of election observation's touted effects. In particular, studies have found evidence that election monitors deter ballot stuffing (Hyde 2007) and that monitored elections are generally of higher quality and more likely to result in government turnover than are unmonitored elections (Kelley 2012, ch. 7).

Evidence of long-term improvements resulting from election monitoring is scant, however. For instance, Kelley (2012) finds that observers often have limited influence over election quality over time. While recommendations from observers sometimes inform subsequent electoral reforms, many election problems tend to persist, and new problems often emerge. Improvements also usually take a long time, "and when progress does occur, the main role of international monitors usually is to reinforce domestic actors" (Kelley 2012, 141).

Election observation may also have unintended consequences that lower the quality of elections, as incumbents strategically alter their manipulation tactics to avoid condemnation by observers. Observers are more likely to condemn blatant manipulation such as ballot stuffing on election day than administrative problems or irregularities occurring before voting takes place (Hyde 2011, 164–65; Kelley 2012, 66–67). It is particularly difficult for observers to distinguish between administrative limitations and intentional electoral manipulation, when confronted with problems such as incomplete or error-ridden voter registries (Beaulieu and Hyde 2009, 404; Kelley 2012, 81; Simpser and Donno 2012, 503). Thus, indirect tactics of election manipulation – such as inaccurate voter rolls, cumbersome voter registration processes that can be blamed on administrative incompetence, inadequate voter education efforts in opposition strongholds, and so on – may proliferate as observers make more blatant forms of cheating more difficult (Beaulieu and Hyde 2009, 400; Carothers 1997, 22; Hyde 2011, 179; Simpser 2008).[7]

In sum, the literature shows that international election observation influences electoral conduct in monitored countries in the short term, if not in the long term. The impact of monitoring on election administration inclusiveness, however, is less clear. For any given election, the presence of election observers may make certain forms of administrative disenfranchisement (particularly those that occur on election day) less likely, but it may also make disenfranchisement through pre-election manipulation of the voter rolls more likely. Furthermore, it is not clear whether observers generally advocate inclusive election procedures or lean toward restrictive procedures that safeguard against fraud, or whether different observer groups offer a mix of (potentially conflicting) recommendations.

A theory of election administration inclusiveness

The literature reviewed above identifies a number of factors that may shape election administration inclusiveness. But how do these variables combine to explain the adoption of inclusive or restrictive election administration practices? I argue that election administration practices bearing on voter access are shaped primarily by four domestic factors: partisan competition, historical legacies of election fraud, the nature of partisan identification and the party system, and the composition of a country's electoral management body. The first two of these factors provide motives for increasing or decreasing inclusiveness, while the latter two factors condition the ability of actors to do so.

In addition to these domestic factors, international variables, such as international financial and technical election assistance and geopolitical pressures and alliances, affect electoral practices generally and election administration inclusiveness specifically. International technical and financial assistance is often necessary for less developed countries to institute inclusive election administration practices, although such assistance is not sufficient to ensure inclusiveness, while geopolitical factors affect the calculus of incumbents when deciding upon electoral practices.

In this section, I flesh out the argument in greater detail.

Partisan interests, electoral competitiveness, and the party system

Politicians often have partisan interests in increasing or limiting access to the ballot through administrative measures. By designing the procedures for voter registration and casting a ballot, political actors can attempt to sway electoral outcomes by affecting who votes. However, not all elections are marked by partisan attempts to shape the electorate through election administration practices.

I argue that two factors are critical to understanding when political actors will attempt to limit access to the ballot box: the ability to identify voters' partisan loyalties and the level of electoral competitiveness. The ability of parties to identify the opposition's supporters is critical in determining the ability of parties to use voting procedures for partisan gain. Whether or not parties decide to use such tactics is influenced by the competitive environment.

Whether or not parties seek advantage through election administration depends in part on the ability of parties to identify their supporters and the supporters of the opposition. Making voting more difficult through election administration practices for partisan gain requires accurate knowledge of voter preferences (Schaffer 2008). Without such knowledge, parties will not be able to anticipate who will benefit electorally from obstacles to voting.[8] Campbell (2005, 271) notes more broadly how party identification patterns may facilitate cheating: "By fragmenting the electorate into groups with predictable voting behaviors, the parties have an easier job identifying those who will likely vote for and against them, which make vote-buying and vote-suppression much easier tasks."

The ability of parties to identify voter loyalties is often thought of in terms of class or racial markers. We therefore expect less inclusive election administration practices when a ruling party can single out opposition supporters for exclusion, whether due to socioeconomic, ethnic, or geographic factors associated with partisan loyalties (Schaffer 2008, 42–44). Thus, the ability of the dominant Democratic Party to identify Republican and Populist supporters through the identifiers of race and class made disenfranchisement through election administration a viable partisan strategy in the post-Reconstruction American South. More generally, restrictive election administration practices often have their largest impact on citizens of low socioeconomic status (see, e.g., Highton 1997), since those with fewer resources are least able to overcome the increased costs of voting that arise from administrative barriers. This suggests that where partisan loyalties correspond to class cleavages, the relative inclusiveness of election administration practices will depend on the extent to which parties with lower-class constituencies can influence election-related legislation and administrative regulations. Where such parties wield significant influence, we expect fewer barriers to voter participation.

Identifying the partisan loyalties of voters, however, is not always limited to broad group markers of race or class. Rather, in some party systems, parties can identify voter loyalties at a more fine-grained level. This is illustrated by negative vote buying (or buying abstention) in nineteenth-century New York, where

> [b]uying off the opposition (paying voters US$10–25 to stay at home), whose members party canvassers identified in the weeks before election day, worked in a world of stable communities – places where party activists knew every citizen and therefore could reasonably predict the inclinations of voters.
>
> (Lehoucq 2007, 39; see also Schaffer 2007, 187)

The ability to identify rival supporters is also necessary to effectively carry out other voter suppression tactics for partisan advantage, such as purging opposition voters from the voter rolls – a practice facilitated historically in Costa Rica, for example, by the fact that candidates printed the names of their supporters in newspaper ads to demonstrate their popularity (Bowman 2003, 267).

The ability to identify rival voters is a necessary condition for efforts to adopt restrictive election administration practices in order to shape the electorate for partisan advantage. But when will parties be motivated to pursue such a strategy? Here, the competitiveness of the electoral environment is critical, as incumbent parties that perceive themselves to be electorally vulnerable are more likely to resort to voter suppression and similar tactics to stay in power (Bentele and O'Brien 2013; Schaffer 2008, ch. 2). Restrictive election administration measures are more likely to be considered when election contests are highly competitive and raising the costs of voting may have enough impact to sway the election result. However, competitiveness must be considered in the light of the perceptions and goals of the electoral actors themselves. Thus, parties may shape election administration rules in their favor, even when an election outcome is expected to be lopsided if that party seeks not just victory but a large margin of victory (for example, to secure a legislative supermajority). Likewise, a governing party may put in place administrative measures that benefit the opposition if it expects – even incorrectly – to win comfortably.

In sum, partisan interests influence the crafting of election administration practices, but only under certain conditions. My findings build on previous work on partisan interests and electoral practices and extend the scope of analysis beyond the two-party American system often studied in the literature to examine a wider range of party systems. I show that partisan interests often, but not always, affect decisions about election administration rules. The salience of partisan interests depends on the nature of parties and their ability to identify their supporters and opponents in the electorate, as well as the level of competitiveness. Consistent with previous research, I find that parties that cannot identify their likely supporters and opponents in the electorate do not attempt to impede voter participation through administrative means. I extend this finding by showing that lack of knowledge of voter loyalties is likely to be found in certain types of party systems, especially those with catch-all parties or fluid party systems marked by low levels of partisan attachments. Such party systems, which are not based on social cleavages and lack strong ties between party organizations and society, are conducive to inclusiveness, since it is difficult for incumbent parties in such systems to identify opposition supporters. Simply put, where parties lack identifiable social bases, voter access is not a viable weapon in electoral competition.

Furthermore, I show that identifying voter loyalties is not just limited to blunt associations between partisanship and class, race, or ethnicity. Rather, the ability of parties to identify their supporters and opponents depends not just on patterns of party identification in the electorate but on party organization – the extent to which parties penetrate into society at the local level and are able to use local knowledge to monitor partisan loyalties.

Historical legacies of election fraud

The electoral threat faced by political parties comes not only from the competitiveness of elections (in terms of the distribution of voter support) but also from the possibility that opponents will cheat their way to victory. Some – but by no means all – modes of cheating involve voter fraud, including multiple voting by the same person, voting by ineligible citizens, and people voting in jurisdictions where they do not reside. While there are many safeguards available to prevent such voter fraud, some of them involve election administration practices that make voting more difficult.

But when will countries adopt restrictive election administration practices to prevent fraud? I find that historical experiences with election fraud shape subsequent election administration practices. A history of election fraud leads democratizing countries to adopt strict safeguards against fraud, which in turn often impose procedural barriers to voting. Where election fraud under authoritarian regimes had been highly visible and blatant, ensuring the rectitude of the electoral process is a high priority for democratizing regimes. Many of the competitors in democratizing elections were previously on the losing end of rigged electoral processes, and the legitimacy of the elections depends on widespread acceptance of the process by competing parties. Such widespread acceptance is sought partly through strict procedures that seek to make voter fraud difficult to perpetrate. The unintended consequence can be election administration practices that make it difficult for eligible voters to register and cast a ballot.

As concerns about election fraud persist over time, restrictive measures, especially those related to voter registration and identification, are likely to remain in place, while diminishing concerns about large-scale fraud open the door for the adoption of more inclusive election administration rules. Thus, transitional regimes sometimes attempt to inoculate elections against the types of fraud that occurred under authoritarian rule. This is consistent with the more general notion that transitional regimes will often reject authoritarian-era electoral institutions, as post-communist regimes did in the case of single-member districts that had been used under communist rule, for instance (Benoit 2004, 384). I show that potential trade-offs between electoral integrity and voter access shape election administration and identify one condition – democratic transition from a regime characterized by election fraud – under which these trade-offs are likely to be resolved in favor of integrity over access.

Electoral management bodies

While partisan interests affect election administration inclusiveness, those effects are partly mediated by the composition of the country's electoral management body. Consistent with expectations, I find that non-partisan EMBs sometimes promote inclusiveness, although they often do so through an unexpected mechanism: influencing electoral legislation. Aside from direct implementation of administrative rules, non-partisan election commissions often play an active role in electoral reform. As Elmendorf (2006) argues, election commissions may influence electoral reform by shifting public opinion toward their proposed reforms, influencing judicial review decisions by providing independent analysis of election legislation, and gaining endorsements for their proposals from legislators who fear alienating election administrators. While this policy analysis and advocacy role of electoral management bodies has been largely overlooked in the literature, I find that non-partisan EMBs can not only prevent restrictive administrative measures being introduced with partisan intent but also influence election administration inclusiveness by promoting and shaping the content of election law reform.

Additionally, although EMB partisanship can facilitate voter exclusion through administrative measures, partisan EMBs can also carry out highly inclusive practices under some conditions, such as when the dominant party on the EMB expects to be victorious under fair electoral competition or under significant international pressure to legitimize elections. I thus find a more complex relationship between EMB structure and election practices than expected, as well as unanticipated mechanisms of EMB influence.

A model of the domestic politics of election administration inclusiveness

Incorporating these factors into a theoretical framework, I identify multiple pathways to inclusive and restrictive election administration, centered on electoral threat, party capacity, and electoral management body composition. Electoral threat encompasses two sources of threat to the major electoral actors: the specter of election fraud and a competitive opposition. When there is a perceived threat of serious election fraud, and/or the major political parties perceive a serious challenge to their electoral goals from their contenders, those parties will have motive to level the playing field or seek electoral advantage through measures that lower election administration inclusiveness. The absence of such a serious electoral threat is conducive to inclusiveness.

Where the electoral threat is posed by a competitive opposition, the ability of parties to act on their motive to restrict the vote is conditioned by their capacity – namely, their knowledge of voters' preferences and their ability to identify opposition supporters – and their control over the EMB. In contrast, where the electoral threat is in the form of a specter of election fraud, the result is likely to be low election-administration inclusiveness even in the absence of parties' knowledge of voters' loyalties or a partisan EMB. In this case, restrictive administrative practices are likely to be written into electoral legislation and will be adopted by parties that believe that eliminating voter fraud will work to their advantage.

A schematic overview of this theory is presented in Figure 2.1, with the key variables presented dichotomously for the sake of simplicity.[9] This simplified model captures the main elements of the domestic politics of election administration inclusiveness. Exogenous to the model are international pressures, which

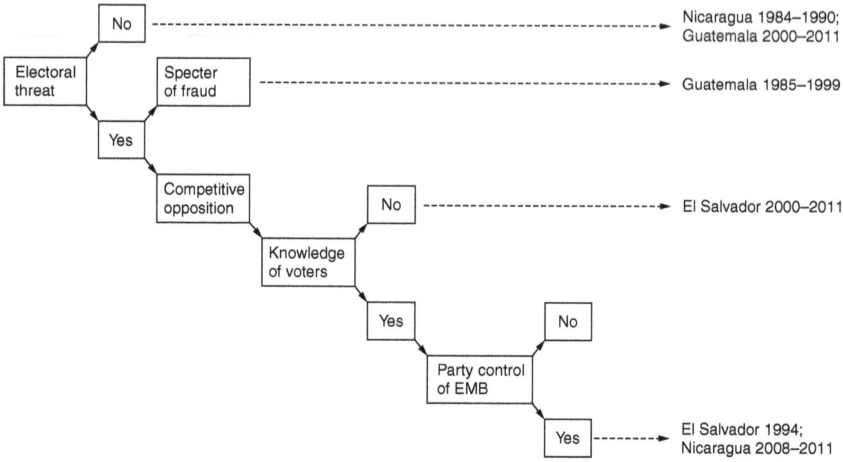

Figure 2.1 Model of the domestic politics of election administration inclusiveness.

may motivate inclusiveness and constrain efforts at disenfranchisement that result from electoral threat. Nevertheless, the model captures several pathways to inclusive or restrictive electoral procedures that are borne out by the case studies.

First, although we should generally expect, almost by definition, an electoral threat to be present in countries with truly open elections, the case studies reveal two distinct patterns in which an electoral threat was perceived as absent by the major political actors. In Nicaragua in 1984 and 1990, there was no perceived electoral threat from opposition parties, as the incumbent party expected to win handily, nor was there a specter of election fraud. Electoral threat was also greatly diminished in Guatemala after fears of widespread election fraud subsided. Due to the extreme instability of the Guatemalan party system and the rapid decline of incumbent parties, the logic of an incumbent party seeking to maintain power and hold off competitive challengers has not been applicable. Instead, it has generally been the incumbent party that is no longer competitive by the time the next election comes around. In these two cases, the absence of electoral threat (in both forms) coincided with moderate to high election administration inclusiveness.

A second pathway illustrated by the cases involves the presence of electoral threat but limited capacity of parties to identify their opponents' supporters in the electorate. In the case studies, the result for inclusiveness differed depending on the nature of the electoral threat. In El Salvador in the 2000s, closely competitive elections represented an electoral threat to incumbents, but the limited ability of parties to identify opposition voters coincided with the adoption of more inclusive practices. In contrast, during Guatemala's political transition, the electoral threat took the form of the specter of election fraud. The result was low inclusiveness, even in the absence of incumbent parties seeking to limit the vote of the opposition.

A final pathway illustrated by the cases involved the presence of electoral threat and two conditions facilitating restrictiveness: the ability to identify (to a greater or lesser degree) opposition supporters, and partisan control (again to a greater or lesser degree) of the electoral management body. This combination of electoral threat and party capacity resulted in low inclusiveness. In El Salvador's pivotal 1994 election, electoral threat was present in both the specter of fraud and a competitive opposition party and was combined with some ability to identify opposition supporters and partisan control over the electoral body. In Nicaragua's 2008 and 2011 elections, the perceived electoral threat was to the incumbent party's supermajority control and coincided with that party's ability to identify opposition supporters and its total control of the electoral body.

The model also identifies a combination of conditions that does not match any of the cases: the presence of an electoral threat and party capacity to identify opposition supporters, along with a non-partisan electoral management body. Under these conditions, we might expect a non-partisan body to act as a bulwark against attempts to impede voter access by parties targeting the supporters of their opponents. However, considering EMB institutional design as endogenous to the dynamics of electoral competition, we should also expect electoral threat (in the form of a competitive challenge) to lead incumbent parties to attempt to politicize the EMB in order to bring the electoral body under its control.

International election observation, technical assistance, and geopolitics

While the model presented above addresses the domestic factors affecting election administration inclusiveness, international variables also matter. Much of the literature in this area has focused on international election observation and, in order to address the gap in our understanding of election observation's effects on inclusiveness, I examine the specific recommendations which observers make related to election administration inclusiveness. I find that observers overwhelmingly (though not unanimously) endorse inclusive practices. But consistent with prior research, I find that the recommendations of international observers have fairly limited impact on processes of electoral reform. While full observer reports, issued long after election day, often contain more detailed and critical remarks on election administration than observers' immediate post-election statements, "by the time the longer report comes out both the media and the world's attention have moved on, and details in the reports frequently escape attention" (Kelley 2012, 61). Pressure from observers also eases between elections, and thus long-term recommendations are often neglected (Kelley 2012, 177). Consistent with previous work on election observation, I argue that international observer recommendations play only a modest role in shaping domestic election-administration practices, at least absent significant domestic pressures for electoral reform (see also Birch 2011, 154; Kelley 2012, 148–49).

International influences on domestic election administration are not limited to election observation alone, however. Of equal or greater importance are the geopolitical interests of foreign powers and the host country's desire for cooperation with the West. Where foreign powers favor electoral reform and the country desires good relations with the West, the influence of observers should be strengthened as the host country seeks to enhance its democratic legitimacy. Where foreign donors have other priorities or where a host country is not dependent on Western favor, pressures for holding high-quality elections will be lessened (Kelley 2012, 145–47). Evidence shows that conditionality exercised by democracy-promoting countries in response to flawed elections is associated with improvements in the following election (Donno 2013). More broadly, linkages with the West are associated with the democratization of competitive authoritarian regimes, while close ties to "black knights," or "counter-hegemonic powers whose economic, military, and/or diplomatic support helps blunt the impact of U.S. or EU democratizing pressure," are associated with the persistence of authoritarianism (Levitsky and Way 2010, 41).

I illustrate the implications of such international political dynamics for election administration inclusiveness. I reveal how international pressure can lead governing parties that expect electoral victory to make election administration as inclusive as possible (while avoiding other forms of manipulation and irregularities as well). Conversely, I show that reduced international pressures and the availability of resources from "black knights" can result in electoral manipulation, including decreased inclusiveness as a method for impeding the participation of opposition voters.

Finally, I also demonstrate the importance of an international influence on election administration beyond election monitoring that is scarcely addressed in the literature: the extensive technical assistance that international organizations, bilateral donors, and NGOs offer to election administrators worldwide. Organizations such as the International Foundation for Electoral Systems (IFES) and the Center for Electoral Promotion and Assistance (CAPEL) offer financial and technical assistance in carrying out a wide range of electoral tasks, including voter education and voter registry modernization. I show that such assistance contributes to inclusive election administration by enhancing the capacity of the electoral bureaucracy in recipient countries. International financial and technical assistance is not sufficient for inclusiveness: measures such as decentralizing polling places and modernizing voter registries depend on domestic political will, and the content of election administration reform is primarily determined domestically. But international assistance is often necessary to make inclusive election administration practices possible.

Conclusion

Although election administration inclusiveness has not been the subject of systematic investigation, previous research suggests a number of factors that influence inclusiveness, as the above discussion indicates. Research on election administration, electoral systems, voting rights, and the international dimensions of democratization suggest that partisan interests, the composition of electoral management bodies, concerns about voter fraud, the activities of civil society, and international democracy promotion efforts will influence how countries administer their elections. Despite the long list of potential influences on election administration, however, little is known about how, to what extent, and under what conditions these factors influence the adoption of specific election administration rules and practices in different countries. A good deal of research has focused on the determinants of overall election quality, rather than the determinants of variation in particular electoral procedures. By examining variations in administrative rules that facilitate or impede voting among eligible citizens, the case studies in the following chapters find support for some pieces of the conventional wisdom about electoral conduct, while challenging and adding nuance to others. I also identify some important causal factors that have been overlooked in prior research.

Notes

1 On early voting, see Burden et al. (2014) and Gronke, Galanes-Rosenbaum, and Miller (2007), and sources cited therein. Some studies also find no effects of early voting on partisan outcomes (Alvarez, Levin, and Sinclair 2012). On voter ID, different studies have come to different conclusions, and there is no consensus on the effects of ID laws on turnout (see among others Erickson and Minnite 2009; GAO 2014; and Mycoff, Wagner, and Wilson 2009). Voting by mail has been found to increase turnout in low-stimulus elections, although it has little effect in high-profile contests (Kousser and Mullin 2007; Southwell 2009; Southwell and Burchett 2000).

2 Some liberalizing registration reforms – such as mail-in registration, prohibitions against purging people from the voter rolls for failure to vote, and "motor voter" programs – have not been shown to boost turnout (Brown and Wedeking 2006; Highton 2004, 510; Knack 1995; Martinez and Hill 1999). But the evidence is clear that some voter registration requirements within the United States have had substantial effects on voter participation.

3 Quantitative cross-national studies of turnout generally do not incorporate election administration variables into their models, with the occasional exception of voter registration requirements – though see Franklin (2002), who finds that voting on a Sunday and postal voting are each associated with higher voter turnout in a sample of 31 countries.

4 *Electoral systems* are conceived as rules for translating votes into seats and for structuring voters' choices on the ballot, as distinct from election administration rules.

5 Many countries fall in between these EMB types, with some election commissioners selected by political parties and others selected by less partisan actors such as the judiciary (see Hyde and Pallister 2015).

6 Prominent international organizations involved in election observation include the Organization of American States (OAS), the Organization for Security and Cooperation in Europe (OSCE), and the African Union. Important NGOs involved in monitoring include the Carter Center, the National Democratic Institute (NDI), and the International Republican Institute (IRI).

7 There is no consensus on the evidence of election observation leading to different forms of electoral manipulation. For contrasting views, see Kelley (2012) and Simpser and Donno (2012).

8 The same is true of designing electoral systems for partisan advantage. As Renwick (2010, 11–12, 56–57) suggests, when parties are unable to predict the partisan implications of different electoral rules, they may choose electoral systems behind a Rawlsian "veil of ignorance."

9 It should be emphasized that the dichotomous treatment of variables in the model does not allow for distinctions in the degree of electoral threat, the degree of party knowledge of voter loyalties, and whether partisan control of the EMB is exercised by one party or several. These nuances are treated in the empirical analysis in the following chapters.

References

Alvarez, R. Michael, and Thad E. Hall. 2006. "Controlling Democracy: The Principal-Agent Problems in Election Administration." *The Policy Studies Journal* 34 (4): 491–510.

Alvarez, R. Michael, Ines Levin, and Andrew Sinclair. 2012. "Making Voting Easier: Convenience Voting in the 2008 Presidential Election." *Political Research Quarterly* 65 (2): 248–62.

Beaulieu, Emily, and Susan D. Hyde. 2009. "In the Shadow of Democracy Promotion: Strategic Manipulation, International Observers, and Election Boycotts." *Comparative Political Studies* 42 (3): 392–415.

Benoit, Kenneth. 2004. "Models of Electoral System Change." *Electoral Studies* 23 (3): 363–89.

Benoit, Kenneth. 2007. "Electoral Laws as Political Consequences: Explaining the Origins and Change of Electoral Institutions." *Annual Review of Political Science* 10: 363–90.

Bentele, Keith G., and Erin E. O'Brien. 2013. "Jim Crow 2.0? Why States Consider and Adopt Restrictive Voter Access Policies." *Perspectives on Politics* 11 (4): 1088–116.

Birch, Sarah. 2008. "Electoral Institutions and Popular Confidence in Electoral Processes: A Cross-National Analysis." *Electoral Studies* 27 (2): 305–20.

Birch, Sarah. 2011. *Electoral Malpractice*. New York: Oxford University Press.

Boix, Carles. 1999. "Setting the Rules of the Game: The Choice of Electoral Systems in Advanced Democracies." *American Political Science Review* 93 (3): 609–24.

Boix, Carles. 2010. "Electoral Markets, Party Strategies, and Proportional Representation." *American Political Science Review* 104 (2): 404–13.

Bowler, Shaun, and Todd Donovan. 2008. "Barriers to Participation for Whom? Regulations on Voting and Uncompetitive Elections." In *Designing Democratic Government: Making Institutions Work*, Margaret Levi, James Johnson, Jack Knight, and Susan Stokes, eds. New York: Russell Sage Foundation.

Bowler, Shaun, Todd Donovan, and Jeffrey A. Karp. 2006. "Why Politicians Like Electoral Institutions: Self-Interest, Values, or Ideology?" *Journal of Politics* 68 (2): 434–46.

Bowman, Kirk. 2003. "The Causes and Consequences of Electoral Reform." *Election Law Journal* 2 (2): 263–69.

Brady, Henry E., and John E. McNulty. 2011. "Turning Out to Vote: The Costs of Finding and Getting to the Polling Place." *American Political Science Review* 105 (1): 115–34.

Brians, Craig Leonard, and Bernard Grofman. 2001. "Election Day Registration's Effect on U.S. Voter Turnout." *Social Science Quarterly* 82 (1): 170–83.

Brown, Robert D., and Justin Wedeking. 2006. "People Who Have Their Tickets but Do Not Use Them: 'Motor Voter,' Registration, and Turnout Revisited." *American Politics Research* 34 (4): 479–504.

Burden, Barry C., David T. Canon, Kenneth R. Mayer, and Donald P. Moynihan. 2014. "Election Laws, Mobilization, and Turnout: The Unanticipated Consequences of Election Reform." *American Journal of Political Science* 58 (1): 95–109.

Campbell, Tracy. 2005. *Deliver the Vote: A History of Election Fraud, an American Political Tradition—1742–2004*. New York: Carroll & Graf Publishers.

Carothers, Thomas. 1997. "The Observers Observed: The Rise of Election Monitoring." *Journal of Democracy* 8 (3): 17–31.

Donno, Daniela. 2013. *Defending Democratic Norms: International Actors and the Politics of Electoral Misconduct*. New York: Oxford University Press.

Dyck, Joshua J. and James G. Gimpel. 2005. "Distance, Turnout, and the Convenience of Voting." *Social Science Quarterly* 86 (3): 531–48.

Elklit, Jorgen, and Andrew Reynolds. 2002. "The Impact of Election Administration on the Legitimacy of Emerging Democracies: A New Comparative Politics Research Agenda." *Commonwealth and Comparative Politics* 40 (2): 86–119.

Elmendorf, Christopher S. 2006. "Election Commissions and Electoral Reform: An Overview." *Election Law Journal* 5 (4): 425–46.

Erickson, Robert S., and Lorraine C. Minnite. 2009. "Modeling Problems in the Voter Identification–Voter Turnout Debate." *Election Law Journal* 8 (2): 85–101.

Fenster, Mark J. 1994. "The Impact of Allowing Day of Registration Voting on Turnout in U.S. Elections from 1960 to 1992." *American Politics Quarterly* 22 (1) 74–87.

Franklin, Mark N. 2002. "The Dynamics of Electoral Participation." In *Comparing Democracies 2: New Challenges in the Study of Elections and Voting*, Lawrence LeDuc, Richard G. Niemi, and Pippa Norris, eds. London: Sage Publications.

Fukumoto, Kentaro, and Yusaku Horiuchi. 2011. "Making Outsiders' Votes Count: Detecting Electoral Fraud through a Natural Experiment." *American Political Science Review* 105 (3): 586–603.

GAO (U.S. Government Accountability Office). 2014. Issues Related to State Voter Identification Laws. www.gao.gov/products/GAO-14-634.

Gimpel, J.G., and J.E. Schuknecht. 2003. "Political Participation and the Accessibility of the Ballot Box." *Political Geography* 22 (5): 471–88.

Gronke, Paul, Eva Galanes-Rosenbaum, and Peter A. Miller. 2007. "Early Voting and Turnout." *PS: Political Science & Politics* 40 (4): 639–45.

Hanmer, Michael J. 2009. *Discount Voting: Voter Registration Reforms and Their Effects*. New York: Cambridge University Press.

Hartlyn, Jonathan, Jennifer McCoy, and Thomas M. Mustillo. 2008. "Electoral Governance Matters: Explaining the Quality of Elections in Latin America." *Comparative Political Studies* 41 (4): 73–98.

Hasen, Rick. 2012. *The Voting Wars: From Florida 2000 to the Next Election Meltdown*. New Haven: Yale University Press.

Haspel, Moshe, and H. Gibbs Knotts. 2005. "Location, Location, Location: Precinct Placement and the Costs of Voting." *Journal of Politics* 67 (2): 560–73.

Highton, Benjamin. 1997. "Easy Registration and Voter Turnout." *Journal of Politics* 59 (2): 565–75.

Highton, Benjamin. 2004. "Voter Registration and Turnout in the United States." *Perspectives on Politics* 2 (3): 507–15.

Hyde, Susan. 2007. "The Observer Effect in International Politics: Evidence from a Natural Experiment." *World Politics* 60 (1): 37–63.

Hyde, Susan. 2011. *The Pseudo-Democrat's Dilemma: Why Election Observation Became an International Norm*. Ithaca and London: Cornell University Press.

Hyde, Susan, and Kevin Pallister. 2015. "Election Administration, Election Observation, and Election Quality." In *Routledge Handbook of Comparative Political Institutions*, Jennifer Gandhi and Rubén Ruiz-Rufino, eds. New York: Routledge.

International IDEA (International Institute for Democracy and Electoral Assistance). 2006. *Electoral Management Design: The International IDEA Handbook*. Stockholm, Sweden: International Institute for Democracy and Electoral Assistance.

Kelley, Judith. 2008. "Assessing the Complex Evolution of Norms: The Rise of International Election Monitoring." *International Organization* 62 (2): 221–55.

Kelley, Judith. 2012. *Monitoring Democracy: When International Election Observation Works, and Why It Often Fails*. Princeton: Princeton University Press.

Keyssar, Alexander. 2001. *The Right to Vote: The Contested History of Democracy in the United States*. New York: Basic Books.

Knack, Stephen. 1995. "Does 'Motor Voter' Work? Evidence from State-Level Data." *Journal of Politics* 57 (3): 796–811.

Knack, Stephen. 2001. "Election-Day Registration: The Second Wave." *American Politics Quarterly* 29 (1): 65–78.

Kousser, J. Morgan. 1974. *The Shaping of Southern Politics: Suffrage Restriction and the Establishment of the One-Party South, 1880–1910*. New Haven: Yale University Press.

Kousser, Thad, and Megan Mullin. 2007. "Does Voting by Mail Increase Participation? Using Matching to Analyze a Natural Experiment." *Political Analysis* 15 (4): 428–45.

Lean, Sharon F. 2007. "Democracy Assistance to Domestic Election Monitoring Organizations: Conditions for Success." *Democratization* 14 (2): 289–312.

Lehoucq, Fabrice Edouard. 2000. "Institutionalizing Democracy: Constraint and Ambition in the Politics of Electoral Reform." *Comparative Politics* 32 (4): 459–77.

Lehoucq, Fabrice Edouard. 2007. "When Does a Market for Votes Emerge?" In *Elections for Sale: The Causes and Consequences of Vote Buying*, Frederic Charles Schaffer, ed. Boulder: Lynne Rienner Publishers.

Lehoucq, Fabrice Edouard, and David L. Wall. 2004. "Explaining Voter Turnout Rates in New Democracies: Guatemala." *Electoral Studies* 23 (3): 485–500.

Levitsky, Steven, and Lucan A. Way. 2010. *Competitive Authoritarianism: Hybrid Regimes after the Cold War*. New York: Cambridge University Press.

López-Pintor, Rafael. 2000. Electoral Management Bodies as Institutions of Governance. Bureau for Development Policy, United Nations Development Program. www.eods.eu/library/UNDP.Electoral%20Management%20Bodies%20as%20Institutions%20of%20Governance.pdf.

Lyons, Terrence. 2004. "Post-conflict Elections and the Process of Demilitarizing Politics: The Role of Electoral Administration." *Democratization* 11 (3): 36–62.

Martinez, Michael D., and David Hill. 1999. "Did Motor Voter Work?" *American Politics Quarterly* 27 (3): 296–315.

McNulty, John E., Conor M. Dowling, and Margaret H. Ariotti. 2009. "Driving Saints to Sin: How Increasing the Difficulty of Voting Dissuades Even the Most Motivated Voters." *Political Analysis* 17 (4): 435–55.

Merriam, Charles Edward, and Harold Foote Gosnell. 1924. *Non-voting: Causes and Methods of Control*. Chicago: University of Chicago Press.

Mitchell, Glenn E., and Christopher Wlezien. 1995. "The Impact of Legal Constraints on Voter Registration, Turnout, and the Composition of the American Electorate." *Political Behavior* 17 (2): 179–202.

Mycoff, Jason D., Michael C. Wagner, and David C. Wilson. 2009. "The Empirical Effects of Voter-ID Laws: Present or Absent?" *PS: Political Science and Politics* 42 (1): 121–26.

Pastor, Robert. 1999. "The Role of Electoral Administration in Democratic Transitions: Implications for Policy and Research." *Democratization* 6 (4): 1–27.

Reilly, Benjamin. 2003. International Electoral Assistance: A Review of Donor Activities and Lessons Learned. Working Paper 17, Netherlands Institute of International Relations 'Clingendael,' Conflict Research Unit.

Renwick, Alan. 2010. *The Politics of Electoral Reform: Changing the Rules of Democracy*. New York: Cambridge University Press.

Rosenstone, Steven J., and Raymond E. Wolfinger. 1978. "The Effects of Registration Laws on Voter Turnout." *American Political Science Review* 72 (1): 22–45.

Schaffer, Frederic Charles. 2007. "Lessons Learned." In *Elections for Sale: The Causes and Consequences of Vote Buying*, Frederic Charles Schaffer, ed. Boulder: Lynne Rienner Publishers.

Schaffer, Frederic Charles. 2008. *The Hidden Costs of Clean Election Reform*. Ithaca: Cornell University Press.

Schaffer, Frederic Charles, and Tova Andrea Wang. 2009. "Is Everyone Else Doing It? Indiana's Voter Identification Law in International Perspective." *Harvard Law & Policy Review* 3 (2): 397–412.

Simpser, Alberto. 2008. "Unintended Consequences of Election Monitoring." In *Election Fraud: Detecting and Deterring Electoral Manipulation*, R. Michael Alvarez, Thad E. Hall, and Susan D. Hyde, eds. Washington, DC: The Brookings Institution.

Simpser, Alberto, and Daniela Donno. 2012. "Can International Election Monitoring Harm Governance?" *Journal of Politics* 74 (2): 501–13.

Southwell, Priscilla. 2009. "Analysis of the Turnout Effects of Vote by Mail Elections, 1980–2007." *The Social Science Journal* 46 (1): 211–17.

Southwell, Priscilla, and Justin Burchett. 2000. "The Effect of All Mail Elections on Voter Turnout." *American Politics Quarterly* 28 (1): 72–80.

Stein, Robert M., and Greg Vonnahme. 2008. "Engaging the Unengaged Voter: Vote Centers and Voter Turnout." *Journal of Politics* 70 (2): 487–97.

Stewart, Charles, III. 2011. "Voting Technologies." *Annual Review of Political Science* 14: 353–78.

3 Electoral integrity and inclusiveness in the Americas

Since the 1980s, Latin America has seen profound changes in the conduct of elections. As countries democratized, new electoral laws were drafted, electoral systems were revised, and new electoral management bodies established. Over time, many countries repeatedly amended their election laws and reformed their election administration practices. Reforms have been wide-ranging, addressing such areas as political party registration, initiatives and referenda, and campaign finance. Many reforms have also addressed issues related to voter access, including identity documents, voter registration, and the accessibility of polling places.

Table 3.1 summarizes some of the current election practices in Latin America that bear on voter access. The data are drawn from the most recent election laws in each country and supplemented with information from the websites of each country's electoral management body, election observer reports, and secondary sources.

The data show the degree of cross-national variation in election administration inclusiveness across the region. In terms of voter registration, automatic registration is the regional norm, although five countries have voter-initiated systems. In the latter cases, the difficulty of registering varies: some countries require more than one trip to a registry office to complete the process, while others require only one, and some countries employ mobile registration units to facilitate voter registration. The situation is similar for obtaining the identity documents needed to register and to vote, where the number of registry visits needed varies from country to country. In at least ten countries, citizens must pay a fee to obtain the identity documents needed to register to vote in at least some circumstances.

The regional norm is a closing date for voter registration that is well in advance of election day. The shortest deadline in the region is 90 days (in Honduras and Paraguay), while several countries close voter registration some 6 months prior to election day (Argentina, El Salvador, Mexico, Panama, and Uruguay). Some countries set an even earlier deadline for changes of residence on the voter registry, imposing particularly strict residency requirements in El Salvador (1 year before election day) and Guatemala (some 17 months before election day). The method of demonstrating residence for electoral purposes also varies across countries: in most cases a sworn statement suffices, but some

Table 3.1 Election administration inclusiveness in Latin America

	Automatic or voter-initiated registration	*Registration process*	*Obtaining ID documents required for registration or voting*	*Registration closing date*	*Residency requirement*	*Proof of residence*	*Registry consultation*	*Removal from registry for not voting*
Argentina	Automatic	–	Obtained in one registry trip; financial cost (~$2.30)	180 days	180 days	New ID card needed, entailing financial cost	Available	No
Bolivia	Voter-initiated	In-person using ID card; mobile registration units used	Obtained in person; financial cost for ID	135 days	135 days	None	Available	Yes (for failure to vote in two consecutive elections)
Brazil	Voter-initiated	In-person using birth certificate or ID card	*No information available*	150 days	150 days	Proof of residence required	Available	Yes (for failure to vote in three consecutive elections without justification or payment of fine)
Chile	Automatic	–	Two registry trips needed; financial cost (~$3.80)	120 days	120 days	None	Available	No

continued

Table 3.1 Continued

	Automatic or voter-initiated registration	*Registration process*	*Obtaining ID documents required for registration or voting*	*Registration closing date*	*Residency requirement*	*Proof of residence*	*Registry consultation*	*Removal from registry for not voting*
Colombia	Automatic	–	Two registry trips needed (3–6 month waiting period to process ID application); voter provides photos for ID	4 months	2 months	None	Available, but registry not sent to political parties	No
Costa Rica	Automatic	–	Two registry trips needed (1–8 day waiting period); some mobile units used; no cost for ID	4 months	4 months	None	Available	No
Ecuador	Automatic	Mobile units used to update residence	Obtained in person; financial cost for ID ($5–$15)	150 days	80–180 days	Proof of residence required	Available, but registry not sent to political parties	No

El Salvador	Automatic	–	Obtained in person in one registry trip; mobile units available for the disabled; financial cost for ID card renewals ($10.31)	180 days	1 year	New ID card needed, entailing financial cost	Available	No
Guatemala	Voter-initiated	In-person using ID card; mobile registration units used	Obtained in person; financial cost for ID (~$11)	120 days	17 months	None	Available	No
Honduras	Automatic	–	Two registry trips needed; mobile units used; no cost for ID	90 days	3.5 months	Proof of residence required	Available	No
Mexico	Voter-initiated	In-person; two registry trips needed (approximately 20-day waiting period); mobile units used	Proof of nationality, photo ID, and proof of residence needed	Approximately 6 months	Approximately 6 months	Proof of residence or two witnesses required	Available	No

continued

Table 3.1 Continued

	Automatic or voter-initiated registration	*Registration process*	*Obtaining ID documents required for registration or voting*	*Registration closing date*	*Residency requirement*	*Proof of residence*	*Registry consultation*	*Removal from registry for not voting*
Nicaragua	Automatic	–	Two registry trips needed; financial cost for ID	90 days	90 days	None	Available	Yes (for failure to vote in two consecutive elections)
Panama	Automatic	–	Obtained in person; mobile units used; no cost for ID	6.5 months	1 year	None	Available	Yes (for failure to vote in three consecutive elections)
Paraguay	Automatic	–	Obtained in person with birth certificate; no cost for first ID, but financial cost for renewals (~$1.50)	90 days	90 days	None	Available	No

Peru	Automatic	–	Obtained in person using birth certificate or minor's ID card; two registry trips needed; mobile units used in remote areas; financial cost for ID card (~$8.50); voter provides photo	120 days	120 days	Utility bill needed and financial cost (~$6.20)	Partially available (only 5-day period for voters to request corrections)	No
Uruguay	Voter-initiated	In person with birth certificate and photo ID; two registry trips needed	Voter ID card obtained in person	6 months	6 months	No proof of residence needed; financial cost to change electoral residence (~$2)	Available but not online	No
Venezuela	Voter-initiated	In person with ID card	Obtained in person with birth certificate; no cost	Approximately 145 days	Approximately 145 days	None	Available	No

continued

Table 3.1 Continued

	Polling place accessibility	*Electoral calendar*	*Mail voting**	*Early voting*	*Absentee voting*	*Voter ID required*	*Provisional/tendered ballots allowed*	*Accessibility of ballots for illiterate voters*
Argentina	Decentralized, residential voting	Voting on Sunday	No	No	Absentee polling stations in prisons only	Yes	No	Ballots include candidate photos
Bolivia	Decentralized, residential voting	Voting on Sunday	No	No	None	Yes	No	Ballots include candidate photos; ballots not provided in indigenous languages, but poll workers must speak local languages
Brazil	Decentralized, residential voting	Voting on Sunday	No	No	In-person absentee voting in large municipalities; pre-registration required	Yes	No	Voting machines include candidate photos
Chile	Decentralized, residential voting	Voting on Sunday	No	No	None	Yes	No	Ballots include party symbols but no candidate photos
Colombia	Decentralized, residential voting	Voting on Sunday	No	No	None	Yes	Yes	Ballots include candidate photos and party symbols
Costa Rica	Decentralized, residential voting	Voting on Sunday	No	No	Absentee polling stations in prisons only	Yes	No	Ballots include candidate photos

Ecuador	Decentralized, residential voting	Voting on Sunday	No	No	Absentee polling stations in prisons; small pilot program of mobile voting units for disabled voters	Yes	No	Ballots include candidate photos and party symbols
El Salvador	Decentralized, residential voting	Voting on Sunday	No	No	None	Yes	No	Ballots include candidate photos and party symbols
Guatemala	Decentralized, residential voting	Voting on Sunday	No	No	None	Yes	No	Ballots include candidate photos and party symbols; ballots not provided in indigenous languages
Honduras	Decentralized, residential voting	Voting on Sunday	No	No	None	Yes	No	Ballots include candidate photos and party symbols
Mexico	Decentralized, residential voting	Voting on Sunday	No	No	In-person absentee voting available to all voters	Yes	No	Ballots include party symbols but no candidate photos
Nicaragua	Decentralized, residential voting	Voting on Sunday	No	No	None	Yes	Yes (until after 2016)	Ballots include candidate photos and party symbols
Panama	Decentralized, residential voting	Voting on Sunday; employers must allow employees time off to vote	No	No	Absentee polling stations in some prisons and hospitals	Yes	No	Ballots include candidate photos and party symbols

continued

Table 3.1 Continued

	Polling place accessibility	*Electoral calendar*	*Mail voting**	*Early voting*	*Absentee voting*	*Voter ID required*	*Provisional/tendered ballots allowed*	*Accessibility of ballots for illiterate voters*
Paraguay	Decentralized, residential voting	Voting on Sunday	No	No	Small pilot program of mobile voting units for disabled voters	Yes	No	Ballots include candidate photos
Peru	Decentralized; incomplete use of residential voting (voters in some places are not assigned to nearest polling place)	Voting on Sunday	No	No	In-person absentee voting available to all voters who register absentee at least 90 days before election day	Yes	Yes (only in limited cases when most information on voter's ID matches the data in the registry)	Ballots include candidate photos and party symbols; ballots not provided in indigenous languages
Uruguay	Decentralized, residential voting	Voting on Sunday; employers must allow employees time off to vote	No	No	In-person absentee voting available for rural areas only (absentee voters must vote within their department of residence)	Yes	No	Ballots include candidate photos
Venezuela	Decentralized, residential voting	Voting on Sunday	No	No	None	Yes	No	Voting machines include candidate photos

Note
* Does not include voting from abroad.

countries require that the voter obtain a new identity document listing the new address, which usually entails payment of a fee. There is less variation on other practices, such as providing ways for voters to consult their status on the voter registry, which is provided to some degree in all Latin American countries.

While many countries have some restrictive voter registration practices, the particular rules vary significantly across countries. The region is more uniform when it comes to reaching a polling place and casting a ballot. All countries in the region now have decentralized polling places that are fairly accessible to most voters, and all countries hold voting on Sundays. While these practices are inclusive, the region is uniformly more restrictive when it comes to convenience-voting measures. No country holds early voting or voting by mail (except for citizens living abroad), and the availability of absentee voting is quite limited, with Mexico and Peru having the most extensive absentee balloting provisions. All countries require voter ID at the polls, but the ID required is usually the national identity card that is needed to become a registered voter and to carry out a wide range of daily transactions. All Latin American countries provide some mechanisms for disabled and illiterate voters to cast a ballot – for instance, by allowing a person of confidence to assist a disabled voter and by using ballots that include party symbols and candidate photos. More restrictive is the dearth of provisions for casting a provisional or tendered ballot when a voter's name does not appear on the voter roll or when there is a discrepancy between the voter's ID and information on the voter roll. Only Colombia, Nicaragua, and Peru allow some form of provisional ballots, and Nicaragua has passed a reform that will eliminate this measure in future elections.

Electoral integrity and EMB partisanship

While the descriptive data in Table 3.1 summarize a subset of election administration practices in Latin America, they do not give a comprehensive understanding of the quality of elections in the region. The broader quality of elections in Latin America can be gauged with data from the Electoral Integrity Project, which conducts expert surveys to assess the quality of electoral processes throughout the world as part of its Perceptions of Electoral Integrity (PEI) project. The PEI dataset includes 21 elections from 15 countries in Latin America.[1] Table 3.2 reports PEI data for Latin America, as well as Canada and the United States for comparison. The PEI Index gives an overall score of an election's quality,[2] with higher scores indicating higher-quality elections, while the PEI Index Rank indicates where the election ranks among all 180 elections for which there is data.

There is a wide range of electoral performance in the region. While Latin America averages 57.9 (out of 100) on the PEI Index, individual countries range from a high of 80.8 (Costa Rica's 2014 presidential election) to a low of 39.6 (Venezuela's 2013 presidential election). Costa Rica and Uruguay perform as well as Canada, while a number of Latin American countries outscore the United States.

Table 3.2 PEI data on electoral integrity

Country	*Year*	*Office*	*PEI Index*	*PEI Index Rank*
Argentina	2013	Legislative	65.49	48
Argentina	2015	Legislative	62.99	56
Bolivia	2014	Presidential	55.63	90
Brazil	2014	Presidential	67.68	39
Chile	2013	Presidential	66.38	44
Colombia	2014	Legislative	61.16	67
Colombia	2014	Presidential	58.60	79
Costa Rica	2014	Presidential	80.81	5
Ecuador	2013	Presidential	54.78	92
El Salvador	2014	Presidential	59.03	76
El Salvador	2015	Legislative	49.08	122
Guatemala	2015	Presidential	47.95	125
Honduras	2013	Presidential	45.20	134
Mexico	2012	Presidential	62.28	63
Mexico	2015	Legislative	52.08	113
Panama	2014	Presidential	60.44	70
Paraguay	2013	Presidential	55.04	91
Uruguay	2014	Presidential	75.48	17
Venezuela	2012	Presidential	54.09	98
Venezuela	2013	Presidential	39.63	153
Venezuela	2015	Legislative	42.15	144
Regional average			57.90	79*
Canada	2015	Legislative	74.73	20
United States	2012	Presidential	62.81	58
United States	2014	Legislative	61.67	65

Note

* The median is reported for the PEI Index Rank variable.

While these variables tell us about the overall quality of elections, Table 3.3 reports regional scores on PEI variables related to voter access. The variables include the extent to which experts agreed that: some citizens were not listed in the voter register; the process of voting was easy; information about voting procedures was widely available; and the authorities distributed electoral information to citizens. All variables are coded so that higher scores indicate higher levels of voter access and information. The scores suggest that Latin American countries on average have fairly inclusive voter registries, especially compared to the United States. The region also scores well on the ease of the voting process and the availability of information about voting procedures, although there is wide variation within the region. For instance, Costa Rica scores highly on all measures, while Colombia's 2014 legislative election scores poorly on the voting process and El Salvador's 2015 legislative election scores poorly on the availability of information for voters.

Unfortunately, cross-national quantitative measures of key independent variables, such as the nature of political parties and historical legacies of election fraud, are nonexistent, making comprehensive statistical tests of the determinants

Table 3.3 PEI data related to voter access

Country	*Year*	*Office*	*Citizens not listed in voter registry*	*Ease of voting process*	*Availability of information about voting procedures*	*Information distributed to citizens by authorities*
Argentina	2013	Legislative	3.57	3.88	4.25	3.86
Argentina	2015	Legislative	3.71	4.14	4.00	3.70
Bolivia	2014	Presidential	2.90	3.82	3.80	3.60
Brazil	2014	Presidential	4.00	4.25	4.38	4.38
Chile	2013	Presidential	3.83	4.37	4.42	4.58
Colombia	2014	Legislative	2.50	2.50	3.38	4.13
Colombia	2014	Presidential	2.00	3.86	4.14	4.14
Costa Rica	2014	Presidential	4.17	4.75	4.86	5.00
Ecuador	2013	Presidential	3.18	3.69	4.00	3.85
El Salvador	2014	Presidential	3.08	4.43	4.07	4.21
El Salvador	2015	Legislative	3.11	2.56	2.78	2.67
Guatemala	2015	Presidential	2.00	3.67	3.56	3.89
Honduras	2013	Presidential	2.25	3.25	3.75	3.50
Mexico	2012	Presidential	3.86	4.57	4.57	4.21
Mexico	2015	Legislative	3.33	4.09	4.09	4.09
Panama	2014	Presidential	3.83	4.13	4.14	3.88
Paraguay	2013	Presidential	2.36	4.00	4.00	3.92
Uruguay	2014	Presidential	4.17	4.25	4.50	4.13
Venezuela	2012	Presidential	3.50	4.36	4.36	4.36
Venezuela	2013	Presidential	3.00	4.29	3.14	2.86
Venezuela	2015	Legislative	2.95	3.95	3.50	3.09
Regional average			*3.21*	*3.94*	*3.99*	*3.91*
Canada	2015	Legislative	2.71	4.38	4.50	4.46
United States	2012	Presidential	1.92	3.33	3.80	4.07
United States	2014	Legislative	1.38	3.44	3.78	4.11

of election administration inclusiveness impossible. Reliable global data on the composition of electoral management bodies are also lacking.[3] However, data are available on the partisanship and professionalism of electoral management bodies in Latin America. Thus, the PEI data can be used to offer a preliminary test of the relationship between EMB structure and inclusiveness.

I use Rosas' (2010) measures of the partisan autonomy and professional autonomy of Latin American EMBs. Rosas employs a three-point scale of partisan autonomy, based on the extent to which parties have a role in nominating and selecting top EMB officials. Those EMBs whose members are chosen by the judiciary are scored most autonomous, while EMBs are scored least autonomous where parties directly select election commissioners. Cases where parties play a role in selecting EMB members through confirmation in the legislature are scored as intermediate (Rosas 2010, 79–80).

Rosas (2010) also employs a measure of professional autonomy, with EMBs scored as more autonomous when a greater number of political actors are involved in the appointment of EMB members, when the judiciary or civil society play a role in nominating EMB members, and when EMB members enjoy longer tenure compared to the tenure of the legislative and executive officials who appoint them (Rosas 2010, 79). Both the partisan autonomy and professional autonomy variables are coded so that higher scores indicate greater autonomy.

We would expect that more autonomous EMBs would be associated with more inclusive electoral practices, other things being equal. The limited number of observations makes multivariate testing of this hypothesis infeasible, so I limit the analysis to simple bivariate regression models of the effect of EMB autonomy on the PEI variables related to inclusiveness. The regression results are reported in Table 3.4.

In all cases, the regression coefficients are in the expected positive direction, indicating that higher levels of EMB autonomy are associated with more inclusive voter registries, an easy voting process, and accessible information for

Table 3.4 Bivariate regression models of EMB autonomy and election administration inclusiveness

	Information distributed to citizens by authorities		*Availability of information about voting procedures*		*Ease of voting process*		*Some citizens not registered*	
EMB partisan autonomy	0.193	–	0.254	–	0.342*	–	0.300	–
EMB professional autonomy	–	0.075	–	0.082*	–	0.138**	–	0.061

Notes
* p-value < .05 (two-tailed test)
** p-value < .01 (two-tailed test)

voters to learn about the voting process. However, the coefficients reach statistical significance in only three of the eight models. Partisan autonomy is significantly associated with the easiness of the voting process, while the professional autonomy measure is significantly associated with the easiness of the voting process and information about voting procedures.

This test is quite preliminary given the small sample size and data limitations, but the results are consistent with previous findings that non-partisan electoral management bodies are associated with higher-quality elections in Latin America (Hartlyn, McCoy, and Mustillo 2008). The PEI data suggest that this relationship applies more specifically to election administration inclusiveness: countries with non-partisan EMBs appear more likely to make the voting process easier, and possibly to be more inclusive in other ways as well.

What this rudimentary quantitative test cannot tell us is the conditions under which non-partisan EMBs produce more inclusive election practices and the mechanisms through which they do so. The detailed case studies in later chapters take up that task. First, however, the remainder of this chapter briefly examines two cases to assess the plausibility of the theory presented in Chapter 2.

Election administration inclusiveness in the United States

Unlike the other cases examined in this study, the United States did not undergo a transition to democracy in the late twentieth century. Yet, the evolution of election administration practices over the past several decades can be explained at least in part with the theoretical framework developed in Chapter 2.

It is impossible to measure the election administration inclusiveness of the United States as a whole, given the country's federal system and decentralized election administration. Election rules are determined to a significant degree at the state level, yielding 50 distinct election administration systems. In general, recent decades have seen a trend toward greater inclusiveness in the United States, with early voting, no-excuse absentee voting, and voting by mail becoming more widespread. Automatic voter registration has spread more recently, with five states adopting it between March 2015 and July 2016. But, at the same time, many states adopted election practices that pose obstacles to participation for some voters. Such measures include cutbacks in early voting, strict rules on third-party voter registration, and especially the introduction of voter identification laws. These developments, as well as earlier efforts to restrict the vote through administrative means, are explicable in terms of the specter of election fraud and, even more so, partisan competition and partisan control over election management.

While the United States is not a newly democratized country with a recent past of authoritarianism and election rigging, the country does have a long history of election manipulation (Campbell 2005), and the historical record is replete with efforts to make voting more difficult that were motivated, or at least justified, by the desire to eliminate election fraud. Such efforts include the introduction of voter registration requirements and lengthy residency periods to vote within a jurisdiction (Hayduck 2005, 21; Keyssar 2001, 103–4, 122–23). As Keyssar (2012) explains, many tedious bureaucratic procedures enacted in the late-nineteenth and early-twentieth centuries were justified by the desire "to 'preserve the purity of the ballot box.' "

However, in recent decades, electoral fraud has been confined to local cases of absentee ballot fraud and the occasional case of dishonest poll workers. Widespread irregularities, such as ballot box stuffing, altering vote tallies, and voter fraud, have been absent or exceedingly rare (e.g., Minnite 2010). However, the lack of a specter of fraud has not prevented the issue of election fraud from being brandished by partisan actors who have sought to shape election administration practices for partisan benefit. It has been these partisan interests that have most shaped election administration rules in the United States.

This is seen historically in the post-Reconstruction South, where a slew of procedural impediments to the vote – including stringent voter registration laws, literacy tests, and poll taxes – were erected after outright disenfranchisement became untenable. While racism was central to these disenfranchising moves, the partisan interests of the Democratic Party in the South were also behind laws to eliminate the African-American and poor white vote (Campbell 2005, 102–3; Kousser 1974). The adoption of voting procedures ostensibly aimed at reducing fraud, such as the secret ballot and voter registration, was also in part intended to disenfranchise some voters for partisan advantage (Campbell 2005, 97–100; Keyssar 2001, 126–27).

Partisan conflicts have also been central to more recent election administration reforms in the United States. The 1993 National Voter Registration Act (NVRA), which mandated voter registration services to be offered in motor vehicle and public assistance offices, was passed by a unified Democratic government over Republican opposition (Martinez and Hill 1999, 296–97), and Democrats have generally supported election day registration while Republicans have opposed it (Carbó and Wright 2008, 68, 71; Hanmer 2009). Discussion of automatic voter registration has also tended to fall along partisan lines, with Democrats supporting the measure and Republicans generally opposing it (NPR 2016). Similarly, partisan divisions over voter identification requirements and other election administration procedures have been intense since 2000, with Republicans usually endorsing more restrictive rules ostensibly to prevent voter fraud and Democrats supporting more inclusive rules to ensure access for voters likely to support the party (Hasen 2012).

These partisan divides over election administration practices are facilitated by patterns of party identification in the electorate, with African-American, Latino/Latina, and low-income voters more likely to support the Democratic Party than the Republican Party (see, e.g., Pew Research Center 2015). With race, ethnicity, and social class correlated with partisanship, the parties are able to craft administrative practices that facilitate or impede the participation of particular social groups. For instance, voter ID laws often require voters to show forms of identification that African Americans and Latinos/Latinas are less likely to possess than whites are – and, for this reason, some such laws have been struck down by the courts as discriminatory (The Economist 2016). Indeed, statistical analyses have linked higher levels of turnout among African-American and low-income voters to the adoption of more restrictive election administration measures in Republican-controlled states (Bentele and O'Brien 2013).

While the social correlates of partisan identification facilitate the use of election administration practices as partisan weapons, highly competitive electoral environments give parties incentive to deploy those weapons. In the US context, this is seen in partisan conflict over voting procedures in highly competitive "swing" states, such as haggling over early voting in Ohio and Florida in 2012, with Republicans in both states attempting to cut back on early voting hours.

Several studies find statistical evidence of the effect of competitiveness on election administration inclusiveness. Bentele and O'Brien (2013) find that increasing competitiveness at the state level in presidential elections is associated with the adoption of less inclusive practices where Republicans hold a majority in the state government, but not in states with Democratic majorities. Increasing turnout among African-American and low-income voters was also associated with a greater likelihood of adopting voting restrictions by Republican-controlled states. Hicks and colleagues (2015) similarly find that highly competitive election outcomes and Republican majorities in state government are associated with higher probabilities of adopting strict voter ID laws.

Partisan control over election management has also affected inclusiveness. While most election administration practices bearing on voter access in the United States are determined through legislation, some are determined by election administrators. Unlike in most countries, the United States does not have a national electoral management body; instead, electoral management is a patchwork of state and local election officials. In many cases, the top state election official and county election officials are partisans, opening the door to charges of partisan motives behind election administration decisions, such as where to locate polling places, the hours available for early voting, and the methods used to purge voters from the voter registry.

Such controversies are particularly sharp in highly competitive states. Leading up to the 2016 election, for instance, some Republican officials on county election boards in North Carolina pushed for reducing early voting hours and eliminating polling places on college campuses (Campbell 2016). In Ohio, the Republican secretary of state attempted to remove voters from the registry if they had not voted for six years and did not respond to a mailing from his office; the move was blocked by a federal court (Graham 2016). Both North Carolina and Ohio are closely contested states in presidential races.

Because of the country's complex federal system of election administration, the effects of partisan control over electoral management are limited to those jurisdictions where the party controlling the electoral machinery has motives to restrict the vote. Most provisions related to voter access are contained in state and federal legislation, but partisan control of electoral management impacts election administration inclusiveness in some jurisdictions, particularly those where electoral competition is fierce.

In sum, the pattern of election administration inclusiveness in the United States appears to be consistent with the theory presented in Chapter 2, at least in broad outline. Patterns of party loyalties, electoral competitiveness, partisan control over electoral management, and (to a lesser extent) concerns about fraud all affect inclusiveness in the expected ways. This suggests that these variables are relevant not only in newly democratized countries but also in established democracies.

Election administration inclusiveness in Honduras

The case of Honduras offers a radically different context to study election administration. The country began its transition to democracy at the outset of the 1980s after a prolonged period of political instability following the caudillo rule of Tibucio Carías (1933–1949). Elections had been eliminated under Carías (Morris 1984, 9), while the period following his fall from power saw civilian governments replaced by elections and military coups. From 1972 through 1981, the military directly controlled the presidency, and during this period the military regime formed an advisory council tasked with producing a new electoral law, although the two main political parties – the Liberals and Nationalists – refused to participate (Morris 1984, 50). The transition back to civilian government proceeded in 1980, when the military convoked constituent assembly elections, and in 1981 when a civilian government was elected in a clean election. This marked the transition to a formal electoral democracy, although the military retained extensive prerogatives and human rights abuses persisted (Schulz and Schulz 1994, 80–85).

In this early period of Honduran electoral democracy, election administration inclusiveness was generally low. Persistent obstacles were posed by voter registration. Honduras' voter registry suffered from a number of shortcomings, to the point where municipal elections in 1983 were postponed because a new electoral census to replace the old voter registration lists had not been completed (Morris 1984, 70; Rosenberg 1989, 49). In subsequent elections, the Liberal and Nationalist parties frequently exchanged accusations of voter roll manipulation, such as removing eligible voters (IFES 1993, 9).

Many Hondurans were disenfranchised by registration problems despite the fact that voter registration is automatic, with the National Registry of Persons (or RNP, by its Spanish acronym) issuing the national ID card needed to vote and compiling the voter lists (IFES 1993, 5; OAS 2002, 5). The most common problems were delays in delivering ID cards to citizens and citizens with ID not appearing on the voter lists.[4] For the 1993 election, many citizens were on the voter list but had not yet received their ID card and were therefore unable to vote, while many thousands who had ID cards were disenfranchised because they were not on the voter list. Still others found themselves transferred to a different polling station at the request of political parties (IFES 1993, 9, 23).

Obtaining the national ID card could be time consuming, with one study reporting a four- to six-month process and that "people have tired of continually returning to RNP offices to find the card not yet available and therefore have stopped trying" (Carter Center 2013, 26, 73). The process is especially difficult for those who lack a birth certificate, who must go through several bureaucratic steps (Carter Center 2013, 23–24). In addition to these obstacles, an early registration closing date – two months in 1993 (IFES 1993, 5) and four months in 2001 (OAS 2002, 8, note 11) – added to the restrictiveness of voter registration.

Over time, these obstacles abated somewhat. In 2001, the RNP made efforts to improve the accuracy of the voters list and to expedite issuing birth certificates. For the first time, preliminary voter lists were also publicized before election day to allow voters to verify and correct their information (IFES 2001b, 3–4), and the lists were sent to political parties for inspection (OAS 2002, 5). Despite these improvements, delays in distributing identity cards persisted (IFES 2001b, 6), and political parties distributed some ID cards to their supporters. As election observers noted, "[b]y having access to voters ID, in a way, political parties have direct control as to who can and cannot vote" (IFES 2001b, 11).[5] During the 2013 election, efforts to distribute ID cards were improved, including the use of mobile brigades to receive applications and deliver identity cards. Observers noted shortcomings in publicizing the use of these brigades, however (EUEOM 2013, 16).

Aside from shortcomings in delivering identity cards, other voter registration practices have been fairly inclusive. The country's electoral laws have required provisional voter lists to be distributed to political parties and posted in public places for voters to consult; purging of the voter rolls has been prohibited during the 120 days before an election (later shortened to 90 days); and those turning 18 years old by election day are able to register in advance of the closing date. The most recent electoral law requires the Supreme Electoral Tribunal (TSE) to establish a permanent electronic system for citizens to consult the electoral census, and anyone not appearing on the electoral census can solicit their inscription up to 90 days before the election.

In addition to voter registration, the location of polling places posed obstacles to voting. Until 1997, polling places were located only in municipal centers (*cabeceras municipales*), and voters in each municipality were assigned to polling places alphabetically, rather than being assigned to the polling station closest to their residence (IFES 1993, 16, 36). Subsequently, voters were able to vote closer to home and the number of polling places increased in 2001 (IFES 2001b, 4; US Department of State, 2000). While reaching a polling place became easier, the country still lacks any system of absentee voting.

Finally, voter education efforts were minimal in the 1990s and early 2000s. Prior to the 1993 election, "only one announcement was shown on television explaining electoral procedures, four days before the actual day of the elections" (IFES 1993, 5). In 2001, observers again noted the paucity of public information campaigns to inform voters of voting procedures or the location of polling places (IFES 2001a, 1; OAS 2002, 19, 21). The country's new electoral law of 2004 included civic-electoral education among the TSE's duties (Art. 15 and 155–57), and voter education efforts improved in subsequent elections (OAS 2008, 8), although observers were critical of the failure to provide voting materials and information campaigns in indigenous languages (EUEOM 2013, 5, 22).

The restrictive voter registration and polling-place practices adopted during Honduras' democratic transition are consistent with the argument developed in Chapter 2, as the country had a history of extensive election fraud, political parties that had some ability to identify opposition supporters, and a partisan electoral management body.

Honduran politics in the mid-twentieth century was marked by election rigging. Elections held in 1956 resulted in the incumbent president's party receiving an implausible 90 percent of the vote; in response, the military carried out a coup and nullified the election results (Morris 1984, 11–12). A 1963 coup brought to power an air force colonel who was later elected president in an election marked by widespread fraud allegations in rural areas (Rosenberg 1986, 9). Constituent assembly elections held in 1965 have been described as "a carefully orchestrated fraud" (Schulz and Schulz 1994, 33) and "obviously fraudulent," as the National Party ensured that "thugs and compliant army men were at the polling places to insure the proper result" (Anderson 1988, 131). Similar tactics were used in municipal elections in 1968 (Anderson 1988, 132; Morris 1984, 40).

Fears of fraud continued during the transition to civilian government. The 1980 constituent assembly election was held while the military was in power and the National Party was prevalent in government positions. There was widespread anticipation of election fraud and complaints of irregularities with voter registration, and some elements in the military called for a delay of the voting and considered a coup to prevent a fraudulent election (Anderson 1988, 146; Morris 1984, 52; Schulz and Schulz 1994, 59).

As it turned out, the 1980 elections were conducted fairly (Anderson 1988, 146), but elections the following year were marked by accusations of voter registration fraud, with the National Party claiming "that the Liberal-dominated TNE had discriminated against Nationalist party members in its purge of the polling lists" (Morris 1984, 56). Concerns about fraud surfaced again for the 1985 presidential election, with charges that the voter rolls were inflated with foreigners and multiple registrations, while "[i]t was rumored that ballots existed with [the incumbent president's favored candidate] Mejía's name already checked" (Schulz and Schulz 1994, 130). Nevertheless, the election turned out to be free of significant fraud. But mutual accusations between the Liberal and National parties recurred during the 1989 election, with accusations that the parties were registering foreigners to vote (Schulz and Schulz 1994, 131, 269).

In sum, Honduras has a long history of electoral fraud and partisan recriminations over electoral manipulation. As Morris (1984, 69) puts it, "Both of the traditional political parties have utilized corrupt electoral practices, and both have complained of unconscionable fraud and manipulation, each accusing its historical rival. Pejoratively, Hondurans have ridiculed themselves by referring to such elections as Honduran style."

Yet, for the most part, Honduran elections were conducted fairly in the 1980s, and subsequent elections in 1990 and 1997 were clean (Booth, Wade, and

Walker 2015, 219, 220). The 1997 and 2001 elections saw the introduction of measures to safeguard the voter registry from manipulation, such as requiring the voter's fingerprint on requests for address changes (IFES 2001a, 2; IFES 2001b, 3). By 2001, election observers reported that "there was a clear consensus among Honduran political actors that no serious fraud or manipulation was expected for the voting" (IFES 2001b, 6). Subsequent observer reports note the generally transparent nature of the voting process (EUEOM 2013, 5), although some problems with election integrity remain: the voter registry is bloated and vote buying is thought to be common, as are fraudulent changes of address for voting purposes (EUEOM 2013, 4, 9, 15).

As Honduras transitioned to democracy under the cloud of election fraud, it did so with a two-party system that had existed for most of the twentieth century and a tradition of strong party identification. According to Taylor-Robinson (2003, 558), "voters were considered to be born with their party loyalties." The two major parties, the Liberals and Nationalists, are clientelistic and generally conservative parties, with the Liberal Party including some left-leaning factions (Taylor-Robinson 2011, 369) and the Nationalist Party historically aligning itself closely with the military. At least during Honduras's transition to democracy, the Liberal Party's strongest support came from more developed and urban regions, while the National Party was stronger in rural areas (Morris 1984, 71).

The well-formed partisan preferences of individual voters, along with the geographic differences in party support, no doubt facilitated attempts to purge the voter rolls of opposition supporters. At the same time, the centralization of polling places meant that transportation on election day was important in rural areas; as one author put it, "the party that can marshal the most buses for its known supporters is the one most likely to win in the backward regions of the country" (Anderson 1988, 168). At the same time, the two major parties may have shared an interest in limiting the turnout of independent voters. As a foremost scholar of Honduran politics points out, "[i]t has even been suggested that traditional parties may see abstention as useful, since 'independents' are thought more likely to abstain than partisans" (Taylor-Robinson 2007, 522).

The major political parties also controlled the electoral management body. The National Elections Tribunal (TNE) was established by the 1978 election law (Morris 1984, 69). In 1982, Congress created the National Register of Persons, which was to issue ID cards and compile an electoral registry (Morris 1984, 69–70). The TNE was partisan in composition, with each political party naming a member to the national tribunal as well as to departmental and local tribunals and polling tables. The Supreme Court also named a representative to the national electoral tribunal. Political parties could remove their members from electoral tribunals at will (IFES 1993, 3–4, 36). Partisanship was so pervasive that political parties rather than the TNE conducted poll-worker training, as poll workers were selected by the parties themselves (IFES 2001a, 5; 2001b, 10). A 2004 reform transformed the TNE into the Supreme Electoral Tribunal. All three members of the national tribunal have party affiliations (OAS 2008, 5). As of the 2013 elections, the TSE still did not directly train poll workers, instead training party trainers who in turn trained their poll workers (EUEOM 2013, 14). Along with party identification, partisan control of the EMB no doubt facilitated partisan attempts at purging voters from the rolls – or at least led to concerns of such purging.

In summary, the general pattern in Honduras is consistent with other cases examined in later chapters: a history of election fraud was followed by restrictive election administration measures, exacerbated by party loyalties in the electorate and partisan control of the EMB that facilitated restrictive practices. Over time, concerns about election fraud subsided, although the electoral body remained staffed by partisan appointees. The experience of holding several electoral processes free of significant fraud was followed by efforts to make voting easier, for instance by decentralizing polling places. Yet, the distribution of identity cards, and therefore voter registration, remained largely in partisan hands.

Conclusion

This chapter has presented descriptive data on election administration in Latin America, as well as some very preliminary evidence that non-partisan electoral management bodies are associated with inclusive election administration practices. Brief case studies of the United States and Honduras also suggest that recent histories of election fraud, the ability of parties to identify their opponents' supporters in the electorate, and partisan control over election management contribute to restrictive election administration practices. The following chapters provide more detailed case studies that trace the causal connections between these variables and election administration inclusiveness in Central America.

Notes

1 I use the PEI 4.0 dataset, which covers elections in 139 countries held between July 1, 2012, and December 31, 2015. The data are available at Harvard University's dataverse site at https://dataverse.harvard.edu/dataverse/PEI.

2 I use the PEI Index (Imputed) variable.

3 For a discussion of the challenges in measuring EMB partisanship, see Hyde and Pallister 2015.

4 Due to errors on the voter lists, in 1989 the National Elections Tribunal (TNE) employed a system of provisional balloting for those voters with a valid ID whose names did not appear on the voter list. This system was considered again for the 1993 election but ultimately was not employed following a Supreme Court decision (IFES 1993, 9–10).

5 The same observer mission noted, however, "that problems with the identity card process affected all political parties equally and in no way involved fraud or manipulation" (IFES 2001a, 4).

References

Anderson, Thomas P. 1988. *Politics in Central America: Guatemala, El Salvador, Honduras, and Nicaragua*. Westport, CT: Praeger Publishers.

Bentele, Keith G., and Erin E. O'Brien. 2013. "Jim Crow 2.0? Why States Consider and Adopt Restrictive Voter Access Policies." *Perspectives on Politics* 11 (4): 1088–116.

Booth, John A., Christine J. Wade, and Thomas W. Walker. 2015. *Understanding Central America: Global Forces, Rebellion, and Change*. Boulder: Westview Press.

Campbell, Colin. 2016. "NC Republican Party Seeks 'Party Line Changes' to Limit Early Voting Hours." *The News & Observer*, August 17. www.newsobserver.com/news/politics-government/election/article96179857.html.

Campbell, Tracy. 2005. *Deliver the Vote: A History of Election Fraud, an American Political Tradition—1742–2004*. New York: Carroll & Graf Publishers.

Carbó, Steven, and Brenda Wright. 2008. "Promise and Practice of Election Day Registration." In *America Votes! A Guide to Modern Election Law and Voting Rights*, Benjamin E. Griffith, ed. American Bar Association Section of State and Local Government Law.

Carter Center. 2013. Voter Identification Requirements and Public International Law: An Examination of Africa and Latin America. www.cartercenter.org/resources/pdfs/peace/democracy/des/voter-identification-requirements.pdf

The Economist. 2016. "North Carolina Voter ID Law Is Struck Down as Racially Discriminatory." August 1. www.economist.com/blogs/democracyinamerica/2016/08/its-duck.

EUEOM (European Union Election Observation Mission). 2013. Honduras: Final Report, General Elections 2013. www.eods.eu/library/EUEOM%20FR%20HONDURAS13.02.2014_en.pdf.

Graham, David A. 2016. "Ohio Can't Purge Infrequent Voters from Its Rolls." *The Atlantic*, September 23. www.theatlantic.com/politics/archive/2016/09/ohio-voting-purge/501404/.

Hanmer, Michael J. 2009. *Discount Voting: Voter Registration Reforms and Their Effects*. New York: Cambridge University Press.

Hartlyn, Jonathan, Jennifer McCoy, and Thomas M. Mustillo. 2008. "Electoral Governance Matters: Explaining the Quality of Elections in Latin America." *Comparative Political Studies* 41 (4): 73–98.

Hasen, Rick. 2012. *The Voting Wars: From Florida 2000 to the Next Election Meltdown*. New Haven: Yale University Press.

Hayduck, Ronald. 2005. *Gatekeepers to the Franchise: Shaping Election Administration in New York*. DeKalb: Northern Illinois University Press.

Hicks, William D., Seth C. McKee, Mitchell D. Sellers, and Daniel A. Smith. 2015. "A Principle or a Strategy? Voter Identification Laws and Partisan Competition in the American States." *Political Research Quarterly* 68 (1): 18–33.

Hyde, Susan, and Kevin Pallister. 2015. "Election Administration, Election Observation, and Election Quality." In *Routledge Handbook of Comparative Political Institutions*, Jennifer Gandhi and Rubén Ruiz-Rufino, eds. New York: Routledge.

IFES (International Foundation for Electoral Systems). 1993. Honduras 1993 Elections: Election Observation Mission Report.

IFES. 2001a. Report of the Second IFES Pre-Electoral Mission to Honduras, November 6–10, 2001.

IFES. 2001b. Election Observation Mission, Honduras General Elections, November 25, 2001, Final Report.

Keyssar, Alexander. 2001. *The Right to Vote: The Contested History of Democracy in the United States*. New York: Basic Books.

Keyssar, Alexander. 2012. "The Strange Career of Voter Suppression." *New York Times*, Campaign Stops Blog, February 12. http://campaignstops.blogs.nytimes.com/2012/02/12/the-strange-career-of-voter-suppression/.

Kousser, J. Morgan. 1974. *The Shaping of Southern Politics: Suffrage Restriction and the Establishment of the One-Party South, 1880–1910*. New Haven: Yale University Press.

Martinez, Michael D., and David Hill. 1999. "Did Motor Voter Work?" *American Politics Quarterly* 27 (3): 296–315.

Minnite, Lorraine C. 2010. *The Myth of Voter Fraud*. Ithaca: Cornell University Press.

Morris, James A. 1984. *Honduras: Caudillo Politics and Military Rulers*. Boulder and London: Westview Press.

NPR. 2016. "Automatic Registration Is the Latest Chapter in Fight over Voting Rights." February 17. www.npr.org/2016/02/17/466986646/automatic-registration-is-the-latest-chapter-in-fight-over-voting-rights.

OAS (Organization of American States). 2002. Report of the Electoral Observation Mission in Honduras, 2001.

OAS. 2008. Informe de la Misión de Observación Electoral en la República de Honduras, Elecciones Generales, 27 Noviembre 2005.

Pew Research Center. 2015. Party Identification Trends, 1992–2014. www.people-press.org/2015/04/07/party-identification-trends-1992-2014/.

Rosas, Guillermo. 2010. "Trust in Elections and the Institutional Design of Electoral Authorities: Evidence from Latin America." *Electoral Studies* 29 (1): 74–90.

Rosenberg, Mark B. 1986. "Honduras: An Introduction." In *Honduras Confronts Its Future: Contending Perspectives on Critical Issues*, Mark B. Rosenberg and Philip Shephard, eds. Boulder: Lynne Rienner.

Rosenberg, Mark B. 1989. "Can Democracy Survive the Democrats? From Transition to Consolidation in Honduras." In *Elections and Democracy in Central America*, John A. Booth and Mitchell A. Seligson, eds. Chapel Hill and London: University of North Carolina Press.

Schulz, Donald E. and Deborah Sundloff Schulz. 1994. *The United States, Honduras, and the Crisis in Central America*. Boulder: Westview Press.

Taylor-Robinson, Michelle M. 2003. "The Elections in Honduras, November 2001." *Electoral Studies* 22 (3): 553–59.

Taylor-Robinson, Michelle M. 2007. "Presidential and Congressional Elections in Honduras, November 2005." *Electoral Studies* 26 (2): 521–24.

Taylor-Robinson, Michelle M. 2011. "The Honduran General Elections of 2009." *Electoral Studies* 30 (2): 369–72.

U.S. Department of State. 2000. Honduras. Country Reports on Human Rights Practices, 1999. www.state.gov/j/drl/rls/hrrpt/1999/392.htm.

4 Guatemala

Raising obstacles to voter participation, 1983–2003

Guatemala has held relatively free and fair elections since the country's return to civilian rule in 1985. Prior to that transition, Guatemalan politics was marked by direct and indirect military rule following the 1954 coup that ended a brief democratic period. While elections were held regularly throughout the 1960s and 1970s, contestation was limited by the banning of leftist parties, the permitted parties' nomination of active military officers as presidential candidates and, in later years, election fraud. By the early 1980s, in the context of economic crisis, rigged elections, and massive state violence against a guerrilla insurgency, the military regime found itself lacking legitimacy both domestically and internationally. In this context, the military sought a return to civilian rule, and during the military-led transition a new electoral regime was constructed.

The transition began with a military coup in 1982, before the fraudulently elected winner of that year's presidential election took office. The new government formed a committee on electoral matters, tasked with drafting a new electoral law, and the committee's work resulted in a series of laws issued by the government in March 1983.

One of these laws created an independent electoral management body – the Supreme Electoral Tribunal (TSE) – made up of five non-partisan magistrates to be chosen from candidates (all lawyers) put forward by a nominating committee consisting of university rectors and law faculty deans. Other laws created the Citizens Registry (charged with overseeing the voter lists) under the control of the new TSE and established less restrictive rules for forming political parties.[1] Another law was to create a new national identity card to replace the old *cédula de vecindad*; however, this law never went into effect, as the government gave in to public pressure generated by concerns about the military regime gathering personal information through the new registration process (Escobar Armas 1987, 17–18; Gálvez Borrell 2008, 135; Interview 16; Medrano 2005, 42). Consequently, a new law on voter registration was put into place, and more than 20 years would pass before a new identification card was finally introduced.[2]

With this structure in place, elections were held in 1984 for a national constituent assembly, with a temporary election law put in place to govern the process. The constituent assembly was tasked with drafting a new electoral law, which was promulgated in 1985. The assembly used the 1983 and 1984 electoral laws as a template when combining the various decrees into a unified Electoral and Political Parties Law (LEPP) (Interview 19).[3] The 1985 electoral law established the framework for Guatemala's electoral regime up to the present. As a law of constitutional rank, any amendments must be approved by a two-thirds vote in Congress and pass a prior review by the Constitutional Court. The law has been amended a number of times but, until 2004, the reforms consisted of relatively minor changes.[4]

The 1983–1985 electoral laws and the establishment of a non-partisan electoral commission marked a profound departure from the electoral regime that had been in place previously. The electoral body created by the 1965 constitution – the *Registro Electoral* – had been under the executive branch's control, which facilitated election rigging. Additionally, contestation had been limited by onerous requirements for the registration of political parties and the arbitrary application of those requirements, in addition to an outright ban on leftist parties (Gálvez Borrell 2008, 72–73, 88, 132; Interview 19). Under the new legislation, the selection of non-partisan election officials, nominated by a committee of legal experts and approved by at least two-thirds of Congress, resulted in a technocratic and neutral electoral management body.

However, the electoral laws and subsequent regulatory decisions of the TSE also included provisions that presented significant obstacles to voter participation. In fact, these two features of the new electoral regime – ensuring fair elections free of fraud and raising substantial barriers to voter participation – were intimately related. In order to inoculate the electoral system against fraud, the act of voting was in many ways made more difficult. These administrative and procedural restrictions ranged from getting registered to vote, to finding information about voting procedures, to reaching the polling station and casting one's ballot. This chapter documents the barriers put in place, discusses the effects of those barriers on voter participation, and explains why procedural barriers to participation were put in place as Guatemala's electoral system was restructured during the country's democratic transition.

Election administration and procedural barriers to voting

Voter registration

The administrative barriers faced by voters began with voter registration, which has been described as "a long road of obstacles" (Boneo and Torres-Rivas 2000, 105) and "unduly bureaucratic" (NDI 1995, 9). Unlike countries that use some form of automatic registration, voter registration in Guatemala is voter-initiated and requires several steps. The process for registering required the citizen to go to one of the delegations of the Citizens Registry located in each municipal center. The need to travel to the centrally located registry, often a great distance from one's residence, created a burden for many people, especially in rural areas and for those lacking transportation (OAS 1997, 30; UNDP 2005, 198).

The process required two trips to the registry on the part of the citizen: one visit to fill out the registration form and a second visit (after the registry had checked the applicant's information) to have his or her identity document stamped with the voter registration information (Boneo and Torres-Rivas 2000, 109). When initiating the process, the citizen would present an identity document and fill out a long form, requiring extensive information. As an election observer report noted,

> if one considers that the information required during the registration process has already been supplied by the citizen during the process of inscription in the civil registry after turning 18 years old, this proceeding constitutes in reality a duplication of the civil registration process.
>
> (OAS 1997, 31)

Thus, rather than automatically adding citizens to the voter rolls from the information available in the civil registries – which issued the identification documents – citizens were required to initiate and carry out a separate process to register to vote. Had plans for a new identification document been carried out in 1983, greater coordination between the civil registry and voter registry would have resulted.[5] Instead, the country maintained its municipal-based civil registry system, with the issuance of identification documents controlled by the municipalities, and instituted a separate voter registry.

For the many citizens lacking an identity document, prior trips to the municipal capital were required in order to register in the civil registry and obtain a *cédula.* Obtaining a *cédula* in turn required a birth certificate, which could require multiple trips to the registry office and payment of a fee (Boneo and Torres-Rivas 2000, 106–8; Sieder et al. 2002, 30). Only after obtaining the correct identification could a citizen then register to vote. Traveling to the municipal center to carry out these transactions could require citizens to spend an entire day away from their home or farm and pay for transportation, while a further financial burden was imposed by requiring citizens to purchase photographs for their *cédula.* These procedures could also alienate indigenous people who "often wish to avoid taking photographs or signing their names, fearing they will be manipulated by unscrupulous people" (NDI 1995, 9; see also López-Pintor and Urrutia 2002, 38).

Another obstacle to voter registration was the de facto adoption of a residency requirement in 1987. Whereas, for the 1984 and 1985 elections, citizens could register to vote in the jurisdiction in which they were living at the time, after 1987 citizens could only register to vote in the municipality where their *cédula* had been issued. For instance, a person from the municipality of Cobán (in the country's north) living in Guatemala City in 1985 could register and vote in Guatemala City; after 1987, the citizen would either need to obtain a new identity document issued in Guatemala City or return to Cobán to vote (Conde Rada 2003, 38; Interview 13). No system of absentee voting was in place to accommodate such circumstances. This change to a voter roll based on *vecindad,*[6] as it is known, was a decision of the TSE rather than a provision in the electoral law and was included in its 1987 regulation (*reglamento*) of the electoral law. By requiring voters to hold a *cédula* from the municipality in which they register to vote, the TSE essentially adopted a quite restrictive residency requirement, since one year of residency was required to obtain that ID in a given municipality (Interview 14). Thus, when moving to a new municipality, the citizen would need to carry out two separate time-consuming proceedings – obtaining a new *cédula* and registering to vote – or return to their old municipality to vote (which would also involve voting for local officials in a jurisdiction in which the citizen no longer lived).[7]

These obstacles to voter registration were compounded by the limited opportunities for voters and political parties to review the preliminary voter register and rectify errors or omissions (Boneo and Rivas 2000, 53–54; NDI 1991, 44). Although the voter roll is formally a public document that interested parties may consult (LEPP, Art. 225), citizens had to visit a registry office to do so, as the lists were not posted in public places prior to election day. However, in recent elections, the TSE has distributed the voter register to political parties, while also being criticized for including minimal information in the distributed lists, thereby making it difficult to rectify errors (EUEOM 2003, 11; OAS 2005, 11; 2009, 23–24).

In addition to what citizens must do to register to vote is the issue of when they must do it. The electoral law requires voter registration to end 90 days prior to election day (LEPP, Art. 9), meaning voters must register before campaigns and civic education programs reach their most intense stages (OAS 1997, 31). The 90-day closing date is relative to the first round of elections; because Guatemala employs a run-off election for the presidency if no candidate receives a majority in the first round (which has been the case in every presidential contest since the return to democratic rule), voters cannot participate in the final election of president without registering some 5 months ahead of time. One observer mission to the 1995 elections noted that many citizens tried to register to vote during this period between the closing of registration and election day (OAS 1997, 31), and many people apparently also try to register between the first and second rounds of presidential elections as well (Prensa Libre 1985a [hereafter PL]). It should be noted that, for the 1985 elections, which were held under a temporary electoral law, the deadline for voter registration was only 2 months before election day and, for the 1984 constituent assembly elections, the deadline was an even shorter 30 days.[8] A reform to the election law in 1987 pushed the deadline back to three months.[9]

In short, as an OAS observer mission put it, "the registration process in Guatemala, given the socioeconomic characteristics of the country, is long and costly, both in terms of time and money" (OAS 2005, 18). And while the voter registration process became easier in later years (as discussed in the following chapter), it continued to be burdensome for potential voters.

Getting to the ballot box

In addition to registering to vote, citizens also face the task of getting to their polling place in order to cast their ballot. Until 2007, this task presented a significant barrier for many eligible voters in Guatemala. Voting centers were limited to the capitals (*cabeceras*) of each of the country's 330 municipalities,[10] each of which is roughly equivalent to a US county; the location of polling sites outside of these capitals was prohibited, first by the 1984 decree calling for the election of a constituent assembly and by the temporary law governing the 1985 elections, and more forcefully in the 1985 electoral law.[11]

As a result of this centralization, many voters – mainly those residing in rural areas – would need to travel long distances to reach their polling site. Each polling site, known as a voting center (*centro de votación*), contains a number of voting tables (*Juntas Receptoras de Votos*, JRV), ranging from just one or two JRVs to several dozen. While the electoral law fixes a maximum of 600 voters assigned to each JRV, the important factor is the concentration of JRVs within a limited number of voting centers. Thus, there were 5,142 JRVs in 1985, and this gradually increased to 8,885 by 2003.[12] However, the number of voting centers was much more limited: for the 2003 elections, for example, there were roughly 1,245 voting centers (López-Pintor 2005, 122)[13] – a relatively small number for the country's 5 million registered voters, averaging over 4,000 registered voters per voting center.

For those residing in rural areas – about 60 percent of the population in the mid-1990s and 52 percent a decade later (OAS 1997, 11; 2008, 44) – traveling to the municipal center to vote could pose a substantial burden. Citing an extreme case, Horacio Boneo (2001, 80) notes that "the inhabitants of the village of Xocolá must travel 160 kilometers to arrive at their JRV located in the municipal capital of their municipality of Nahualá." Others have pointed out examples of villagers traveling three to four hours on foot just to reach public transportation that could bring them to their municipal center (Ramirez Barrios 2002, 56). While the required travel was less extensive for most voters, the required trip from a rural village to the municipal center was a burden for many citizens.

While centralized voting raised barriers for rural voters, the method of assigning voters to polling stations also posed obstacles for urban voters. Voters were assigned to a polling station based on their registration number rather than their residence. Thus, a voter in the capital city might be required to travel not to the nearest voting center, but to one across town to which he or she had been assigned.[14] Consequently, family members often voted in different parts of the city based on their registration numbers (ASIES 1997, 61–62; Boneo 2001, 80).

Compounding these barriers to voting was the lack of free public transportation on election day, posing obstacles especially to lower-income urban voters (EUEOM 2007, 59). While the issue of election day transportation would arise during later debates over electoral reform, the delays in reform prevented the government from offering free public transport to facilitate travel to polling sites

(Acción Ciudadana et al. 1999, 164). Election day transportation became an issue in the 1999 elections, as the OAS observer mission noted receiving complaints over "an allegedly deliberate stoppage of public transit in the metropolitan district of Guatemala City, with the intention of preventing certain sectors of the population from going to the polls" (OAS 2000, 19). As discussed below, the unavailability of public transportation, in the context of centralized voting and failure to assign urban voters to polling places based on residence, led to political parties playing a large role in transporting voters to the polls.

A final hurdle for many voters in getting to the ballot box prior to 2004 was the fact that elections were held during the labor migration season, when many rural laborers migrate to different municipalities to work on harvests. Since there is no system for absentee voting, tens of thousands of migrant workers (and perhaps more) were effectively unable to vote (Boneo and Torres-Rivas 2000, 115–23).[15] The lack of absentee voting procedures also meant that no provisions existed to allow the hospitalized or prisoners awaiting trial to vote (EUEOM 2007, 23).

Casting a ballot

Once registered and after traveling to one's assigned polling place, the actual process of voting presented further obstacles. Before receiving a ballot, a voter would need to show his or her identity card to the poll worker and, if the document wasn't stamped with the voter registration information, he or she would be asked for a registration ticket; without the registration stamp in the *cédula* or a registration ticket, the voter could not vote – even if their name were on the voters list. A voter would also be turned away if his or her name was not on the list, even if the registration number on their *cédula* corresponded to the range of registration numbers assigned to that voting table. Minor mismatches between the registration number listed on the voter roll and the number on the voter's *cédula* could also prevent a voter from casting a ballot (CAPEL and CEDEP 1986, 39–40, 45–46; TSE 1995, 20).

There were thus multiple ways a voter could be prevented from casting a ballot at the polling place: not having either a registration stamp on their identity card or a registration ticket, or having these but not appearing on the voter list, or a mismatch between their identity document number and the number listed on the voter roll – situations likely to be common where voter registrations were processed manually. There is little systematic evidence regarding how many voters were affected by such rules, and it is possible that poll workers sometimes applied the rules leniently. But in 2003, when problems with the voter rolls were particularly severe because of technical problems resulting from a new method for updating voters' residences,[16] the domestic election observer group Mirador Electoral estimated that between 44,200 and 57,400 people "turned out to the polls but could not vote" (NDI n.d., 29).[17] Similar problems reappeared in the 2007 elections (EUEOM 2007, 50). Most likely, fewer voters were affected by similar problems in prior elections, but the potential existed in the rules for minor errors in the voter rolls to result in disenfranchisement of voters, in marked contrast to Nicaragua's more permissive rules (see Chapter 6). Guatemala also lacks a system of provisional ballots that could alleviate such problems.

An additional obstacle to participation in indigenous areas was the failure to staff polling stations with poll workers who spoke the local languages.[18] With some 22 indigenous languages spoken in the country in addition to Spanish, and an estimated 43 percent of self-identified indigenous people speaking only their native Mayan language (Moreno 2008, 11), the linguistically unrepresentative makeup of polling station staff has posed a further barrier to participation for some indigenous peoples. As one observer noted, the lack of representativeness results in cases of voters getting to the voting table after waiting in line only to find that the poll workers do not speak their language and cannot explain any problems that might occur with the person's registration or documentation (Interview 12). The lack of instructional assistance to voters in indigenous languages has been a particular problem, considering that five different ballots are used for the country's concurrent elections (EUEOM 2003, 11).[19]

Voter education

The obstacles of onerous voter registration procedures, centralized polling locations, and restrictive procedures for allowing voters to cast a ballot were compounded by voter education efforts that were generally characterized as insufficient, given Guatemala's socioeconomic and cultural context. Numerous observers noted the insufficiency of efforts by the state to provide voters with information concerning the registration and voting process (Azpuru 2004; Boneo and Torres-Rivas 2000, 166), an evaluation shared by even the TSE itself (CRE 1997, 4–5, 8). The effectiveness of voter education programs was limited by their uneven territorial coverage, the lateness with which education campaigns were launched, and the challenges of translating voter information into indigenous languages.

The TSE has carried out voter-information campaigns since its first elections, such as publishing lists of voting stations in the capital city with corresponding voter registration numbers in the country's largest daily paper and establishing phone lines for voters to call for information (PL 1985b; 1985c). Over time, the TSE devoted increasing resources to such efforts but, at least before the mid-2000s, the TSE's efforts were widely considered insufficient to inform the country's diverse population of the voting process. An observer mission to the 1995 elections noted the efforts of the TSE to promote voter registration, but emphasized "the lateness … as well as the limited geographical reach of the effort" (NDI 1995, 19). Another observer team similarly noted that the TSE conducted an intensive voter education campaign in the days prior to the election, but it did not have the resources to carry out a long-term effort (OAS 1997, 32–33); thus, the voter education campaign was minimal prior to the close of voter registration.

Evaluations of voter education campaigns were more positive after 1999 (e.g., OAS 2000, 10–11), but many remained critical, especially regarding the insufficiency of information provided in indigenous languages, despite improved efforts on the part of election officials (EUEOM 2003, 9, 11; López-Pintor 2005, 126–27; MIOE 2003, 43; OAS 2005, 13, 16). The lateness of voter-information campaigns was also a problem. Given the early closing date for voter registration, information and publicity campaigns were sometimes launched too late to impact those people not registered to vote – as was the case in 2003, when the information campaign began on October 1 (OAS 2005, 13), after voter registration had ended. More generally, Mirador Electoral's evaluation in 2003 was that "[t]he TSE is not effectively disseminating information to the public on such things as voting places, ballots, and tables" (Mirador Electoral 2003). The National Democratic Institute (n.d., 25) offered a similar evaluation regarding the inadequate publicity surrounding the updating of the voter rolls in 2003. As discussed in the following chapter, efforts to provide voters with necessary information improved for the 2007 and 2011 elections.

Guatemala's restrictive election administration measures during this period are summarized in Table 4.1. The following section discusses the effects of these measures.

The effects of procedural barriers to voting

These procedural obstacles to voting had several effects on Guatemalan electoral politics, particularly the level of voter turnout, the composition of the electorate, the quality of the voter rolls, and even the success of particular parties and the patterns of partisan mobilization.

The system of voter registration led to a situation of both under- and over-registration: difficult registration procedures kept many eligible citizens from registering, while the separation of civil and voter registries and ineffective collaboration between the two resulted in voter rolls bloated with deceased and emigrated people. While precise rates of registration are unknown due in part to the unreliability of census data, all estimates suggest relatively low rates of voter registration, typically in the 65–75 percent range from 1985 to 1995 (ASIES 1986, 6, 9; NDI 1991, 51; OAS 1997, 28–29). Voter registration rates among women, indigenous, and rural citizens were particularly low (see, e.g., UNDP 2005, 199). Difficulties acquiring an identity document played a role in under-registration, as an estimated 15 percent of Guatemalans did not possess a *cédula* in 1995, due in part to the destruction of some civil registry offices during the civil war (OAS 1997, 29). While possession of identity documents increased over time, even by the mid-2000s significant numbers still did not possess identification, with women, indigenous, and rural residents particularly affected (UNDP 2005, 199).

As might be expected, the level of voter registration, particularly among women and indigenous citizens, increased alongside the gradual improvements in the accessibility of voter registration after 1999 (see Chapter 5). In absolute

Table 4.1 Election administration inclusiveness, Guatemala 1983–2003

Dimension	*Description*	*Inclusiveness*
Voter registration		
Extent of state responsibility for registering voters	Voter-initiated, no state efforts to register citizens	Low
Difficulty of registration process	Complex process involving multiple trips to centralized registration offices (partially decentralized after 2001); cost of providing photograph	Low
Ease of access to ID documents required for registration	Difficult; obtaining *cédula* required birth certificate, travel to centrally located offices, and financial cost	Low
Registration closing date	30 days (1984); 2 months (1985); 3 months (1986–present)	Medium
Residency requirement	De facto 1 year (1987–2002), 6 months after 2002; updating registration required	Low
Provisional registration	None	Low
Registry consultation	Limited opportunities to review and verify registry data, expanding over time	Low/medium
Purging of voter rolls	Voters not purged from the rolls for failure to vote	High
Getting to the ballot box		
Accessibility of polling places	Polling places centralized in municipal centers; limited public transportation	Low
Assignment of voters to polling places	Numerical (not based on residence)	Low
Convenience voting measures	Not used	Low
Electoral calendar	Voting held on Sunday, but during labor migration season	Medium
Casting a ballot		
Voter ID requirement	*Cédula* required; exact match between information on ID and voter rolls required	Low
Provisional or tendered ballots	Not used	Low
Voter education		
State efforts to inform voters of where and how to register and vote	Limited in territorial and linguistic coverage (but increasing over time); limited duration, beginning late in electoral cycle	Medium
Overall inclusiveness		Low

terms, the voter roll increased by 12 percent between 1999 and 2003 and by 18 percent from 2003 to 2007 (OAS 2008, 36). The number of registered women increased by 24 percent from 2003 to 2007 (compared to an increase of 12 percent for men); as a result, women came to account for 46.02 percent of the voter rolls in 2007 (OAS 2008, 38), and in 2011 women made up more than half of the voter roll for the first time in the country's history (PL 2011e).

Alongside low rates of voter registration, the voter registry accumulated errors due to incomplete purging and the failure to update voters' residences when they moved to a new municipality, and the inclusion of people who had initiated the registration process but never completed it by making the final trip to the registry office (Boneo and Torres-Rivas 2000). Independent audits of the voter rolls have found extensive problems with the accuracy of the data (Erazo 2007; NDI n.d., 25).

Besides the impact on voter registration rates, the most frequently noted effect of restrictive election administration practices has been the low level of voter participation. Measured turnout rates in Guatemala were among the lowest in the world through the mid-1990s, with abstention concentrated among women, young people, and seasonal migrant workers (Torres-Rivas and González 2001, 45–46). Before 2011, voter turnout ranged from a high of over 60 percent of registered voters in the first round of the 1985 transitional elections (ASIES 1986, 6) to under 47 percent in the first round of the 1995 elections (International IDEA 2011).[20] Taking into account the relatively low levels of voter registration among eligible voters, turnout as a proportion of the voting-age population has actually been much lower, below 50 percent even for the first round of presidential elections (when legislative and municipal offices are concurrently elected). While socioeconomic factors and disaffection from political parties also contribute to low turnout, administrative hurdles have been important as well.

Election observers and analysts have often noted that the restriction of voting to municipal capitals, burdensome voter registration procedures, scheduling elections during the migration season, and insufficient voter education efforts have lowered participation (Azpuru 2004; EUEOM 2003, 59; OAS 1997, 20; OAS 2000, 42; Spence 2004, 81). Observing the 1990 elections, the National Democratic Institute suggested centralized polling places reduced participation among women, as "[m]any men who had made the long walk from their homes to the polling sites said their wives had stayed home with the children or had gone to the market rather than vote" (NDI 1991, 50). Examining the issue quantitatively, a UNDP report (2005, 202–3) found a positive correlation between the proportion of the population living in urban areas and voter turnout, consistent with the notion that traveling to municipal capitals in rural areas hindered voter participation. Comparing turnout across Guatemala's municipalities from 1985 to 1995, Lehoucq and Wall (2004) found that larger municipality size and higher numbers of voters assigned to each voting station (a measure of voter waiting time) were associated with lower turnout. Studies drawing on surveys also found that procedural barriers such as those involving voter registration lowered participation (Boneo and Rivas-Torres 2000; Nevitte, Cruz, and Estok 2007). Thus, while the methodologies and emphases differ, studies of voter turnout in Guatemala agree that procedural barriers – from the complexities of voter registration to the distances traveled to reach one's polling station – are important in keeping turnout low.[21] And low turnout has been concentrated among women and rural voters who are most affected by procedural barriers.

While administrative obstacles contributed to a heavily male electorate, they also gave greater electoral weight to urban areas. From 1985 to 1999, municipal-level turnout was negatively associated with the proportion of municipal residents living in rural areas (Sáenz de Tejada 2005). Partly as a result of higher turnout in urban areas, the election results in the largest municipalities, such as Guatemala City, were often decisive in determining presidential contests until the decentralization of polling places changed this pattern in 2007 (see, e.g., Sáenz de Tejada 2005, 161, 176–77, 196, 235).

Procedural barriers may also have affected the composition of the electorate through the practice of *acarreo* (carriage) – the provision of transportation by political parties on election day. The practice was widespread, with observers estimating that 15 percent of voters reached their polling station in a political party vehicle for the 1995 elections (OAS 1997, 47). Observers frequently expressed concern over the potential for parties to pressure voters that they transport, as well as the disadvantages for smaller parties that lack resources to mobilize voters in this way (EUEOM 2003, 56; OAS 1997, 20), although others have emphasized the ineffectiveness of *acarreo* as a means of capturing votes (Escobar A. 2000, 182; Interview 27). At the margins, the practice may have helped shape the composition of the electorate by ensuring access for some party supporters, while leaving others to find their own means of reaching their voting center.

It is difficult to determine whether these effects on the composition of the electorate had consequences for policy preferences – in other words, whether non-voters differed from voters in their opinions or preferences. However, one geographically limited study suggests that such differences existed, finding non-voters were "significantly more likely than voters to identify economic matters – the lack of job opportunities and poverty – as the most serious problems facing the country" (Nevitte, Cruz, and Estok 2007). As the 2007 presidential election would also show, greater participation among rural voters could sway election results and affect campaign strategies (see Chapter 5).

"Certidumbre fue la primera cosa":[22] procedural barriers to protect the integrity of the vote

As the preceding sections show, Guatemala adopted highly restrictive election administration practices that contributed to low rates of voter participation. This raises the question of why such restrictive rules and practices were put in place. The primary motive behind the choice of administrative rules and procedures was the desire to prevent election fraud. This motive influenced election administration practices, such as centralized polling places, how voters were assigned to polling stations, voter registration, and voter education.

The origins of centralized polling places

Numerous sources indicate that polling sites were limited to municipal capitals in Guatemala as a response to past electoral fraud which, according to the conventional wisdom, tended to occur at polling stations in rural zones. Accordingly, polling places were centralized to provide election authorities greater control over the voting process and prevent coercion of rural voters by landlords or local political bosses (ASIES 1997, 61; Boneo and Torres-Rivas 2000, 131–32; López-Pintor and Urrutia 2002, 38; NDI 1995, 9; Núñez 2008, 14). The idea that polling centralization was intended to prevent fraud is shared widely by knowledgeable political actors in Guatemala. Former TSE magistrate Hugo Maul Figueroa has noted more broadly that the country's electoral law was "concentrated fundamentally in avoiding manipulation and fraud. Therefore, some writers have defined our electoral law as an anti-fraud electoral law" (ASIES 1997, 59).

There were instances of election fraud throughout Guatemalan history. For instance, after the 1954 coup, Castillo Armas was "elected" with 95 percent of the vote in a referendum in which "citizens voted orally in the presence of security personnel" (Trudeau 1993, 36). After Armas was assassinated in 1957, an election was held that "was so overtly fraudulent that it was annulled" (Jonas 1989, 135). These were followed by more procedurally honest contests in 1966 and 1970, which one scholar attributes to the confidence of the incumbent party's candidate in winning a clean contest (Anderson 1988, 25, 28).

But it wasn't until the elections of 1974 (and then again in 1978 and 1982) "that the alteration of voting results became systematic and global" (Gálvez Borrell 2008, 120). All of these presidential elections were contested almost entirely by military candidates representing different elite and military factions, but election fraud (and increasingly, over time, violent repression) was used by the right-wing parties in power against their more moderate opponents. The 1974 election has been described as "a blatant farce" (Anderson 1988, 28), with the military-aligned parties' candidate being declared the victor over the Christian Democratic candidate Efraín Ríos Montt, who was widely believed to have won the vote. By 1980, some parties threatened to boycott municipal elections because of expectations of fraud, resulting in a one-month postponement of the contests (Anderson 1988, 46).

These instances of election fraud contributed – along with the continuing guerilla insurgency, the state's counterinsurgency violence, and economic crisis – to delegitimizing the military regime and prompting a slow transition to constitutional civilian rule. Following the 1982 election fraud, "Guatemala witnessed the unusual spectacle of a protest march led jointly by members of such disparate political parties as the extreme right-wing National Liberation Movement and the Christian Democrats" (Trudeau 1989, 98). When a coup brought General Ríos Montt to power in March of that year, before the fraudulently elected president took office, the coup plotters pointed to electoral fraud and the attendant loss in legitimacy of the country's political institutions to justify their actions (Fuentes Destarac 2008, 572; Gálvez Borrell 2008, 110–11). It was during Ríos

Montt's brief rule, with previous election frauds fresh in mind, when transitional electoral laws were written to construct a new election administration.

Yet, despite the widespread denouncement of fraud in the three elections between 1974 and 1982, and the consensus that the subsequent centralization of polling places was a direct response to how those frauds were carried out, the existing historiography offers few details on how those episodes of election fraud occurred. Trudeau (1993, 39) identifies a wide range of fraudulent practices, "including buying votes; issuing false identification documents; social pressure, especially on the large haciendas; ballot recounting and re-marking; and preelection fraud centering on illegal registration and harassment of opposition candidates." More generally, the literature is suggestive that centralization of vote counting and government control of the electoral body were key mechanisms for perpetrating fraud (Gálvez Borrell 2008, 72, 109). For instance, in 1974, the official announcement of election results was interrupted, "feeding the idea that results were being altered in favor of the government's candidate ... It was only after a week that the official data appeared, when, we can suppose, the numbers had already been conveniently manipulated" (Sabino 2008, 141). A similar process unfolded during the 1978 election, with the televised vote count being interrupted and several days passing before it was announced that General Lucas García – who had been in third place during the vote count – had won (Trudeau 1993, 39–40). Based on his interviews with people involved, Sabino (2008, 142, 299) concludes that vote totals from the provinces were altered by the government in the capital city.

At the same time, there is little documented evidence of vote manipulation in rural areas. However, several knowledgably Guatemalans suggest that landlords and local political bosses (*caciques*) exercised control over the votes of their workers (Interview 01) and that ballot stuffing occurred in rural areas where there was little presence of opposition parties or election authorities (Interviews 09, 14, 15). Voting in far-flung rural areas also meant that the process of transporting materials from rural areas to the capital could result in "lost ballot boxes" (Interview 07). The centralization of voting sites was a means to prevent these types of manipulation and fraud, by making it easier for parties to monitor the election process and also lending more control to (now independent) election authorities over the transmission of election results (Interviews 09, 19). While many people emphasize fraud that occurred in rural areas, the person charged with drafting the transitional electoral laws in 1983 suggested that fraud occurred at all levels – from the voting tables in rural areas, to the transport of votes to departmental capitals (when votes would be diverted to someone's house to be modified), to the vote tallying at the national level in Guatemala City. Other problems included voters arriving at their polling site to find that someone had already voted in their place, or that their name was not on the voter list. Such fraud was facilitated by the absence of party poll watchers or their exclusion from voting centers (Interview 19).

Disagreement over the locus of fraud is also evident in the records of the National Constituent Assembly that drafted the 1985 electoral law.[23] Article 231 of the draft bill, which dealt with the location of voting sites, generated vigorous debate. In the draft bill, the article read simply, "The Municipal Electoral Juntas are obligated to install polling stations in the respective Municipal capitals." Assembly members debated whether centralizing polling places would prevent the types of fraud that had occurred in previous elections and whether centralization would put an undue burden on voters.

Representative Carlos González Quezada of the center-right National Renewal Party (PNR), who was on the committee that drafted the bill, opened the discussion by noting that the purpose of limiting voting sites to municipal capitals was to "maintain the purity of the suffrage, in view of the sad experiences that we have had, of the location of [voting] tables in rural areas." In contrast, representative Scheel Montes of the center-right UCN party raised the issue of voter exclusion, noting that some rural areas had larger populations than some municipal *cabeceras*, and argued that centralization "wouldn't be protecting the purity of the electoral suffrage, but limiting it." Scheel suggested amending the article to allow for polling stations "in those places in which, in the judgment of the corresponding persons, there is a sufficient turnout of voters to merit the location of [voting] tables."

Those supporting centralization raised several points. Representative Recinos Figueroa of the UCN argued that, if voting were held in villages, landlords and *caciques* would be able to influence the votes of workers, and local authorities would be able to intimidate voters, whereas voting in municipal capitals would help ensure a free vote. By this logic, centralized voting might be an obstacle to exercising one's right to vote, but it would ensure that one's vote was made freely. Representative Luis Alfonso López of the right-wing Anticommunist Unification Party (PUA), defending the original text of the article, argued that allowing for polling sites to be placed anywhere deemed "adequate," "we'll know that, as adequate places will be selected, in the first place, by the incumbent government, those that are precisely the places adequate to commit fraud…" Here and elsewhere in the legislative debate, the equating of the Supreme Electoral Tribunal with the government reveals the lack of trust in the independence of the new electoral authority that prevailed at the time.

Others – including representatives López (PUA) and Fuentes Sandoval (of the rightist MLN party) – suggested that centralization would not place an undue burden on voters. Some deputies even suggested that party provision of transport to "their voters" would help alleviate the burden of distance and that, with public campaign financing allotted based on the number of votes parties received, parties would be motivated to mobilize voters and get them to the polls.[24]

Representative Scheel Montes (UCN) was more skeptical, asking "If we believe there is going to be pressure [on voters] in a hamlet or a village, why won't there be that pressure in the municipal capital?" Scheel also foreshadowed later criticisms from election observers by arguing that the political parties offering transportation to the polls would exercise undue influence on voters. Interestingly then, while some feared that local bosses would pressure voters if polling were conducted in remote rural areas, others expressed the inverse fear that political parties would pressure voters by controlling transportation if voting were centralized.

In debating the efficacy of centralization as a means of combating fraud and the consequences for voter inclusion, the central issues were the locus of prior electoral fraud and the normative issue of whether ensuring clean elections was worth the price of the exclusion of some voters. On the locus of prior election frauds, representative Fuentes Sandoval (MLN) articulated the rural fraud thesis: in the "elections of 1982 and before, the electoral authorities always located voting tables in the parcels, in the villages, on the farms, etc., etc., that history reminds us, that there is where the popular will of the people was changed." Representative López (PUA) bolstered the case for centralization by referring anecdotally to ballot boxes found thrown out "in a street in Alta Verapaz" and of ballot boxes being stuffed "in a certain departmental capital" – seemingly unaware that this latter example of fraud occurring in a departmental capital did little to justify limiting voting sites to such areas.

The rural fraud thesis did not go unchallenged. Representative Castellanos of the UCN argued "that the majority of fraud is done in the departmental governorships, and not in the [municipal] capitals, nor in the farms, nor the hamlets." Representative Scheel concurred:

> Gentlemen, let's not deceive ourselves any more, we know Guatemala, and we know that electoral fraud isn't done at the voting tables, it's done where they count the votes, it's done in the departmental capitals, where they bring the ballot boxes…

Scheel offered his own anecdote to bolster his case:

> Who commits fraud, has to be a well known person, let's remember that famous case … of a mayor of Jacaltenango, that for being very honorable and very honest, carried the ballot box to deliver it personally in the departmental capital, and his fright that, at arriving at the municipality of Huehuetenango, found that the voting of the municipality whose votes he was carrying on his back were already tallied on the blackboard; that is to say, that that isn't done in the [local] places or hamlets or villages.

If there was disagreement among the deputies about whether past instances of electoral fraud occurred at polling places in rural villages, at the vote-counting sites in the departmental capitals, or all of the above, there were also differences among the deputies in striking a balance between clean elections and voter inclusion. Two members of the committee that drafted the bill put the issue starkly: representative González Quezada stated flatly, "… we [in the committee] prefer that some citizens don't participate in the process, because they are far from the voting station, than that the vote can be utilized, as an instrument, for fraud," while representative Recinos Figueroa noted "that there will be abstention, but we believe that a minimal abstention is preferable to having a spurious government." Representative López (PUA) similarly articulated the normative issue at stake quite clearly:

> We shouldn't be romantic, let's be practical, let's defend Guatemalan democracy in the face of abstention; what is more sinful, that in the elections the will of the people is mocked, or that a certain quantity of citizens don't show up to vote because the place is very distant? … I know municipalities, for example, one in Petén, that's called Piedras Negras, that to travel from Piedras Negras to Poptún, it's two days on the road; however, I ask myself, is it a sufficient argument that, because a group of citizens of Petén don't go to vote, we will permit fraud in the rest of the departments of the Republic?

Others expressed more preoccupation with the barrier that centralization would represent. For instance, the president of the constituent assembly Roberto Carpio Nicolle (of the Christian Democratic Party, DCG) noted the great distances that some would have to travel on foot to reach their voting site and expressed reticence to centralize voting centers, "supposing that there was always fraud, that there always could be fraud, that in Guatemala there isn't going to be democracy."

But on the heels of three consecutive fraudulent elections, the arguments for centralizing voting sites ultimately won the day. As the assembly debates show, legislators understood that centralizing polling stations would be an impediment to some prospective voters, but most felt that the threat of fraud in far-flung voting sites outweighed this consideration. Opponents of centralization introduced an amendment to allow for the departmental electoral councils, in agreement with political party representatives, to place voting sites outside of municipal capitals.[25] Ironically, this proposal was almost identical to the solution ultimately settled on over 20 years later, after fierce battles between Congress and the TSE. But at the time, the amendment made no headway, with representative Gonzalez Quezada arguing that many parties lacked the ability to place poll watchers at more polling stations and suggesting that some parties would be at an advantage in deciding where to locate the polling stations.

It is worth noting that one deputy in the constituent assembly suggested the need for Guatemala to experience two or three elections with centralized voting sites in order to consolidate the (democratic) electoral system, and that the issue of decentralization could be revisited in the future.[26] Despite the later consensus on the need to decentralize voting sites, many observers hold the opinion that centralization was appropriate at the time it was adopted and served its purpose. As one person put it, using an analogy of a child's growth, the country's electoral system needed to first learn to crawl, then learn to walk, then to talk – i.e., to hold elections free of fraud, then find ways of including more voters (Interview 06). In any case, the system set up in the early to mid-1980s did effectively rid the country of the blatant fraud common in prior periods,[27] whether as a result of centralization or (more importantly) through the establishment of an independent electoral management body.

There are other possible explanations for the centralization of polling places to consider. Perhaps the centralization of voting sites was not intended to reduce the chances of election fraud but to impede rural (and especially indigenous) voters from casting ballots, and talk of preventing fraud was a smokescreen for this ulterior motive. Such a motive could have been based on partisan goals for parties that enjoyed stronger support in urban areas, or based on general prejudice of the predominantly male non-indigenous (Ladino) legislators. Several considerations give this interpretation plausibility. First is the absence of leftist or ethnic-based parties in the constituent assembly that might have had a natural base among the country's indigenous *campesinos*; the elite-dominated parties that crafted the electoral rules may have been relatively unconcerned with or even hostile to participation among rural, indigenous, and poor voters. Second, the centralization of polling stations (and other barriers) would give parties a gatekeeping function, ensuring access to their supporters by providing transportation on election day and helping them to register to vote (see, e.g., Carter Center 2003), while independent voters or supporters of small parties with limited resources could potentially be left to their own devices to navigate procedural obstacles. Finally, several legislators made a reasonable case that the greater risk of fraud existed at the departmental level, where vote counts were tallied, rather than at rural voting stations.

However, there are several reasons to accept the fraud-prevention hypothesis at face value. First is the tremendous influence that election rigging in the three prior elections had in the country. These frauds contributed to the "total delegitimation" of the military regime and the consequent transition to nominally democratic rule (Interview 19). One of the expressed motivating factors for the 1982 coup that initiated the transition from military rule was the repeated electoral frauds, with the junta referring to "the fraudulent electoral practices" in its proclamation to the people (Castillo Milla 2006, 6). Not surprisingly, the major political parties that had been victimized by fraudulent electoral practices endorsed the coup (Trudeau 1993, 60). It is therefore reasonable to conclude that ensuring fair elections free of fraud was the overriding priority of the staff and legislators who crafted the 1983–1985 electoral laws.

Second, the fraud-prevention thesis was accepted by all political analysts and participants interviewed by the author; no respondents, even former guerrillas, suggested that disenfranchisement for partisan gain was the motivation behind the centralization of voting sites. Similarly, the 1985 legislative debate on centralization was free of accusations of partisan motivations, despite opposing views of some of the deputies. The absence of partisan motives is partly understandable in light of the political uncertainty at the time: some parties lacked clear social bases and therefore had no partisan reasons to try to include or exclude particular segments of the population from the ballot box. One of the strongest parties in the assembly, the UCN, had just recently formed, and one of the party's representatives spoke in favor of centralization while two others were the most vocal opponents of centralization. The UCN had, in fact, performed more strongly in more urbanized municipalities than rural areas in the 1984 constituent assembly elections (Sáenz de Tejada 2005, 121, 127), but that did not prevent some of its members from advocating less stringent polling centralization.

Older parties had slightly more clearly defined social bases. One of the largest parties in the assembly, the right-wing MLN (which had been in power during parts of the authoritarian period) had a strong presence in rural areas (Sáenz de Tejada 2005, 126). Yet, one of the party's representatives was a strong supporter of centralization. The social base of the Christian Democracy party (DCG) was even clearer. The DCG had a strong rural organization and had particularly strong support in indigenous communities, where it performed well in 1984 and in subsequent elections (Sáenz de Tejada 2005, 124, 126, 160, 162). Of all the parties represented in the constituent assembly, it would have been the DCG that might have opposed centralizing polling places. And, in fact, several DCG representatives supported an amendment to the elections bill to allow polling places outside of municipal capitals. However, the party also had strong reason to safeguard the system against fraud, having been the victim of fraud in the 1974 presidential election. One former assembly deputy (for the left-leaning PR party) noted that in the assembly

> … [t]here was really no talk of anything else but preventing election fraud, it was a priority subject, since there had been a permanent frustration in the parties, especially in Christian Democracy, that had suffered those constant election robberies. There was a desire to stop fraud by all means.
>
> (ASIES 2005, 88)

It is not clear if all DCG deputies opposed polling centralization, as the legislative records do not contain vote totals for the measure. All that can be concluded is that, given the alignment of forces in the assembly, the measure could not have been approved without the support of some centrist deputies. Given the available evidence, it appears that the desire of parties to have a level playing field free of ballot stuffing was the priority of the day, overcoming potential partisan motives to facilitate or impede the participation or rural voters.

But if partisan motivations didn't drive the decision to centralize voting, another consideration may have been the ongoing armed conflict between the government and guerrillas. Certainly, ensuring security for voting would have been difficult in some rural areas where guerrilla forces were active. Some people note that putting polling stations in all villages wasn't feasible in the context of armed conflict (Interviews 06, 19). However, these same people were clear that avoiding election fraud was the motivation for centralization: "there was no other reason for it," in the words of one respondent (Interview 06). Rather than a competing explanation, the armed conflict might be thought of as an additional security consideration for lawmakers who wanted to avoid irregularities and fraud at all costs.

Assignment of voters to polling places

While the installation of voting sites only in municipal capitals was intended to prevent election fraud, other measures affecting where voters were assigned to vote also responded to a desire to prevent election irregularities, although other factors also played a role.

Requiring citizens to vote in the municipality where they received their *cédula*, rather than in the municipality of their current residence (which was often different), was a decision of the TSE rather than a provision in the electoral law and was included in its 1987 regulation of the law. In the 1984 and 1985 elections, as a new voter list was drawn up, the voter rolls were based on voters' current residence. The decision by the TSE to switch to a more restrictive system was motivated by a desire to avoid manipulation of the voter rolls and to better organize the registration process. As the director of the voter registry at the time put it when discussing the change, "this is something we fixed," emphasizing the "certainty" and "order" of the process that this ensured (Interview 16). In particular, limiting voting to the municipality where one holds an identification document would help prevent the transfer of voters to different municipalities for strategic electoral purposes (Interview 16) – a problem that is at the root of many contemporary electoral conflicts, particularly after the switch back to a residence-based system. In a system with voter lists based on residence, a candidate for mayor might arrange for supporters from a neighboring municipality to fraudulently register to vote in his own jurisdiction, and on election day the candidate or his party would bus in these outside voters – the famous *traslado* (transfer) of voters. Requiring an identity document issued in the municipality where one registered to vote would make this practice more difficult.

Like voting centralization, this measure represented a significant obstacle for some citizens living far from their place of birth, who (in the absence of any form of absentee balloting) would need to travel cross-country to vote or go through the process of obtaining a new identification document. And, like centralization, this measure responded to the overriding objective of assuring clean election processes free of fraud. It also apparently encountered little opposition: while the measure was a TSE initiative, the political parties did not oppose it, according to one person involved (Interview 16). By the mid-1990s, an initiative was proposed within the TSE to loosen the requirement by instituting a limited form of absentee balloting, allowing voters living outside of their *cédula* municipality to vote for national offices in the municipality where they were residing (holding a *cédula* in the new municipality would still be needed to vote for local offices). The idea was to facilitate the vote for those living away from their homes, while not complicating (or opening up for abuse) municipal and district elections (Interview 14). However, the proposal made no headway within the TSE, and it wouldn't be until 2001 that the TSE moved back to a voter roll based on residence (see Chapter 5).

Another aspect of voter assignment to polling places was the division of the voter lists in urban areas by voters' registration numbers rather than by residence, so that voters would not necessarily be assigned to the polling site closest to their home. This method of assigning voters was carried over from the military-era electoral codes (Interview 19), but it is not clear why it was maintained when the electoral system was revised in the 1980s. A former TSE official suggested that the TSE simply lacked the technical capacity to divide the voter lists cartographically within municipalities (Interview 24), and this is plausible considering the significant external technical assistance needed to carry out polling-site decentralization after 2004. However, others suggested that the lack of technical cartographic tools was not insurmountable (Interviews 16, 19). Whatever the case may be, it is clear that this aspect of the voting process did not receive much attention at the time, unlike the centralization of voting sites, and the issue did not elicit debate among the legislators approving the electoral law. As a holdover from the previous electoral system, this method simply seemed the easiest way of ordering the voter lists, while the effects on voter convenience were apparently not foreseen (Interviews 16, 19).

Voter registration and casting a ballot

If the centralization of polling sites is explicable as a means of controlling the election process and making fraud more difficult, "[t]he reasons and the logic for [the] administrative complexities" surrounding voter registration "are difficult to explain" (López-Pintor and Urrutia 2002, 42). This is because to some extent the complexities resulted from administrative inefficiencies and inadequate coordination between the voter and civil registries. Yet, to some extent the voter registration obstacles are also explicable in terms of protecting against election fraud.

With regard to the closing date of registration, the move from one month prior to election day in 1984 to three months prior in 1987 responded to the need for more time to prepare the voter lists (Interviews 04, 16, 19). This preparation involves compiling the registration data, verifying the data and purging the registrations of those ineligible to vote (such as active police and military personnel, who are not legally allowed to vote), and printing and distributing the lists to the departmental and municipal election boards and voting centers. The extension of the closing date also responded in part to concerns of fraud: according to the director of voter registration at the time, this three-month period between the closing of registration and election day was needed to avoid irregularities with the voter lists (Interview 16). The 1985 electoral law required the voter roll to be purged and printed no later than 30 days before elections (LEPP, Art. 225), a measure surely intended to protect against manipulation of the voter lists (e.g., strategic transfers of registrations across municipal lines).

Extending the closing date to three months was probably also intended to allow more time to verify the information on the voter register, particularly given the insecurity of the *cédula* which citizens used when registering to vote (Interview 19). The *cédula*'s lack of safeguards – it was an easily forged paper document – also meant that the voter registration process involved security checks that resulted in applicants making multiple trips to the registry office. After receiving a voter registration application, the voter registry checked the applicant's information against the municipal civil registry (a check against falsified identity documents), and the civil registries were required to notify the voter registry if they received verification requests for a single person from more than one voter registry office (a check against multiple voter registrations).[28]

Thus several restrictive aspects of the voter registration process – an early closing date and a long process involving multiple trips to the registry – were the result of concerns about voter registration fraud. But the system put in place was not particularly effective at preventing such problems. For instance, a lack of communication between the country's decentralized civil registries (where citizens report births, deaths, and changes to civil status) and the TSE's Citizen's Registry (which produces the voter roll) posed obstacles to purging the voter lists. Although the civil registries were obligated to share information with the Citizen's Registry, this often didn't happen in practice, and the problem was often compounded by family deaths not being reported to the civil registries in the first place (OAS 1997, 31; 2005, 17). Furthermore, the TSE historically did not have the technology available to adequately cross-check information in the registries (OAS 1997, 32). Until recently, many registration offices lacked computers and entered voter registrations manually, which slowed down the process of compiling the voter rolls and was another reason for the TSE to prefer an early registration closing date (Interview 14). Thus, the decentralized and fragmented registry system resulted in the worst of both worlds: restrictive voter registration procedures and security checks that relied on inaccurate civil registries and thus provided imperfect protection against manipulation of the voter rolls.

After lengthening the voter registration closing date in 1987, changes were not considered until recently (Interviews 04, 13, 14). Despite improvements in technology in registration offices, the TSE has recently proposed not to move the closing date closer to election day but to end voter registration even earlier – six months before election day. According to the director of voter registration, the TSE considered the three-month period to be inadequate to purge, print, and distribute the voter rolls (Interview 21). Surprisingly, despite the recognition that many people try to register after the closing date, and the widely noted Guatemalan cultural characteristic of doing things at the last minute, the early closing date has received practically no attention from election observers or civil society groups as an obstacle to participation. One exception is the study by Boneo and Torres-Rivas (2000), who suggested shortening the closing date to 30 days and noted that no technical obstacles impede doing so (151). In general, according to a former TSE magistrate, the TSE has prioritized the integrity of the voter lists and has not considered under-registration of eligible voters to be a significant problem (Interview 13).

Voter education

In providing voters with the information necessary to participate, two related factors were critical: the low priority given to voter education and the limited resources available to carry out voter education activities. According to a long-time TSE staff person, voter education was a lower priority in the past than it is today, as the imperative of establishing clean elections absorbed the attention of election administrators (Interview 22). As a result, the educational efforts of the TSE were aimed at training poll workers and party poll watchers – actors with a direct impact on election integrity – more than voter-information campaigns (CRE 1997; TSE and CAPEL 1986).

Voter education gained higher priority in the late 1990s with the electoral reform process, and the funding devoted to voter education increased over time and was supplemented by international aid. However, funding limitations remained a constraint. A former TSE magistrate noted that funds had been a constraint in translating and providing informational materials in all indigenous languages, leading the TSE to focus only on a handful of the most common languages (Interview 17). Observers have also pointed to the lack of resources as an impediment to long-term voter education efforts (OAS 1997, 32–33). But funding shortages were not the only problem. The social and cultural context presents enormous challenges: for instance, the Academy of Mayan Languages (ALMG) translates TSE educational materials, but there have been problems with the translations being in a formal style of indigenous languages that people do not understand. And in the face of such challenges, the TSE was not always effective at utilizing low-cost alternatives, such as coordinating with local community radio stations to disseminate voter information in indigenous languages (Interview 22). Initially a low priority hampered by funding constraints, voter education became a much more high-profile concern of the TSE beginning in the late 1990s, and funding constraints lessened considerably. As discussed in Chapter 5, the result was more intensive voter-information campaigns.

Conclusion

When Guatemalan lawmakers and election administrators crafted the country's election administration in the 1980s, the past weighed heavily on their choice of rules and procedures. After experiencing three consecutive fraudulent elections, they sought above all else to safeguard Guatemalan elections against fraud in order to secure a democratic electoral system. To deter ballot stuffing and manipulation of rural voters, voting sites were limited to municipal capitals. To protect against voter registration fraud after the failure in 1983 to introduce a more secure identity document, a system of registry checks was put in place that resulted in a complex process of voter registration. And in the focus on rooting out election fraud, other issues such as voter education received lower priority. The result was a complex of administrative rules and procedures that was highly restrictive for voter access to the ballot box.

Other factors influenced election administration as well, such as financial constraints and simple administrative holdovers from the previous electoral system. But concerns about election fraud had the biggest impact on electoral administration rules and procedures. The weight of the past influenced the electoral code in other ways as well: the minimal barriers for forming political parties adopted in 1983–1985, for instance, responded to the limited contestation that had been permitted under the military regime (El Periódico 2011; Gálvez Borrell 2008, 133–34).[29] Thus, while voter access was restricted, electoral competition also became freer and fairer.

The electoral administration set up in the 1980s would prove difficult to reform in later years. Some technical components of the system would prove susceptible to path dependence, making change costlier as time went on. Other aspects would be subject to partisan and inter-institutional battles. During the reform process, the roles of partisan interests, civil society groups, and international election assistance become more prominent. It is to that process that we turn in Chapter 5.

Notes

1 These laws were, respectively, Decreto 30–83, Decreto 31–83, and Decreto 32–83.
2 Decree Law (*Decreto*) 33–83 gave the TSE's Citizens Registry oversight over what was to be the new ID document. Later debates over a new identification document would see fierce battles over whether the TSE or another agency would oversee the process of issuing ID cards.
3 General elections held in 1985 were governed by a temporary election law, Decreto 47–85. The Electoral and Political Parties law approved in 1985 went into effect the following year.
4 See Decretos 74–87, 10–89, and 35–90.
5 Decreto 31–83 called for coordination and information-sharing between the voter registry (*Registro de Ciudadanos*) and the civil registry (*Registro General de la Población*). While the legislation did not clearly spell out the division of responsibilities between the two registries, it is easy to imagine that a system of automatic voter registration would have resulted had the government not backtracked on plans to introduce a new identification document.
6 Based on the municipality where the voter has received his or her *cédula de vecindad* (ID card), rather than based on the voter's current residence.
7 In 2003, the TSE returned to residence-based registration, as discussed in the following chapter.
8 See Decreto 47–85, Art. 19 and 21, and Decreto 3–84, Art. 13 and 15.
9 Decreto 74–87, Art. 3. The electoral law approved in 1985 went into effect the following year, and it did not specify a registration closing date. However, elections were not held under the new law until after the 1987 reform.
10 The number of municipalities later increased to 332.
11 See Decreto 3–84, Art. 30; Decreto 47–85, Art. 36; and LEPP, Art. 231.
12 For the number of polling tables in various election years, see ASIES 1986, 6, 9; Mirador Electoral 2007; OAS 1997, 11; and TSE n.d.[b], 115.
13 Different sources report slightly different numbers of voting centers; see OAS 2005, 15 and Ortiz Loaiza et al. 2008, 24.
14 A similar system was employed in El Salvador, but with voters assigned to voting centers alphabetically rather than by the order of their registration number (Boneo 2001, 80).
15 CRE (1998, 59) gives an estimate of 500,000 migrant workers in the country, although it is not certain how many would have been working a significant distance from their home municipality to be effectively unable to vote.

16 This updating of the voter rolls was part of the process of allowing people to vote in their municipality of residence and preparing for the decentralization of polling sites, discussed in Chapter 5.

17 The EU and OAS observer missions also reported widespread problems with the voter lists on election day (EUEOM 2003, 9; OAS 2005, 66).

18 Even as recently as 2007 – after reforms to the electoral law had required the TSE to take diversity into account when staffing polling stations and other levels of the electoral bureaucracy (Article 172) – an indigenous observer mission noted that in 40 percent of the districts they visited, staff did not speak the local indigenous language (MIOE 2007, 127–28). The TSE has generally opted to retain temporary staff at local and departmental levels from one election to the next, in order to benefit from their experience and training; the trade-off has been failure to make these levels of the election administration bureaucracy more representative of the population.

19 Voters cast separate ballots for president, congressional representatives for the national district, congressional representatives for departmental districts, municipal councils, and the Central American Parliament.

20 For some elections, the turnout figures vary significantly in different sources. For instance, some sources give a 69 percent turnout figure for the first round in 1985 (OAS 1997, 48), while others give a figure of 61 percent (ASIES 1986, 6). While the sources are often not clear on this point, it appears that the lower figures only include valid votes. Given the large number of null or blank ballots cast, this can result in substantially different reports of voter turnout.

21 Effective turnout is even lower if the high proportion of null and blank ballots cast is considered. Such ballots often exceed 10 percent of all ballots cast (OAS 1997, 48; TSE n.d.[a], 213; n.d.[b], 36). Many null and blank ballots may represent protest votes or cases where a voter turns out to vote for their local officials and chooses to leave their ballots for national offices (often considered less important) blank. However, lack of knowledge about how to mark one's ballot (reflecting inadequate voter education efforts) may also cause many null votes (see Boneo and Torres-Rivas 2000, 113).

22 "Certitude was the first thing." One interview respondent (Interview 19) used this phrase when discussing the priority given to ensuring the security and transparency of the electoral process when designing the country's electoral administration system in 1983.

23 This section draws on the debates of the National Constituent Assembly published in *Diario de las Sesiones de la Asamblea Nacional Constituyente*, Tomo II, No. 117, August 28, 1985, and No. 118, August 29, 1985. All quotes in the following paragraphs are taken from these sources.

24 As representative López (PUA) put it: "I ask myself, if the place is distant, what do the political parties do, they can't contribute to transport their electors?" Representative González Quezada of the PNR raised the issue of public campaign funds.

25 The amendment was introduced by representatives German Scheel Montes (UCN), Tomás Ayuso (DCG) and Abel Ordóñez (DCG). Roberto Carpio Nicolle also expressed support for it during the legislative debate.

26 As representative González Quezada put it:

> … if we are legislating under the phantom of the great electoral frauds, it is preferable that this society holds some three or two more elections, so that we consolidate democracy in Guatemala, and in the future the road remains open to us for constitutional reform of this same law … but today the circumstances oblige us to maintain, in every respect, to put a lock on any possibility of electoral fraud, because only the purity of the electoral process can consolidate the beginning of democracy in Guatemala.

27 While large-scale fraud is a thing of the past, reports of vote buying at local levels are still common (see Carter Center 2003; Mirador Electoral 2003; NDI 1995, 10).

28 See Decreto 138–83, Art. 5 and 12; and Reglamento 1987, Art. 2.
29 The number of signatures required to form a political party was reduced from 50,000 to 4,000.

References

Acción Ciudadana, Centro de Estudios para el Desarrollo y la Democracia (CEDAPE), Consejo de Investigaciones para el Desarrollo de Centroamérica (CIDECA), Fundación Friedrich Ebert, International Institute for Democracy and Electoral Assistance (IDEA), and Instituto de Enseñanza para el Desarrollo Sostenible (IEPADES). 1999. *Quién es Quién: Catálogo Electoral 1999*. Guatemala: Magna Tierra Editores.

Anderson, Thomas P. 1988. *Politics in Central America: Guatemala, El Salvador, Honduras, and Nicaragua*. Westport, CT: Praeger Publishers.

ASIES (Asociación de Investigación y Estudios Sociales). 1986. *Guatemala 1985 Elecciones Generales*.

ASIES. 1997. *XIII Seminario Sobre El Rol de Los Partidos Políticos: Régimen Electoral y Organización Política: Instrumentos de Transformación Democrática en Guatemala. Guatemala.*

ASIES. 2005. *El Sistema de Partidos Políticos de Guatemala a 20 Años de la Ley Electoral y de Partidos Políticos.*

Azpuru, Dinorah. 2004. "International Electoral Assistance to Guatemala." Paper presented at the International Studies Association Meeting, Montreal, Canada.

Boneo, Horacio. 2001. "Consideraciones Sobre Voto Residencial, Documento Único de Identitad y Cartografía Electoral." In *Construyendo la Democracia Electoral en Guatemala*, Edelberto Torres-Rivas, Secundino González M., Horacio Boneo, Fabrice Lehoucq, and David L. Wall, eds. Guatemala: FLASCO.

Boneo, Horacio and Edelberto Torres-Rivas. 2000. *Por Qué No Votan Los Guatemaltecos? Estudio de Participación y Abstención Electoral*. Guatemala City, Guatemala: IDEA, Tribunal Supremo Electoral, and UNDP.

CAPEL (Centro Interamericano de Asesoria y Promocion Electoral) and CEDEP (Centro de Estudios Politicos). 1986. *Elecciones Generales Guatemala, 1985, Programa de Capacitacion Político-Electoral*. Guatemala: CAPEL-CEDEP.

Carter Center. 2003. Postelection Statement on Guatemala Elections. December 19. www.cartercenter.org/news/documents/doc1567.html.

Castillo Milla, Felix. 2006. Proceso de Reforma de la Ley Electoral y de Partidos Políticos. Cuadernos de Trabajo No. 4. Guatemala: FLACSO.

Conde Rada, César Augusto. 2003. *El Padrón Electoral en Guatemala: Antecedentes y Situación Actual*. Guatemala: FLACSO.

CRE (Comisión de Reforma Electoral). 1997. Documento Para Discusión: Tema General: Campañas de Información Pública. (TSE Centro de Documentación document #370).

CRE. 1998. *Compilación de Documentos Técnicos de Análisis*. Guatemala: Organization of American States.

Decreto 3–84. Ley Electoral Específica Para La Elección De Asamblea Nacional Constituyente. January 19, 1984.

Decreto 10–89. 1989.

Decreto 30–83. La Ley Organica del Tribunal Supremo Electoral. March 23, 1983.

Decreto 31–83. La Ley del Registro de Ciudadanos. March 23, 1983.

Decreto 32–83. La Ley de Organizaciones Políticas. March 23, 1983.

Decreto 33–83. La Ley del Registro General de Población. March 28, 1983.

Decreto 35–90. June 6, 1990.

Decreto 47–85. Ley Específica Para Las Elecciones Generales de 1985. June 3, 1985.

Decreto 74–87. November 10, 1987.

Decreto 138–83. Ley de Inscripción y Empadronamiento de Ciudadanos. November 9, 1983.

Erazo María, Alejandra. 2007. "The Guatemalan Electoral Roll Key to Citizen Participation." *Focal Point* 6 (5). www.focal.ca/publications/focalpoint/fp0607/?lang=e&article=article5. (Accessed June 3, 2010).

Escobar Armas, Carlos. 1987. *La Ley Electoral y de Partidos Políticos de Guatemala, 1985: Sufragio y Democracia*. San José, Costa Rica: IIDH-CAPEL.

Escobar A., Carlos. 2000. "Sistemas de Elección de Parliamentarias en América Central y República Dominicana: El Caso de Guatemala." In *Sistema de Elecciones Parliamentarias y su Relación con la Gobernabilidad Democrática*. Instituto Interamericano de Derechos Humanos.

EUEOM (European Union Electoral Observation Mission). 2003. Final Report on the Parliamentary and Local Elections.

EUEOM. 2007. Final Report on the General Elections.

Fuentes Destarac, Mario. 2008. "Análisis de las Reformas Políticas en Guatemala." In *Reforma Política y Electoral en América Latina, 1978*–2007, Daniel Zovatto and J. Jesús Orozco Henríquez, eds. International Institute for Democracy and Electoral Assistance/Universidad Nacional Autónoma de México.

Gálvez Borrell, Víctor. 2008. *Política y Conflicto Armado: Cambios y Crisis del Régimen Político en Guatemala (1954–1982)*. Guatemala City: Postgrado Centroamericano de Ciencias Sociales de FLACSO.

International IDEA (International Institute for Democracy and Electoral Assistance). 2011. "Voter Turnout Data for Guatemala." www.idea.int/vt/country_view.cfm?CountryCode=GT. (Accessed February 7, 2012).

Jonas, Susanne. 1989. "Elections and Transitions: The Guatemalan and Nicaraguan Cases." In *Elections and Democracy in Central America*, John A. Booth and Mitchell A. Seligson, eds. Chapel Hill and London: University of North Carolina Press.

Lehoucq, Fabrice, and David L. Wall. 2004. "Explaining Voter Turnout Rates in New Democracies: Guatemala." *Electoral Studies* 23 (3): 485–500.

LEPP (Ley Electoral y de Partidos Políticos), Decreto Número 1–85 de la Asamblea Nacional Constituyente.

López-Pintor, Rafael. 2005. "Case Study: Guatemala." In *Getting to the CORE: A Global Survey on the Cost of Registration and Elections*. International Foundation for Electoral Systems and the United Nations Development Program.

López-Pintor, Rafael, and Edmundo Urrutia. 2002. "Guatemala." In *Voter Turnout since 1945: A Global Report*, Rafael López-Pintor and Maria Gratschew, eds. Stockholm: International Institute for Democracy and Electoral Assistance.

Medrano, Gabriel. 2005. "Retos Para la Reforma del Sistema Nacional de Identificación en Guatemala." In *Encuentro Internacional: La Gestión de Registro Civil y la Emisión de Documentos de Identidad Ciudadana en Centro América*, Tribunal Supremo Electoral (Guatemala). Guatemala: Organization of American States.

MIOE (II Misión Indígena de Observación Electoral). 2003. Informe Final, Elecciones Generales 2003.

MIOE (III Misión Indígena de Observación Electoral). 2007. Informe Final de las Elecciones 2007.

Mirador Electoral. 2003. Fourth Report on the National Electoral Process. September 25.

Mirador Electoral. 2007. Primer Informe de Observación. May 3.
Moreno Morales, Daniel Eduardo. 2008. "Ethnic Identity and National Politics: A Comparative Analysis of Indigenous Identity and Political Participation in Bolivia and Guatemala." Ph.D. diss. Vanderbilt University.
NDI (National Democratic Institute). 1991. *The 1990 National Elections in Guatemala.* Washington, DC: National Democratic Institute for International Affairs.
NDI. 1995. *Report of the NDI Survey Mission to Guatemala.* Washington, DC: National Democratic Institute for International Affairs.
NDI. n.d.[a]. Guatemala: Building Citizen Confidence and Participation, USAID Associate Cooperative Agreement No. 520–03-A-013 under the CEPPS Leader Agreement No. DGC-A-00-01-00004-00.
Nevitte, Neil, José Cruz, and Melissa Estok. 2007. *Barriers to Electoral Participation in Guatemala: Diagnostic of 4 Municipalities.* FLASCO-Guatemala.
Núñez Vargas, Eduardo. 2008. "Las Elecciones Generales 2007: Balance General Sobre un Sistema en Transición." In *Siete Claves Para El Cambio: Análisis Técnico, Político y Normativo del Proceso Electoral Guatemala* 2007, Eduardo Núñez Vargas, coord. Guatemala: Soros Foundation/NDI/NIMD/ASIES/DOSES/FLACSO.
OAS (Organization of America States). 1997. *Observaciones Electorales en Guatemala, 1995–1996.*
OAS. 2000. Report of the Electoral Observation Mission to Guatemala, 1999 Elections.
OAS. 2005. Informe de la Misión de Observación Electoral en Guatemala Elecciones Generales 2003.
OAS. 2008. *Informe Final de Gestión: Asistencia Técnica al Régimen Electoral Guatemalteco.* Secretaría General de la Organización de los Estados Americanos (OEA)/Secretaría para Asuntos Políticos (SAP)/Departamento para la Cooperación y Observación Electoral (DECO).
OAS. 2009. Informe de la Misión de Observación Electoral, Elecciones Generales (9 de Septiembre de 2007) y Segunda Vuelta Electoral Presidencial (4 de Noviembre de 2007), República de Guatemala.
Ortiz Loaiza, Paola, María Alejandra Erazo, Silvia Montepeque, and Sara Sapón. 2008. "22 Años Después: Lo Inédito del Proceso Electoral 2007." FLACSO Cuadernos de Información Política, No. 14. Guatemala: Flacso.
El Periódico. 2011. "No lo Hicieron por Demócratas sino Porque no Tenían Alternativa." June 20.
Prensa Libre. 1985a. "Ninguna Persona Podrá Empadronarse Antes de las Elecciones de Diciembre." November 20.
Prensa Libre. 1985b. [no title]. December 2.
Prensa Libre. 1985c. [no title]. December 6.
Prensa Libre. 2011. "Padrón Electoral Llega a 7 Millones 340 Mil 841, Según el TSE." August 10.
Ramirez Barrios, Ronaldo Enrique. 2002. *Las Limitantes a la Participación Ciudadana Contenidas en la Ley Electoral y de Partidos Politicos.* Tesis para Licenciado, Ciencia Juridicas y Sociales. Universidad Rafael Landívar.
Reglamento a la Ley Electoral y de Partidos Políticos. 1987. Acuerdo Número 181–87. (Guatemala).
Sabino, Carlos. 2008. Guatemala: *La Historia Silenciada (1944–1989), Tomo II, El Dominó que no Cayó.* Guatemala City: Fondo de Cultura Económica de Guatemala.
Sáenz de Tejada, Ricardo. 2005. *Elecciones, Participación Política y Pueblo Maya en Guatemala.* Guatemala City: Universidad Rafael Landívar.

Sieder, Rachel, Megan Thomas, George Vickers, and Jack Spence. 2002. *Who Governs? Guatemala Five Years after the Peace Accords*. Cambridge, MA: Hemisphere Initiatives.

Spence, Jack. 2004. *War and Peace in Central America: Comparing Transitions toward Democracy and Social Equity in Guatemala, El Salvador, and Nicaragua*. Brookline, MA: Hemisphere Initiatives.

Torres-Rivas, Edelberto, and Secundino González. 2001. "Introducción a un Laberinto: Las Elecciones en Guatemala." In *Construyendo la Democracia Electoral en Guatemala*, Torres-Rivas, Edelberto, Secundino González M., Horacio Boneo, Fabrice Lehoucq, and David L. Wall, eds. Guatemala: FLACSO.

Trudeau, Robert H. 1993. *Guatemalan Politics: The Popular Struggle for Democracy*. Boulder and London: Lynne Rienner.

TSE (Tribunal Supremo Electoral – Guatemala). 1995. Instructivo, Juntas Receptoras de Votos.

TSE. n.d.[a] *Memoria de las Elecciones 1990/1991*. Guatemala.

TSE. n.d.[b] *Memoria: Elecciones 95–96*.

TSE and CAPEL (Centro Interamericano de Asesoria y Promocion Electoral). 1986. *Programa de Capacitacion Político-Electoral, Elecciones Generales 1985*. Guatemala.

UNDP (United Nations Development Program). 2005. *Informe Nacional de Desarrollo Humano 2005: Diversidad Étnico-Cultural: La Ciudadanía en un Estado Plural*. Guatemala: United Nations Development Program.

5 Guatemala

Election administration reform and improving voter access, 2004–2011

After establishing highly restrictive procedural barriers to voting in the 1980s, Guatemala held several relatively free and fair elections marked by low levels of voter participation. By the mid-1990s, electoral reform was on the agenda, with many proposals focusing on making voting more accessible. When the country's civil war came to an end in 1996, issues of election administration were included in the peace accords, beginning a long process of electoral reform. This chapter recounts the story of the reform process in Guatemala and explains what made dramatic changes in election administration inclusiveness possible and why the reforms took the particular shape that they did, removing some obstacles to voting while leaving others in place.

Early attempts at reform

By the mid-1990s, Guatemalan political parties, the Supreme Electoral Tribunal (TSE), and observers on all sides acknowledged the obstacles to voting presented by centralized polling sites, the manner of assigning voters to voting centers, and the processes of documentation and voter registration (OAS 1997, 16, 37). A number of amendments to the electoral law were introduced in Congress in the mid-1990s to address these problems.[1] Several bills introduced in 1993 and 1994 would have located polling stations outside of municipal capitals. In 1994, the TSE, using its power to initiate legislation, proposed polling-site decentralization and the creation of a new identification card (to be issued by the TSE), while a collection of civil society groups proposed similar measures. Yet another bill would have decentralized polling stations, provided free public transportation to the polls and instituted an absentee voting system.[2]

However, despite support from various quarters on the desirability of polling decentralization and a new identity card, these reforms made no headway. One obstacle was that most of the proposed amendments to make voting easier were tied up with other, more controversial measures. Several of the proposals would have allowed non-partisan civic committees to run candidates for Congress (they are currently limited to fielding municipal candidates), thus creating more competition for established political parties. One proposal would have instituted compulsory voting and changed a number of party registration and campaign finance rules and was blocked by the Constitutional Court; another sought to circumvent the constitutional prohibition of presidential candidacies of those who had participated in a coup, intended to benefit FRG (Guatemalan Republican Front) party leader Efraín Ríos Montt.

Another obstacle to reform was disagreement over the form that polling-site decentralization should take. Some proposals from legislators called for drastic decentralization of polling stations to any population center of 200 or more registered voters, while the TSE wanted the power to decide where to locate voting centers and actively opposed the more radical decentralization proposals, noting the logistical difficulty of establishing voting centers in the country's 6,000 villages and the need for cartographic studies to choose appropriate sites. The TSE also opposed the proposed plan for absentee voting, fearing multiple voting in the context of weak safeguards against obtaining fake identity cards (TSE n.d.[a], 15). Yet another impediment to reform was the fact that many of the reforms were proposed when a national election was on the horizon, which made reform less likely (CRE 2004, 21) – despite the fact that some reforms would not have gone into effect until after the 1995 elections.

Thus, the mid-1990s saw a number of failed proposals to increase election administration inclusiveness. Ultimately, it took the end of the country's armed conflict and the resulting peace accords to give electoral reform a new boost and place it squarely on the political agenda (Interviews 06, 07, 08).

The electoral accord and the commission on electoral reform

The Guatemala Peace Accords between the government and the URNG guerrillas were wide-ranging and included the Agreement on Constitutional Reforms and the Electoral Regime, signed in December 1996. The sections of the accord that dealt with the electoral regime put the issue of voter participation front and center and recognized

> [t]hat the electoral processes suffer from specific shortcomings which impede the effective enjoyment of the right to vote, and that include citizens' lack of reliable documentation, the absence of technically prepared voter lists, difficulty of access to registration and voting, lack of information and the need for greater transparency in electoral campaigns.
>
> (Section II)

According to two URNG members, issues of electoral administration were included in the peace accords with the aim of opening up and democratizing what they considered to be a discredited political system (Interviews 08, 10).

To boost voter participation and improve the legitimacy of the electoral process, the accord addressed a wide range of issues – the majority of them dealing with election administration inclusiveness – as a minimum agenda for modernizing the electoral regime. Areas identified for reform were voter documentation, voter registration, the voting process (the location of polling places and the access of migrant workers to voting), voter-information campaigns, transparency of parties and campaign finance, and strengthening electoral institutions. On voter documentation, the accord called for replacing the country's antiquated and easily falsified paper identity document (*cédula de vecindad*) with a more modern, general purpose identity card that would also serve as voter identification. The accord indicated that the TSE would issue the identity document – an issue that became deeply contentious later – and that the new document should be used for the next electoral process, in 1999; as it turned out, it would be more than a decade before distribution of the new ID card would begin.

Among the most contentious and challenging election administration matters contained in the accord were voter registration and polling-place decentralization. On the decentralization of polling places, the implementation of which would be hotly debated in the following years, the accord called for the TSE to choose, in consultation with political parties, appropriate polling locations outside of municipal centers which would be accessible to party poll watchers and election observers (section II, par. 12).

To implement decentralization, corresponding changes in voter registration would be needed. In particular, voter rolls would need to include voters' specific places of residence and not just the municipality in which they resided. The accord also recommended facilitating voter access to registration centers, particularly in rural areas, and ensuring that deaths and changes of residence were more fully recorded in the voter rolls. Partly related to these recommendations were the suggestions on institutional strengthening, which included modernizing the national registry to "permit the automation of data and its integration into coordinated networks for the effective cross-checking, maintenance, and updating of electoral rolls" (section II, par. 20). With a primary focus on increasing voter participation but also touching on issues of campaign finance regulations, the accord set an expansive agenda for reform.

To study and elaborate a proposal for the relevant reforms to the electoral law, the accord mandated the creation of a Commission on Electoral Reform (CRE), to be presided by the Supreme Electoral Tribunal and with participation from all parties with representation in Congress (seven parties with one representative each). The commission was to complete its work within six months of being constituted (though its term was subsequently extended twice) and publish a report with the recommended legal reforms.

With its agenda based on the electoral accord, the Commission on Electoral Reform began its work on April 1, 1997. The commission's work was supported by technical studies elaborated by the TSE with support from the Organization of American States (CRE 1998). In addition, the CRE issued a public call for reform proposals, and a wide range of civic groups and individual citizens presented two dozen proposal packages to the commission, most containing multiple recommendations. Many of the proposals reiterated the reforms called for in the electoral accord, including decentralization of voting sites, "domicile voting" (the assignment of voters to the voting center closest to their residence), and a new identity document. Some proposals also called for the provision of free public transportation on election day and voting rights for army and police members and for Guatemalans living abroad (Acción Ciudadana et al. 2005; TSE n.d.[b]).

Other proposals went beyond the CRE's minimal agenda, including requirements for parties to run indigenous candidates in top spots on party lists and allowing civic committees to run candidates for Congress (Cerigua Weekly Briefs 1998; TSE n.d.[b]). Thus the already extensive agenda was widened further through the proposals from civil society.

The CRE's work culminated in a 1998 report titled "Guatemala, Peace and Democracy" and an associated bill introduced in Congress proposing changes to 163 articles of the electoral law.[3] The CRE's president, TSE magistrate Mario Guerra Roldán, urged Congress to enact the amendments swiftly so that they could be implemented for the following year's general election (Cerigua Weekly Briefs 1998).

The election administration measures included in the CRE package included: decentralization of polling sites at the discretion of the TSE; assigning voters in large cities to the polling station closest to their home; state provision of free transportation on election day (and prohibiting parties from transporting voters); moving election day from December to August to facilitate the participation of seasonal migrant workers; and requiring the TSE to carry out ongoing civic and voter education programs (CRE 2004). Changes tightening party registration requirements were also included. Aside from specific legal reforms, the CRE report also called on the TSE to facilitate voter registration by simplifying its procedures, utilizing mobile registration units, and extending hours of operation in registration offices (CRE 2004, 185). Other legal reforms proposed by civil society groups, such as allowing civic committees to run Congressional candidates and party quotas for women and indigenous people, were excluded from the final proposal. According to the CRE's executive secretary, these larger measures were excluded in the hopes of passing the other proposals quickly before the 1999 elections (Interview 06). The final package of proposed reforms thus "reflect[ed] closely those recommended in the peace accords themselves" (Cerigua Weekly Briefs 1998).

According to several CRE members, there had been consensus among the party representatives and the TSE magistrates within the CRE on the major issues of voter access, such as polling-place decentralization (Interviews 06, 07, 16). These reforms were also supported universally by civil society groups, academics, and the recommendations of international election observers. But six years would pass before Congress approved changes to the electoral law. As legal reforms stalled in Congress, the TSE pursued administrative measures to lower barriers to participation.

TSE initiatives to improve voter registration

While changes to the electoral law were delayed, the TSE undertook measures to facilitate the vote that didn't require legal reforms. At this time, the issue of increasing voter participation was high on the agenda and, in the late 1990s, a study being carried out by Horacio Boneo and Edelberto Torres-Rivas and funded by international organizations emphasized the problem of voter registration (Boneo and Torres-Rivas 2000; Interview 13). Two TSE measures thus focused on voter registration: the employment of mobile voter registration units and the switch back to a voter roll based on citizens' residence (rather than *vecindad*).

The use of mobile registration brigades began in 1999. These brigades consist of small teams that visit areas removed from the permanent registry offices (both in rural areas and in commercial centers in cities) for a short period to carry out voter registration. Today their coverage extends to all of the country's departments, with teams generally spending five days or more in a community to carry out registration (Interview 21; Sánchez del Valle 2000, 29; TSE n.d.[c], 828–29). These brigades, combined with greater publicity from the TSE promoting voter registration, resulted in significant increases in the voter rolls, particularly in predominantly indigenous areas (López-Pintor and Urrutia 2002, 39, 41–42). The brigades also serve as a means for voters to update or check their registration status.

Equally significant was the TSE's modification of its regulation of the electoral law in 2001. With this change, citizens could register to vote in the municipality in which they currently resided, even if they did not obtain their identity document in that municipality. Citizens already registered would be able to update their information in order to transfer their registration to their municipality of residence (TSE 2001b). The following year, another modification established a six-month residency requirement to register in a given jurisdiction (TSE 2002) but, in practice, there were few controls in place to enforce this.

This measure returned the voter registration process to what had been in place prior to 1987, with the goal of facilitating the vote in order to boost participation (PL 2001g). The updating of voters' registration data was also used to implement domicile voting, assigning voters to the voting center nearest their residence (Interview 17). While expressing tentative support for the measure, some legislators and civil society observers expressed concern about the potential for voter fraud (PL 2001g), a concern that has remained widespread. Since no documentation of residence in the jurisdiction is required when registering, this change did indeed open the possibility for voter registration fraud. If voters lie about their address when registering – a practice thought to be common – they can register in a different municipality in order to support local candidates in that town. This voter registration fraud – what Fukumoto and Horiuchi (2011) call "preelectoral residential registration" (587) – results in the infamous *traslado* (transfer) of outside voters to support mayoral candidates, often giving rise to election-related conflicts.[4] This administrative measure aimed at increasing inclusion thus also loosened protections against voter fraud. This is particularly unusual given the TSE's tendency to prioritize safeguards against fraud, and subsequently the TSE sought stricter safeguards such as requiring proof of residence when registering, an earlier closing date for voter registration to allow more time to detect anomalies on the voter rolls (Interviews 21, 22), and a longer residency requirement.[5]

Reforming the electoral law

While the TSE reduced administrative barriers related to voter registration, electoral reform was taken up in Congress in early 2000, following the general election in late 1999. Both the TSE and deputies from a range of parties in Congress agreed on the importance of the reforms in order to increase voter participation and concurred that the year following an election would be the ideal time to approve the reforms (PL 2000a; 2000b; 2000c). The TSE magistrates and Congressional deputies agreed that the basis of discussion should be the CRE report, and all signs indicated that all of the party caucuses in Congress were disposed to approve electoral reforms that year (PL 2000c; 2000e).

However, the reform process would follow a torturous path before finally resulting in wide-ranging changes to the electoral law. In October 2003, all but one of Guatemala's political parties subscribed to a Shared National Agenda, an accord promoted by the UNDP and the Netherlands Institute for Multiparty Democracy. One of the priorities of the agenda was to reform the electoral law, which took center stage in the new Congress inaugurated in 2004 (PL 2004a; 2004c). There were many calls – by independent analysts, some Congressional deputies and, above all, the TSE – for further delay of the reforms to take additional proposals into account (especially those emanating from the TSE) (PL 2004b; 2004d; 2004e; 2004f). Ironically, the delays in approving the reforms had led both to a sense of urgency and also the opinion among many that the reforms had already become dated (PL 2004e). Despite continuing disagreements over a number of measures in the reform package, the governing Gran Alianza Nacional (GANA) coalition threw its support behind the electoral reforms, as a result of a "gentlemen's agreement" with other parties over unrelated pieces of legislation pending in Congress. This cleared the path for the electoral reform bill that had been debated in 2001 to be approved (unchanged) on April 21, 2004, over the objections of the TSE, with 135 deputies voting for the amendments and only 10 deputies voting against (PL 2004g; 2004h; 2004j).[6] Many deputies voting for the bill acknowledged that the amendments included errors and omissions, and the passage of the reforms was accompanied by a pledge to approve follow-up changes within 90 days (PL 2004i).

It quickly became apparent that further reforms would not be approved quickly, and the Congressional Committee on Electoral Matters indicated that proposed amendments from the TSE and civil society would be considered. The discussion of additional amendments centered on some of the most contentious issues, such as campaign finance regulation, implementation of a new identity document, and the participation of women and indigenous candidates. At this time, the term "second generation reforms" – meaning the inclusion of themes promoted by the TSE and civil society not treated in the 2004 reforms – gave way in Congress to talk of "harmonizing reforms," limited to correcting errors and inconsistencies included in the first round of amendments (PL 2004k; 2004o). Finally, on October 19, 2006, some two and a half years after its 90-day term to approve a second round of electoral reforms had passed, Congress approved the second set of amendments to the electoral law.

Reform and inclusion: making the right to vote more accessible

The reforms to the electoral law, coupled with the administrative initiatives of the TSE, significantly increased Guatemala's election administration inclusiveness. A centerpiece of the reforms was the decentralization of polling sites (LEPP, Art. 231). This led to the creation of new rural electoral jurisdictions for voting centers outside of municipal capitals and a major increase in polling sites: from 8,885 voting tables in 1,262 voting centers for the 2003 elections to 13,756 tables in 2,060 centers for 2007 (EUEOM 2007, 21; OAS 2008, 54). Decentralization was widely praised by election observers and drew positive evaluations from election officials and party leaders (e.g., EUEOM 2007; OAS 2008, 57). It also proved popular with the public, and rural communities solicited the TSE to set up rural voting centers in their areas (MIOE 2007, 108).

Electoral reform also increased access for urban voters through implementation of domicile voting (LEPP, Art. 224). This began on a limited basis, with the updating of voters' registration information prior to the 2003 elections, with the TSE using voters' residence to geo-code their registration; prior to this, the voter registry contained no codes for residence (since such information did not affect one's assignment to a voting center) (Boneo 2001, 81; OAS 2009, 18–19).[7] With the reforms to the electoral law, urban voters could now avoid traveling across town to reach their polling station. The reforms also moved up election dates from November to September, which served to facilitate the vote of migrant workers employed on the major coffee and sugar harvests from October to February (ASIES 2005, 45; Interview 16; Vargas 2008a).

Finally, the reforms explicitly added civic and voter education to the TSE's responsibilities, formalizing what the TSE already considered part of its duties. This corresponded with more extensive voter education efforts. For the 2007 election season, the TSE carried out voter education campaigns – through radio, television, printed materials, telephone hotlines, and the Internet – directed particularly at informing voters about decentralization and also sent an estimated 3.5 million telegrams to voters informing them of their polling-place assignment (EUEOM 2007, 35–36). In 2011, the TSE distributed 7 million mini-telegrams to registered voters with their voting center information and employed information kiosks in commercial centers, text messages, print and online ads, and an extensive campaign of television and radio spots carried out in Spanish and four Mayan languages (TSE 2011a; 2011b; 2011c).

Election observers acknowledged the improved efforts to inform voters about where to vote and better dissemination of information in Mayan languages, while also emphasizing that voter information in indigenous languages still had limited reach (EUEOM 2007, 35, 49; Jessup, Hayek, and Hällhag 2008, 7; MIOE 2007, 78; Mirador Electoral 2008, 25, 116). Interviews carried out by domestic observers in 2007 with members of two of the largest indigenous language groups revealed that most people in these communities did not have adequate information about the polling-decentralization process (Mirador Electoral 2007, 9). More generally, despite more extensive efforts at informing voters about the electoral process, the TSE's information campaigns were again launched late, thus hindering their effectiveness (EUEOM 2007, 36; Mirador Electoral 2008, 13). The informational campaign leading up to the 2011 elections was massive, but dissemination of information in Mayan languages continued to be slow (PL 2011b; 2011f).

The first elections held after the reforms, in 2007, saw a small increase of 2 percentage points in voter turnout, compared to the previous election. Decentralization appeared to facilitate the rural vote, as turnout in rural areas reached 70 percent, compared to 57 percent for urban areas (EUEOM 2007, 55). The increase in turnout from the prior elections was larger in predominantly indigenous departments than non-indigenous (MIOE 2007, 70). The results were more dramatic in 2011. The voter rolls increased by more than 22 percent since 2007,[8] with a 33 percent increase in registration for women – who for the first time made up more than half the voter rolls at 50.7 percent (PL 2011d; Siglo 21 2011b). Voter turnout reached 69 percent of registered voters (TSE 2012, 151), matching the historic high of the 1985 elections (but with a more inclusive voter roll).

Despite these significant changes, voter registration was left largely untouched by the electoral law reforms. For instance, the closing date for registration was unchanged by the 2004 and 2006 reforms.[9] In practice, however, the bureaucratic complexity that voters faced when registering was reduced, as all voter registry offices were computerized by 2008 and able to complete a voter's registration in one office visit (Interview 21). However, the increases in voter registration rates after 2007 were the result, at least in part, of the requirement put in place by the UNE government that social welfare recipients be registered voters. The departments with the highest numbers of welfare recipients through the program *Mi Familia Progresa* saw particularly large increases in voter registration (see Siglo 21 2011b).

The key part of the legal reforms that would have changed voter registration practices was the introduction of a new national identity document. The 2004 electoral law reforms made reference to the new document that would replace the *cédula*, and the following year Congress passed the National Registry of Persons Law. This created a new civil registry (RENAP) which, for the first time, created a centralized national registry and introduced a new identity card (DPI) to replace the *cédula* that had been issued by municipal registry offices.

Everyone agreed on the need for a new and more secure identity document, but the contentious issue was implementation. Since 1985, the TSE had advocated the creation of a new ID that the TSE itself would oversee, and it lobbied strongly on this point during the reform process; this was also the position of the CRE proposal for electoral reform and the initial decision of the congressional committee on electoral matters (PL 2005a; 2005b). The TSE made a strong case, considering the central role of the ID card in the voting process and the tribunal's established bureaucratic infrastructure (with registry offices in every municipality in the country), as well as its political independence. Moreover, the task of issuing identity cards would have kept the TSE busy during its idle time between elections and likely cost less than setting up a new agency (Interview 14). Yet, Congress ultimately decided to create a new agency in which to vest the new civil registry, to be overseen by one representative each from the TSE, Congress, and the executive branch.

Had the TSE been given control over the new civil registry, voter registration would have become automatic, as the CRE had intended (Interviews 13, 14); since citizens would register for an ID with the TSE, an additional voter registration process would have been unnecessary. Nevertheless, automatic voter registration was planned even with the creation of RENAP. The 2006 amendments to the electoral law aimed partly to reconcile the electoral and registry laws and would have renamed the TSE's Citizens Registry the "Citizens' Electoral Registry" and allowed for direct input of civil registry data into the voter registry – thus eliminating the requirement to carry out two separate procedures to register (Núñez Vargas 2008a, 15, 18). But when the draft of the 2006 reforms to the electoral law was reviewed by the Constitutional Court, the court ruled that the name change was unconstitutional. In short, the court determined that the civil registry, RENAP, could not carry out activities pertaining to the Citizens' Registry (i.e. voter registration), particularly because the civil registry law could not modify the responsibilities of the Citizen's Registry which are laid out in the electoral law, a law of constitutional rank (Corte de Constitucionalidad de Guatemala 2006; Interview 21). Therefore, automatic voter registration would apparently require a constitutional reform (Interview 09).[10]

The consequence of the court ruling was to maintain a two-step process for voter registration: first obtaining an identity card through RENAP, then registering to vote with the TSE. Other ways to facilitate voter registration were sought, such as placing voter registration tables in RENAP offices, so citizens could complete both steps in one place (Interviews 02, 17). But, as of 2011, there were only a handful of voter registration stations located in RENAP offices (Interview 21). This measure for facilitating voter registration (akin to the American motor voter system) was limited by distrust between the TSE and RENAP, in particular the TSE's concerns about contaminating the voter rolls with potentially unreliable data from RENAP and fear of tarnishing the TSE's reputation by offering services in RENAP offices, considering the inefficiencies and controversies of titanic proportions during the new civil registry's first years in operation (Interviews 17, 21, 23). Another obstacle to collaboration was the lack of clarity in the legislation regarding the relationship between RENAP and the TSE (Conde Rada 2008, 47, 52–53; Mirador Electoral 2008, 119; Núñez Vargas 2008a, 39–40), although by 2011 collaboration had improved, with the registries sharing data for verification purposes and RENAP providing fliers from the TSE containing information on voter registration (PL 2011a).

Thus, while the TSE made the voter registration process easier, a host of problems with the new civil registry (including long wait times and delays of weeks or months between soliciting an ID card and receiving it) made the prior step of obtaining an identification document more difficult than before (PL 2009; 2010a). The service was so inefficient in some places that there were reports of people sleeping outside of RENAP offices in order to sell their spots in the morning to people who needed to carry out registry transactions (PL 2010f). Inefficiencies in the civil registry particularly affected young people turning 18 years old shortly before an election, who needed an ID card to register to vote (Interviews 04, 17, 21; El Periódico 2011; Siglo 21 2011a). Thus, while Guatemalans now receive a more modern and secure identity card, it was initially difficult for many people to obtain due to delays and inefficiencies, and they still must carry out an additional process to register to vote, with young citizens particularly disadvantaged.

By the 2011 general election, Guatemala had undergone a series of significant election administration reforms, many of which made voting more accessible. A summary of election administration inclusiveness in Guatemala for the 2004–2011 period is presented in Table 5.1.

Explaining electoral administration reform

The substantial changes in Guatemala's electoral administration beginning in the late 1990s raise a number of questions. What made such reforms possible? Why were reforms, on which all major political actors agreed, delayed for so long? How did different factors – partisan interests, the electoral management body, concerns over election fraud, and international electoral assistance – shape the form that electoral administration took?

Delaying reform

Why did Congress take so long to pass reforms that had been agreed upon by the major political parties by 1998? A number of factors intervened between the 1998 CRE report and the 2004–2006 reforms. One of the most important was the scope of the reforms being considered, which touched on nearly all aspects of the electoral system – including election administration, campaign finance, and internal party governance. Thus, as was the case with many reform proposals in the mid-1990s, election administration measures were tied up with more contentious issues. The number of reforms being considered caused confusion among legislators and proved to be a stumbling block to passage (Interviews 03, 08); as a former Congressional deputy admitted, there is little expertise of technical electoral matters in Congress (Interview 28). The timing of the reforms made matters worse. When the CRE sent its package of proposals to Congress in

Table 5.1 Election administration inclusiveness, Guatemala 2004–2016

Dimension	*Description*	*Inclusiveness*
Voter registration		
Extent of state responsibility for registering voters	Voter-initiated, significant state efforts to facilitate registration	Medium
Difficulty of registration process	Simple registration process completed in one trip to registry office, with decentralized registration services	High
Ease of access to ID documents required for registration	*Cédula* or DPI required; obtaining DPI obstructed by bureaucratic inefficiencies	Low
Registration closing date	3 months prior to 2016; 4 months after 2016	Medium/low
Residency requirement	6 months prior to 2016; 17 months after 2016; no documentation of residence required	Low
Provisional registration	None	Low
Registry consultation	Information available through kiosks and online, mailed to voters; voter rolls distributed to parties	High
Purging of voter rolls	Voters not purged from the rolls for failure to vote	High
Getting to the ballot box		
Accessibility of polling places	Polling places decentralized from 2007 on	High
Assignment of voters to polling places	Residential for voters with updated registry information	High
Convenience voting measures	Not used	Low
Electoral calendar	Voting held on a Sunday prior to labor migration season	High
Casting a ballot		
Voter ID requirement	*Cédula* (or DPI from 2011 on) required	Medium
Provisional or tendered ballots	Not used	Low
Voter education		
State efforts to inform voters of where and how to register and vote	Moderate territorial and linguistic coverage, extensive duration of information campaigns through diverse media	Medium
Overall inclusiveness		Medium

1998, elections were on the horizon for the following year, and there was reluctance to change the rules of the game shortly before an electoral process (Interview 18). After the 1999 elections, the reforms were taken up by a new Congress with a new party in the majority. Turnover of TSE magistrates took place in 2002, and a new Congress took office in 2004 – turnovers which slowed down reforms, according to a former TSE magistrate (Interview 13). As new deputies entered Congress, they needed time to become familiar with the electoral reforms, which included issues with which many legislators were not well versed (Interview 04).

With more than 150 changes to the electoral law being considered, disagreements over the most conflictive issues – particularly campaign finance and political party regulations – held up passage of the reforms that everyone agreed on, such as the decentralization of polling places (Interviews 06, 08). Matters were made worse when the governing FRG party inserted a clause in the reform bill that would have sidestepped the constitutional ban on candidacies of coup makers, allowing their leader Efraín Ríos Montt to run for president – a measure roundly opposed by everyone but the FRG (PL 2001b; 2001c; 2001d; 2001e). Other modifications to the committee bill would have infringed on the TSE's autonomy, which drew fierce opposition from the TSE, opposition parties, civil society, and even other Central American electoral bodies (PL 2000g; 2000h; 2000i; 2000j). While Congress backtracked on the measures that would have infringed on TSE autonomy, and the Constitutional Court blocked the measure to allow Ríos Montt's presidential candidacy, these controversial proposals held up the process long enough to lose the window of opportunity following the 1999 elections. By 2002, the closeness of upcoming elections was added to the reasons that opposition parties offered for not supporting passage (Interview 11; PL 2002a).

Even on issues of consensus, such as decentralizing polling places, there remained disagreement over questions of implementation, as had been the case in the mid-1990s. The CRE proposal had left it in the hands of the TSE to decide the proper locations of polling stations (CRE 2004, 173–74; TSE 2001a, 161). Congress instead opted for a rapid and extensive decentralization, mandating a voting center for any population center (village, hamlet, etc.) containing 500 or more registered voters. The TSE wanted a more gradual decentralization based on its cartographic studies that had identified locations that would meet the criteria of security and adequate infrastructure, as well as voter access – both to ensure control over rural voting centers and so as to not exceed the TSE's capacity. Rather than a mandate to install polling stations based solely on the number of registered voters, the TSE wanted to maintain discretion over polling locations, allowing it to place stations in strategic locations where voters from several villages could converge (Azpuru 2004; EUEOM 2007, 21; TSE 2001a, 161).

The 2004 reforms reflected Congress' preference for a strict requirement based on the number of registered voters. This decision can be attributed to the genuine desire of the political parties to increase participation and facilitate access of their supporters to the polls, as well as to the legislators' lack of familiarity with the technical criteria employed by the TSE (Interviews 13, 16, 25). The 2006 amendments to the electoral law returned discretion to the TSE in locating polling sites after the TSE and Congress reached an agreement, whereby the TSE pledged to establish more rural voting sites for the 2007 elections than it had initially planned, in exchange for the authority to decide their locations and a budget increase in order to carry out the decentralization (Interviews 17, 27).[11]

These disagreements over particular measures, combined with the procedural requirement of a two-thirds vote in Congress to reform the electoral law, slowed down the process. The short post-election window of opportunity to pass reform and the need for court review of any amendments to the electoral law also explain why Congress chose to pass error-riddled reforms in 2004, with a promise to immediately work on another round of changes (Interview 25). Rather than make revisions that would require review by the Constitutional Court, Congress decided to approve the pending 2001 reform bill that had already passed court review, putting off other reforms and corrections for a later date (Carter Center 2004, 17).

The specter of election fraud

What of the concerns of election fraud that had been fundamental to the adoption of restrictive election administration rules in the 1980s? Unlike during the debates surrounding the drafting of the 1985 electoral law, the issue of fraud was a secondary (though still important) theme during the reform process. There was some apprehension within both Congress and the TSE about the decentralization of polling sites resulting in election fraud (Interviews 07, 08, 14), along with general concerns about decentralization causing disorganization in the electoral process (Interview 06). But, ultimately, fears of fraud recurring played a minor role in the reform process (Interviews 27, 28), only arising periodically during the FRG government of 1999–2003, when there were concerns of decentralization being manipulated by the governing party (Azpuru 2004; Interview 11). During the congressional debate over reform, Congressional Deputy Pablo Duarte discussed the issue of fraud colorfully (Congress of the Republic of Guatemala 2001a):

> …the electoral and political parties law was created in that stigma that existed over the fraudulent electoral processes. I'll never forget that they used to say the fraud was committed in the villages, and on the farms the people would go to line up to vote, and the military commissioner would pass by … handing out election papers already folded so that they would put them in the ballot box. The person would ask "…who did I vote for?" And they would answer him: "jackass, don't you know that the vote is secret?" But we can no longer keep legislating over the fears of the past. We can no longer keep legislating over what happened and over all the blood spilled in this country, fraud, etc.…

And indeed, the specter of fraud did not deter legislators from pushing for polling-site decentralization. Rather, concerns about fraud most directly shaped election administration by preventing the implementation of absentee balloting: when such a system was considered to facilitate the vote of migrant workers, it was rejected by the TSE because of such concerns ("Exposición de Motivos…," 25).[12]

That the historical experience of election rigging exercised relatively little influence on the reform process is understandable, considering the country's experience in the intervening years. By the time the peace accords were signed, Guatemala had held three national and several municipal elections[13] that were largely free of fraud; by the time the reforms were finally approved, five relatively clean national elections had been held. Thus, by the time reforms were discussed, the threat of wholesale fraud had been greatly reduced, and confidence in the TSE had grown (Interviews 06, 09). In particular, the safeguards in place – such as party poll watchers receiving copies of the local vote tallies – lessened the risks associated with decentralization (Interviews 14, 27). This does not mean that accusations of fraud are in short supply around election time: they are still common, though generally focused on local rather than national races and concerning vote buying and pre-electoral residential registration (voters falsely swearing to changes of residence when updating their voter registration) rather than wholesale ballot stuffing or alteration of the vote tally.[14] And the Guatemalan public remains deeply preoccupied with election fraud, according to public opinion polls (PL 2010b). But among lawmakers and election administrators, there was confidence that reforms such as decentralization would not lead back to the dark days of ballot stuffing. Lingering fears of fraud colored discussions over the form that polling decentralization would take, with many concerned about the risk of fraud inherent in a drastic decentralization that did not take security conditions into account (e.g., Castillo Milla 2006, 37); but no one suggested that polling stations remain centralized in municipal capitals for fear of fraud. But the late 1990s and early 2000s, low voter participation rather than fraud had become the central problem of election administration.

Partisan interests

Just as purely partisan interests played little role in the initial construction of procedural obstacles to voting, they also explain little of the reform process that made election administration more inclusive. During the debates in Congress, no legislators publicly opposed the inclusionary aspects of reform, although there was disagreement over the form that polling decentralization would take (with some legislators supporting the TSE position). There were few differences along ideological lines: for instance, while the leftist URNG party that emerged from the country's guerrilla movements supported electoral reform throughout, other small leftist parties were consistent critics of some non-administrative elements of the reforms.[15]

Consensus on reform was also long-standing: an election observer mission to the 1999 elections reported that all of the candidates and parties interviewed were

> unanimous in expressing their concern over the high rates of voter abstention recorded in previous elections … and pointed to the legal difficulties that citizens face in attempting to register and vote as one of the factors discouraging a greater voter turnout.
>
> (OAS 2000, 13)

Such contemporaneous public expressions of support were verified in later interviews with observers and participants in the electoral reform process, all of whom agreed that the political parties supported polling decentralization and the goal of increasing voter turnout. While there were differences along party lines that delayed passage of the electoral reforms, there were few if any differences over administrative inclusion.

What is puzzling is that all parties would support administrative reforms that would prove to have significant political consequences. Centralization of polling sites had conferred potential advantages to parties or candidates with the resources to transport rural voters to the polls. Moreover, national elections had often been decisively influenced by the vote in urban areas, above all the department of Guatemala (containing about one-fourth of the country's voters). But in the first elections after reform in 2007, the rural vote was decisive in electing the center-left Álvaro Colóm president (MIOE 2007, 74; Núñez Vargas 2008b, 61–62; Sáenz de Tejada 2005, 161, 188, 235). As an observer mission noted,

> all the areas outside the capital responded to the political proposals that were more focused on rural development (an issue that was repeatedly stressed by Colóm …). On the other hand, the capital proved more receptive to proposals focusing on the fight against citizen insecurity (the clear *leitmotiv* of [Otto] Pérez Molina's campaign).
>
> (EUEOM 2007, 59; see also Mirador Electoral 2008, 49–50)

Again in the 2011 run-off election, there was a noticeable difference between the top two candidates in their support in urban versus rural areas (PL 2011h), although this time the conservative Otto Pérez Molina defeated his opponent Manuel Baldizón. Moreover, increased participation may have contributed to a significant drop in the re-election rate of mayors in 2007, as "mayoral candidates had to be more sensitive to citizens' needs and interests, particularly those of women, youth, and indigenous people in rural areas who were voting for the first time" (USAID 2010). The decentralization of polling sites also reduced (but did not eliminate) the role of party transportation on election day and led parties to increase the territorial coverage of their campaigning and organizational structures in areas outside of municipal capitals, while also requiring parties to field larger numbers of party poll watchers on election day (Blanco 2008, 89; Núñez Vargas 2008a, 17, 20, 27; OAS 2009, 10).[16]

Party support for reform can be explained by a confluence of several factors. Before 2007, voting restrictions were not perceived to confer significant advantages on some parties over others, and most party elites did not foresee the consequences of reform. Also, any advantages that would be lost by larger parties would be compensated through reduced spending on voter transportation and advantages in fielding party poll watchers at more polling places. Finally, the administrative reforms did not threaten the primary sources of power for party elites: campaign financing and the dominance of caudillos inside parties.

First, as might be expected, smaller and particularly leftist parties wanted to ensure the access of their likely supporters through election administration reforms (Interviews 07, 08). However, the desire to facilitate access for potential supporters was not limited to such parties but was universal across the political spectrum (Interview 16). The barriers to participation that polling location and voter registration imposed were not widely perceived to benefit some parties over others (Interviews 18, 26) – with one exception: larger parties with more resources were advantaged by centralized polling sites because they could afford to provide transportation to voters on election day (Interviews 12, 28).

That barriers to voting did not benefit parties of particular ideological stripes is understandable in light of the nature of Guatemala's party system, which is highly fluid and marked by low levels of partisan attachments in the electorate. Most parties are clientelistic, catch-all parties centered on a single prominent personality rather than programmatic organizations with a clearly defined social base (Sánchez 2008). However, modest differences do exist in party support along urban-rural and rich-poor lines, as evidenced by the differences between two of the top contenders in the 2007 and 2011 elections, the National Unity of Hope (UNE) and the Patriot Party. These differences proved decisive in the 2007 elections, but the parties appear to not have anticipated the effects that increased access to the polls for rural voters would have on election results (Interview 09). As Núñez Vargas (2008b, 62) puts it, "[w]hat [the 2007] election teaches is that the model of electoral organization centralized in municipal capitals also had political effects that hadn't been perceived with clarity until the moment of this reform." After 2007, parties appeared to have adapted to this reality, devoting more attention to capturing rural votes.

Second, while larger parties might see their advantage in providing election day transportation reduced, this would be compensated by their greater ability to field party poll watchers for a greatly increased number of voting sites. Fielding a sufficient number of poll watchers has been challenging for smaller parties, and this is seen as an advantage for larger parties (Interviews 01, 08, 16). More important is that the "advantage" of providing transport to voters was increasingly seen as a burden by political parties and candidates. As several people involved in the reform process noted, political parties hoped to save money on providing transportation to the polls, which represented a significant campaign expense (Interviews 07, 27). Moreover, parties recognized that there was no guarantee that the voters being transported to the polls would vote for them, and thus transporting voters wasn't really worth the money (Interview 27). Even after decentralization, party transportation is still provided, but its importance has diminished and it is less expensive. At the same time, more effective means of capturing votes, such as vote buying, are thought to be widespread (Interviews

10, 12). Thus decentralization would shift election day costs from political parties to the TSE, and parties would lose little political advantage in exchange.

Finally, the reforms that passed through Congress ultimately did not infringe on the sources of political power of party elites. Most Guatemalan parties are highly personalistic, built around a single prominent political figure (or caudillo),[17] and election administration reforms did not threaten these caudillos by dispersing political power inside parties. The reforms did little to promote more democratic procedures of decision making within parties, while administrative reforms that facilitated the participation of women and indigenous as voters did nothing to guarantee their participation as candidates (Interviews 10, 18). The increased regulations on campaign finance also fell far short of ensuring transparency or imposing meaningful spending limits.

In sum, personalistic catch-all parties did not foresee significant consequences from making voting easier, while those consequences that were foreseen (reduced costs of transporting voters and increased numbers of party poll watchers) were anticipated to benefit larger parties. Thus, election administration reforms represented a chance to increase voter participation without upsetting the balance of electoral power or threatening the internal control of political parties by caudillos.

However, while purely partisan interests were conducive to reform, the collective interests of Congress in securing patronage resources did have detrimental consequences for election administration inclusiveness. Namely, by creating a new civil registry (RENAP), Congress inadvertently derailed automatic voter registration. Subsequently, the prospects for easier voter registration through TSE–RENAP collaboration were limited by RENAP's inefficiencies, bureaucratic turf struggles, and legal uncertainty over the relationship between the two bodies.

Congress' decision to create RENAP is widely attributed to the desire to control patronage resources, with deputies wanting to "dip their hands in" the "golden goose" that the new agency represented (Interview 25).[18] This patronage takes the form of the distribution of jobs in RENAP and the allocation of contracts related to the production of identity cards. Sure enough, after the creation of RENAP, some of its officials were investigated for anomalies in the awarding of contracts (including a US$114 million contract awarded to a company tied to a campaign supporter of President Colóm), and there were media reports of nepotism in RENAP hiring of family members of Congressional deputies (PL 2008; 2010c; 2010d; 2010e). The creation of a centralized registry essentially transferred a source of patronage and rent-seeking from municipal offices, which had previously controlled the issuance of *cédulas* (and collected associated fees), to the central state, with detrimental consequences for election administration inclusiveness.

EMB structure: the Supreme Electoral Tribunal

While the nature of Guatemala's political party system facilitated election administration reform, the Supreme Electoral Tribunal was a major protagonist of reform. The TSE's independence and professionalism have been more or less constant since its creation, with only some variation in the quality of its top leadership. It therefore might be concluded that the TSE's independence (which has remained constant) cannot explain variation in election administration inclusiveness over time. But such a conclusion based on covariation alone would be overly simplistic. Not only has the TSE's independence prevented the type of partisan capture that could lead to administrative disenfranchisement (as has happened in Nicaragua – see Chapter 7), but it has allowed for the formulation of independent initiatives and the development of the technical capacity necessary to implement polling decentralization and voter registry modernization. As a result, the TSE has played a key role in promoting more inclusive election administration, although it has done so cautiously and, at times, has resisted changes that would facilitate voter access in its efforts to balance voter inclusion and election integrity.

The TSE recognized early on the procedural barriers that inhibited voter participation and, particularly during the 1990s under the leadership of magistrates Mario Guerra Roldán and Felix Castillo Milla, the tribunal worked to prepare the way for more inclusive practices. As early as 1994, it submitted an initiative to Congress that would have allowed the tribunal to establish voting centers outside of municipal capitals.[19] Once the Commission on Electoral Reform was formed in 1997, the TSE conducted technical studies on electoral cartography and a new identification card and planned for the implementation of domicile voting (TSE 1997). The TSE also recognized the insufficiency of prior voter-information campaigns and sought to carry out more extensive efforts through diverse strategies and welcomed the inclusion of voter education among its legal mandates (CRE 1997).

Yet, the TSE has also resisted some measures that would increase inclusiveness and pursued others that would make voting more difficult. The tribunal debated and ultimately rejected a form of absentee balloting, discussed above, in order to protect against potential voter fraud. It also sought an earlier closing date for voter registration, claiming it needs ample time to prepare the voter lists, particularly to purge ineligible citizens and to detect fraudulent residences on voters' registrations (Interviews 04, 21, 22). According to the director of voter registration, the time frame to finalize the voter rolls one month before election day (as stipulated by law) is tight, which led the TSE to propose to Congress an earlier closing date (Interview 21). The tribunal's stance on voter registration can be attributed to the jealousy with which the TSE guards the voter registry, seeing it as a fundamental safeguard of the electoral process and being eager to ensure the accuracy and integrity of its contents (Interview 23).

The TSE has also vacillated between inclusive and exclusive administrative measures. A prominent example is the voter registry for the 2003 elections, when many voters who had updated their registration in order to vote closer to their residence found that their names did not appear on the appropriate voters list. As the extent of these technical problems became clear leading up to the election, the TSE adopted a measure to ensure that duly registered voters would not be disenfranchised. Registered voters who did not appear on the voters list at the table to which they were assigned were able to cast a tendered ballot at another table in the same voting center, where the voter's name would be added to a blank voters list (*padrón en blanco*). Despite the inadequate dissemination of information to voters regarding this measure (which was decided on less than two weeks before election day) and insufficient training of poll workers on its use, this TSE decision allowed some of the people whose names did not appear on the voter rolls to cast their ballots (EUEOM 2003, 9, 11; OAS 2005, 12, 66).

But in the second round of the presidential voting, the TSE did not use the blank voter lists, despite the fact that the OAS observer mission, domestic observers, and both campaigns in the run-off urged the TSE to use the measure again. The TSE argued that the measure had been abused during the first round and suggested that the number of people that would be affected in the second round wouldn't be sufficient to alter the election results (EUEOM 2003, 12; OAS 2005, 59, 61, 69). A TSE magistrate at the time recalled that the magistrates felt that the problems that had given rise to the use of the blank voter roll in the first round had been corrected by the run-off vote, so its use was not needed, while making it a permanent feature would have opened the election process to manipulation (Interview 17).

There have also been limitations in the areas in which the TSE has been more proactive, such as voter education. While the tribunal has devoted more attention and resources to informing voters of when, where, and how to vote, the effectiveness of such programs has been limited. One reason is the conceptualization and focus of publicity campaigns, which include text messages and online consultation of vote center locations – in other words, programs designed by (and for) people with resources such as Internet access (Interview 13). Another challenge is the availability of funding, particularly the timing of when funds are available. Because the TSE's budget for electoral years tends to be approved late, and international financial support tends to come after the convocation of an electoral process, voter-information campaigns generally begin not long before the close of voter registration, if not after (Interview 22). A new challenge is the overlap of responsibilities between TSE departments, with a new Institute for Civic-Electoral Formation with uncertain responsibilities in relation to the Unit for Civic-Electoral Training and Education (now relegated largely to training TSE staff, poll workers, and party poll watchers) and the communications department (which handles TV and radio spots). With such a division of responsibilities, there is not always consistency across the departments in the approach to voter education (Interview 22).

In sum, the TSE has at times been proactive in making election administration more inclusive, but it has generally done so cautiously. Some see it as a conservative institution, aiming to avoid fraud above all other goals (ASIES 2005, 97–98), and a number of observers (including at least one former magistrate) consider the TSE magistrates to be overly cautious – noting how magistrates are lawyers who tend to strictly interpret their powers, lack managerial experience or electoral expertise, and seek to fulfill their duties during their term without attracting controversy (Interviews 02, 07, 14). Cautiousness has led to consideration of restrictive measures like an earlier closing date for voter registration, while resource constraints have hampered voter education activities. However, on balance, the TSE's independence and the accumulated experience of its staff contributed to its ability and willingness to pursue polling decentralization, streamlined voter registration procedures, and other measures to facilitate voter participation. Above all, the tribunal's independence allowed it to play a proactive role in sponsoring and endorsing modifications to the electoral law that increased election administration inclusiveness.

Civil society

Unlike the period when the electoral system was designed, the electoral reform process took place in a context of an active civil society. When the CRE and, later, the congressional committee on electoral matters invited civil society proposals for electoral reform, numerous civic and academic groups submitted formal proposals.[20] Additionally, many groups published reports on electoral issues offering recommendations for reform. And, from 1999 onward, civil society included a particularly relevant form of civic activity: domestic election observation. Dozens of local organizations participated in election observation through a number of national efforts. The largest, *Mirador Electoral*, was first active in 2003 and is composed of several prominent NGOs and academic institutions. It fields thousands of observers throughout the country and receives ample media coverage. Other observer efforts of varying sizes are regularly carried out by the Human Rights Ombudsman's office, organizations of indigenous peoples led by *Organismo Naleb'*, the University of San Carlos, and the peak business association CACIF. Monitoring groups offer recommendations on all types of electoral matters, including administrative inclusiveness, both through post-election reports and through direct contacts with the TSE.

What role did such civil society advocacy have in the reform process and in election administration more generally? On the surface, it may appear that legislators and election administrators were influenced by the advocacy of domestic election observers and other civic groups. These groups had access to policymakers through both the CRE and the congressional committee on electoral matters and, by all accounts, enjoyed cooperative relations with the TSE. Civic groups consistently advocated more inclusive administrative practices,[21] and during the reform process civic groups criticized what they perceived to be a focus on avoiding election fraud, noting that the problem of fraud "has already been surpassed by the work of the Supreme Electoral Tribunal" and recommending that the reforms focus on promoting citizen participation and the strengthening of political parties (PL 2001a). And, indeed, some of the reforms that were proposed by civic groups were subsequently implemented. However, closer analysis reveals that civil society advocacy had little direct effect on election administration inclusiveness or the reform process.

Recommendations from civil society groups at best only added legitimacy to reforms that were already on track to be implemented, rather than resulting in particular measures being adopted (Interview 07). This is evident from a comparison of proposals from civic groups with the reforms proposed by the TSE and those approved in Congress. While civic groups consistently supported polling decentralization and the introduction of a new identification card, these measures were already on the political agenda by the mid-1990s. Other reforms that civil society groups promoted which were not already part of the agenda – including campaign finance regulations and gender and ethnic quotas – were either not included or watered down in the bills passed in Congress.

Leaders of domestic election observer groups agree their influence on election law reform has been limited (Interviews 02, 12). And although Congress invited input on electoral reform from civil society, civic organizations criticized Congress' reluctance to fully consider their proposals (ASIES 2004, 24; PL 2001a); the executive secretary of the CRE suggested that Congress invited input from civil society for appearances only, since the CRE had already solicited reform proposals from civic groups (Interview 06).

While civil society organizations had little impact on Congress, relations between domestic election observers and the TSE have been more collaborative. During election processes, observers provide the tribunal with concrete information on electoral issues[22] and maintain close contact with its magistrates – providing it with allies in its disputes with the political parties and Congress (Interviews 02, 12). And, by all accounts, the TSE is generally receptive to election observer recommendations (Interviews 02, 04, 12). This is in contrast to the relative absence of bilateral relations between observers and political parties (Interview 02).

Yet the close collaboration between observers and the TSE doesn't appear to have had much impact on election administration inclusiveness. The most important observer recommendations that directly address TSE behavior in regard to inclusiveness involve voter education activities, and observers have consistently called for more extensive voter education efforts (MIOE 2003, 133; 2007, 78, 130–31; Mirador Electoral 2003; 2007, 4; 2007c; 2008, 118). But improvements in voter education activities have been slow and are partly due to the electoral reforms that made civic education part of the TSE's mandate. A reasonable assessment would be that pressure from observer groups has played, at best, a modest role in pushing the TSE to slowly expand its voter education activities.

Some notable impacts of civil society groups deserve mention. Civic groups have, on occasion, carried out their own voter education activities (Carter Center 2003; OAS 2005, 26–33) and helped citizens obtain identity cards and register to vote (OAS 2005, 30, 32). Domestic election observers have also helped guarantee the integrity of the electoral process and have built civic networks mobilizing women, youth, and indigenous peoples. Thus, through their activities, they have directly helped some citizens navigate electoral procedures and had other positive effects. Yet in terms of legal reforms and administrative regulations, civil society has had little impact on the shape of electoral administration.

International influences

The process of election administration reform was largely determined by domestic actors, but the international community contributed resources to make more inclusive election administration possible. International involvement took several forms: international election observation, rhetorical support for electoral reform, financial and technical electoral assistance, support for domestic election observation groups, and learning from the experiences of other countries.

International election observers consistently recommended reforms to make voting more accessible, including polling decentralization, improved voter registration procedures, and free transportation for voters on election day.[23] These recommendations are routinely delivered to the TSE during and after electoral processes, and the preliminary statements of international observers receive extensive attention in the Guatemalan media. International actors also offered consistent rhetorical support for electoral reform and for making voting more accessible. The UN mission in Guatemala following the peace accords exhorted Congress to approve reforms to the electoral law (MINUGUA 1999; 2000; 2002), and the US ambassador similarly expressed the United States' support for the reforms (PL 2000d).

International actors have also provided financial and technical assistance for election administration. Bilateral aid has come from a number of countries,[24] often being channeled through international bodies like the Organization of American States (OAS) and the Center for Electoral Promotion and Assistance (CAPEL). While the TSE has received international support since 1985, external assistance expanded drastically with the formation of the CRE in 1997, when the OAS took a lead role in providing technical support for electoral cartography studies, voter registry modernization, and civic education (Azpuru 2004; Jessup, Hayek, and Hällhag 2008, 13; OAS 2008), providing $7 million from 1997 to 2004 for the establishment of cartography and education and training units within the TSE (PL 2004n). The International Institute for Democracy and Electoral Assistance and the United Nations also provided technical assistance to the TSE and the congressional committee on electoral matters (Azpuru 2004; CRE 2004, 5, 8; PL 2000f).

International assistance has been devoted to both long-term institutional strengthening and short-term support for election processes. The international community supplied $9 million for the 2003 elections (supplementing the TSE's budget of $14 million) to support the updating of the voter rolls, equipment purchases, and domestic election observation groups (EUEOM 2003, 12–13). In preparation of the 2007 elections, in which polling sites would be decentralized for the first time, international support poured in. A program funded by Sweden, Norway, the United States, and Britain focused on long-term institutional strengthening as well as immediate logistical support for 2007 elections. The program was implemented by the OAS and CAPEL and focused on improving the voter rolls and promoting voter registration (e.g., helping to digitize the registration process), technical support for polling decentralization, and support for information and training programs (Jessup, Hayek, and Hällhag 2008; OAS 2008). Total funding was $4.6 million (Jessup, Hayek, and Hällhag 2008, 15), while the United States Agency for International Development provided another $2 million for the 2007 elections for a variety of purposes, including technical assistance related to decentralization and voter-information campaigns (USAID n.d.).

Another form of international involvement has been support for domestic election observers. Donor countries have funded domestic observation efforts, with the National Democratic Institute playing a leading role in coordination and advising (NDI n.d.; 2004). Finally, another mode of international influence on domestic election administration comes in the form of learning from other nations. Electoral management bodies increasingly share experiences and best practices, and such cooperation is institutionalized in the Tikal Protocol for Central American electoral bodies. Through biannual conferences and periodic visits to other countries, election authorities are able to address common concerns and learn how things are done in neighboring states.

The impacts of these international influences on the shape of election administration have been variable across types of involvement. Election observation missions, whatever their positive impacts in deterring fraud and increasing confidence in election results, played little role in identifying areas in need of reform. According to former TSE magistrates, election authorities were already aware of the problem areas that international observers pointed out, although observer reports did provide the TSE with external legitimation in its dealings with Congress (Interviews 14, 15). The lack of follow through on international observer recommendations has even garnered media coverage (PL 2011c). More influential has been international support for domestic election observation efforts, which was critical in the establishment of Mirador Electoral, the country's largest observer group. Yet as discussed above, domestic observers had little impact on the legal and administrative reforms that made election administration more inclusive.

Cross-national learning and emulation had a larger impact on the shape of reform. While the TSE drew lessons from other electoral bodies on issues such as party finance oversight and voting abroad (Interviews 3, 4, 23), it was the civil registry reform that was most affected by the models available in other countries. Both the TSE and Congress used international models to bolster their competing proposals for civil registry reform. In 2004, the TSE convoked (with the OAS) a regional conference on civil registries and identity documents, which resulted in international expert proposals – delivered to the congressional committee on electoral matters – that the TSE be the state entity to issue the new identity cards (PL 2004l). Similarly, members of the congressional committee traveled to a number of other countries to learn about their civil registry systems, and a member of the committee reported that the system in place in Peru was influential in deciding to create RENAP (Interview 27). When the congressional committee indicated its preference for the creation of a new state agency, it pointed to other nations – especially Peru – in justifying its decision (PL 2004m). While other motives almost certainly influenced the decision in Congress to create RENAP, the availability of a well functioning model to emulate allowed Congress to more easily justify that decision. Learning from other nations' experiences was thus a double-edged sword, used by different institutions to support competing proposals.

International influence on election administration is most clearly seen in the area of financial and technical assistance. This assistance was especially critical in carrying out polling decentralization, updating the voter registration system, and in voter education campaigns. According to the former coordinator of OAS assistance to the TSE, the extent of reform would have been impossible in the same time frame without the assistance provided by the international community (Interview 06). A former TSE magistrate also emphasized that polling decentralization and advances in voter registration and voter education would not have been possible without international support, noting that the government would likely not have supplied the necessary funding (Interview 17). An evaluation by Sweden's international development agency also concluded that OAS support contributed to the successful decentralization of polling sites (Jessup, Hayek, and Hällhag 2008, 21); a less critical OAS report likewise concluded that the organization's technical assistance to Guatemala helped ensure the success of decentralization and also improved the quality and coverage of the voter registry (OAS 2008, 16, 103).

International financial assistance has also been essential for carrying out a mundane task of voter education: printing informational materials. External financing has been critical for producing everything from informational brochures and posters aimed at voters to instructional manuals for poll workers (Interview 03; Jessup, Hayek, and Hällhag 2008, 23–24). According to the director of the TSE's Unit for Civic-Electoral Training and Education (UCADE), which produces most of these printed materials, the unit's job would be practically impossible without international support (Interview 20).

In sum, international flows of ideas and (more importantly) resources contributed significantly to greater election administration inclusiveness in Guatemala. However, this impact did not occur through the imposition of particular priorities or models; rather, by all accounts, international assistance facilitated reforms that were determined domestically (see, e.g., Azpuru 2004). While the shape of electoral reform was determined by domestic actors and interests, the resources provided by the international community made more inclusive election administration possible by funding polling decentralization, voter registry modernization, and voter education activities.

Conclusion

A confluence of factors came together to produce the Guatemalan electoral reforms. Political parties across the spectrum supported administrative reforms that were expected to have little effect on the parties' electoral competitiveness or party leaders' positions, while reducing the costs of voter mobilization. The

Supreme Electoral Tribunal, independent of partisan interests and seeking to boost the legitimacy of the electoral regime, sought to improve voter access while maintaining the integrity of the election process that it had ensured since the mid-1980s. International actors played a crucial role in providing the financing and technical expertise to implement electoral reform, although it was domestic actors that set the reform agenda. Civil society also pushed for reform, but ultimately had little impact; electoral reform was an elite affair, driven by technocrats and politicians, rather than the result of popular pressures. The complex reform process resulted in an election administration system that presented fewer obstacles to voters wishing to exercise their suffrage, with important (if limited) consequences for campaigning methods and electoral outcomes.

Notes

1 This section draws on compilations of reform initiatives in Catalina Soberanis 1995, OAS 1997 (Annex X), and Acción Ciudadana et al. 2005.

2 In this bill, introduced by a deputy of the FRG party, absentee voting would have taken the form of "national tables" at voting centers where voters, registered in other jurisdictions, could have cast ballots for national (but not municipal or departmental) offices. According to a former TSE magistrate, a similar measure was debated internally within the TSE (Interview 14).

3 The TSE used its initiative power to introduce the bill in Congress. See "Proyecto de Decreto que Contiene Modificaciones a la Ley Electoral y de Partidos Políticos," introduced into Congress, November 5, 1998.

4 According to a long-time TSE staff member, the true extent to which this practice occurs is unknown (Interview 22); however, the TSE verified some 50 cases in 17 municipalities following the 2011 elections (PL 2011g). Presumably, it affects mostly municipal elections rather than Congressional contests, and mayoral candidates (typically incumbents) are thought to orchestrate this type of fraud.

5 Reforms to the electoral law approved by Congress in 2016 incorporated some of these TSE proposals, including an earlier registration closing date and an onerous residency requirement, prohibiting residence changes in the voter registry a full year prior to the convocation of an electoral process, or approximately 17 months prior to election day. See Decreto 26–2016, Art. 2, amending Art. 13 of the electoral law.

6 Thirteen deputies were absent. The gentlemen's agreement was with the FRG, PAN, and UNE parties.

7 While civil and voter registries had voters' addresses on file, these were often outdated, especially since voters moving within a municipality would have no incentive to update their voter registration, as it wouldn't affect where they would be assigned to vote.

8 Calculated from Mirador Electoral 2011, 14.

9 A proposal presented to the congressional committee on electoral matters in 2000 by the union of TSE employees recommended shortening the registration deadline to two months before election day in order to facilitate participation (Sindicato 2000). It appears to be the only organization to have recommended this change in a proposal to Congress.

10 Congress again attempted to make voter registration automatic in a 2013 bill that would have entered RENAP data directly into the voter registry, and the Constitutional Court again struck down this provision. See Expediente 5352–2013, issued by the Court on July 11, 2014.

11 The TSE had developed several scenarios for decentralization, with a maximum of some 687 new rural sites (CEMs), an intermediate scenario of 311, and a minimal scenario of 166 (OAS 2008, 45). Congress pushed for the maximum scenario (PL 2006a; 2006b). The pertinent change was to article 231 of the electoral law.

12 The absentee system considered would have consisted of "national tables," discussed above (note 2). The TSE opted instead to change the date of elections to address the migrant worker issue, and to make changing one's residence for voter registration purposes easier.

13 Some municipal elections were not held concurrently with national elections until the late 1990s.

14 See, e.g., EUEOM 2007. 24–25; MIOE 2007, 77; Mirador Electoral 2008, 19–20; and Prensa Libre 2011e.

15 This draws on legislative records and media coverage at the time. See Congress of the Republic of Guatemala 2001a; 2001b; and Prensa Libre 2002b.

16 These effects were also mentioned by a number of people interviewed by the author (Interviews 01, 08, 10, 26).

17 An observer mission to the 1990 elections noted that most political parties were "relatively new, personalist electoral vehicles without extensive and permanent organizational structures" (NDI 1990, 15), and the same organization reported five years later that most parties "have traditionally been personalistic parties which have been vehicles for the personal ambitions of individual caudillos" (NDI 1995, 7). These observations were still accurate a decade later (see, e.g., EUEOM 2007, 7–8).

18 This view is shared by many other analysts. But others attribute the decision to a desire to emulate Peru's registry system, in which the electoral authority and civil registry are separate, rather than emulate the Mexican or Nicaraguan system in which the electoral authority issues identity cards. This alternative explanation is discussed below.

19 TSE, "Proyecto de Reformas a la Ley Electoral y de Partidos Políticos," submitted to Congress December 1, 1994 (in Acción Ciudadana et al. 2005).

20 Sixteen proposals were submitted to the congressional committee in 2000; 24 were submitted to the CRE.

21 One exception is Mirador Electoral's (2008, 118) proposal to drop citizens from the voter roll if they do not vote in two consecutive elections, a measure also recommended by Conde Rada (2008, 52) and IFES (2004, 9) and proposed by the TSE in a reform bill submitted to Congress. The purpose of this proposal is to address the problem of incomplete purging of deceased and emigrated citizens from the voter rolls; however, such a measure would also mean that some voters would have to re-register if they abstained from two consecutive elections.

22 One of the most important areas in this regard is the information compiled by Mirador Electoral/Acción Ciudadana on campaign spending that exceeds legal limits (Interview 02).

23 Of dozens of observer recommendations regarding election administration inclusiveness, I found only two that called for more restrictive measures: in order to improve the accuracy of the voter rolls, the European Union's mission to the 2007 elections suggested an earlier closing date and a longer residency requirement for voter registration (EUEOM 2007, 61–62). See the Appendix for more detail.

24 Primarily the United States, Canada, Norway, Sweden, Switzerland, the Netherlands, Japan, and Mexico.

References

Acción Ciudadana, Comisión Específica de Asuntos Electorales del Congreso de la República, and the State University of New York. 2005. Base de Datos de Propuestas de Reformas a la Ley Electoral y de Partidos Políticos. CD-ROM.

Agreement on Constitutional Reforms and the Electoral Regime. Stockholm. December 7, 1996.

ASIES (Asociación de Investigación y Estudios Sociales). 2004. *Gobernabilidad Democrática y Reformas de Segunda Generación a la Ley Electoral y de Partidos Políticos.* Seminario Permanente Sobre el Rol de Partidos Políticos, XX Sesión. Guatemala: ASIES.

ASIES. 2005. *El Sistema de Partidos Políticos de Guatemala a 20 Años de la Ley Electoral y de Partidos Políticos.*

Azpuru, Dinorah. 2004. "International Electoral Assistance to Guatemala." Paper presented at the International Studies Association Meeting, Montreal, Canada.

Blanco, Ligia Ixmucané. 2008. "Comportamiento Electoral y Desempeño Institucional de los Partidos Politicos." In *Siete Claves Para El Cambio: Análisis Técnico, Político y Normativo del Proceso Electoral Guatemala* 2007, Eduardo Núñez Vargas, ed. Guatemala: Soros Foundation/NDI/NIMD/ASIES/DOSES/FLACSO.

Boneo, Horacio. 2001. "Consideraciones Sobre Voto Residencial, Documento Único de Identitad y Cartografía Electoral." In *Construyendo la Democracia Electoral en Guatemala,* Edelberto Torres-Rivas, Secundino González M., Horacio Boneo, Fabrice Lehoucq, and David L. Wall, eds. Guatemala: FLASCO.

Boneo, Horacio and Edelberto Torres-Rivas. 2000. *Por Qué No Votan Los Guatemaltecos? Estudio de Participación y Abstención Electoral.* Guatemala City, Guatemala: IDEA, Tribunal Supremo Electoral, and UNDP.

Carter Center. 2003. Postelection Statement on Guatemala Elections. December 19. www.cartercenter.org/news/documents/doc1567.html.

Carter Center. 2004. Financing Democracy in Guatemala, Final Report. www.cartercenter.org/documents/1674.pdf.

Castillo Milla, Felix. 2006. Proceso de Reforma de la Ley Electoral y de Partidos Políticos. Cuadernos de Trabajo No. 4. Guatemala: FLACSO.

Catalina Soberanis, Ana. 1995. *Análisis de los Proyectos de Reformas a la Legislación Electoral y de los Partidos Políticos: Guatemala.* Guatemala. INCEP Centro de Documentación, doc. 1263.

Cerigua Weekly Briefs. 1998 (June 24). www.tulane.edu/~libweb/RESTRICTED/CERIGUA/1998_0618.txt. (Accessed May 1, 2011).

Conde Rada, César. 2008. "Análisis Sobre la Coherencia y Efectividad de la Ley Electoral y de Partidos Políticos." In *Siete Claves Para El Cambio: Análisis Técnico, Político y Normativo del Proceso Electoral Guatemala* 2007, Eduardo Núñez Vargas, ed. Guatemala: Soros Foundation/NDI/NIMD/ASIES/DOSES/FLACSO.

Congress of the Republic of Guatemala. 2001a. Diario de Sesiones del Congreso de la República de Guatemala, Periodo Extraordinaria 2001–2002, Tomo I, Numero 09, July 23.

Congress of the Republic of Guatemala. 2001b. Diario de Sesiones del Congreso de la República de Guatemala, Periodo Ordinario 2001–2002, Tomo I, Numero 011, July 25.

Corte de Constitucionalidad de Guatemala. 2006. Expediente 1106–2005. January 10.

CRE (Comisión de Reforma Electoral). 1997. Documento Para Discusión: Tema General: Campañas de Información Publica. TSE Centro de Documentación, Doc. #370.

CRE. 1998. *Compilación de Documentos Técnicos de Análisis.* Guatemala: Organization of American States.

CRE. 2004. *Guatemala, Paz y Democracia: Informe de la Comisión de Reforma Electoral.* 3rd Edition.

EUEOM (European Union Electoral Observation Mission). 2003. Final Report on the Parliamentary and Local Elections.

EUEOM. 2007. Final Report on the General Elections.
"Exposición de Motivos y Proyecto de Decreto de Modificaciones a la Ley Electoral y de Partidos Políticos." n.d. TSE Centro de Documentación, Doc. "Ley 536."
Fukumoto, Kentaro, and Yusaku Horiuchi. 2011. "Making Outsiders' Votes Count: Detecting Electoral Fraud through a Natural Experiment." *American Political Science Review* 105 (3): 586–603.
IFES (International Foundation for Electoral Systems). 2004. Valoración Técnica de los Procesos Electorales, Elecciones Generales del 2003, República de Guatemala, Informe Final.
Jessup, Francesca, Elisabeth Hayek, and Roger Hällhag. 2008. Asistencia Técnica al Régimen Electoral Guatemalteco. Stockholm, Sweden: SIDA (Swedish International Development Cooperation Agency) Evaluation.
López-Pintor, Rafael, and Edmundo Urrutia. 2002. "Guatemala." In *Voter Turnout since 1945: A Global Report*, Rafael López-Pintor and Maria Gratschew, eds. Stockholm: International Institute for Democracy and Electoral Assistance.
MINUGUA (Misión de Verificación de Las Naciones Unidas en Guatemala). 1999. Cuarto Informe del Secretario General de las Naciones Unidas Sobre la Verificación de los Acuerdos de Paz de Guatemala – A/54/526. December 2.
MINUGUA. 2000. Quinto Informe del Secretario General de las Naciones Unidas Sobre la Verificación de los Acuerdos de Paz de Guatemala – A/55/275. July 26.
MINUGUA. 2002. Séptimo Informe del Secretario General de las Naciones Unidas Sobre la Verificación de los Acuerdos de Paz de Guatemala – A/56/1003. July 10.
MIOE (II Misión Indígena de Observación Electoral). 2003. Informe Final, Elecciones Generales 2003. Guatemala.
MIOE (III Misión Indígena de Observación Electoral). 2007. Informe Final de las Elecciones 2007.
Mirador Electoral. 2003. Fourth Report on the National Electoral Process. September 25.
Mirador Electoral. 2007. Así Marcha el Proceso Electoral: Tercer Informe: Resumen Ejectivo. June 28.
Mirador Electoral. 2008. Proyecto de Observación Nacional Electoral Para Guatemala: Elecciones Generales 2007 Informe Final. Guatemala City, Guatemala.
Mirador Electoral. 2011. Segundo Informe de Observación de 2011. August 30.
NDI (National Democratic Institute). 1991. *The 1990 National Elections in Guatemala*. Washington, DC: National Democratic Institute for International Affairs.
NDI. 1995. *Report of the NDI Survey Mission to Guatemala*. Washington, DC: National Democratic Institute for International Affairs.
NDI. 2004. NDI Reports (Spring). www.ndi.org/files/1709_ndireports_spring2004_0.pdf.
NDI. n.d.[a]. Guatemala: Building Citizen Confidence and Participation, USAID Associate Cooperative Agreement No. 520-03-A-013 under the CEPPS Leader Agreement No. DGC-A-00-01-00004-00.
Núñez Vargas, Eduardo. 2008a. "Las Elecciones Generales 2007: Balance General Sobre un Sistema en Transición." In *Siete Claves Para El Cambio: Análisis Técnico, Político y Normativo del Proceso Electoral Guatemala* 2007, Eduardo Núñez Vargas, coord. Guatemala: Soros Foundation/NDI/NIMD/ASIES/DOSES/FLACSO.
Núñez Vargas, Eduardo. 2008b. "Reforma al Régimen Electoral y de Partidos Políticos en Guatemala: Una Tarea Inconclusa." *Escenarios de la Reforma Política* 2 (1): 51–72.
OAS (Organization of American States). 1997. *Observaciones Electorales en Guatemala, 1995–1996*.
OAS. 2000. Report of the Electoral Observation Mission to Guatemala, 1999 Elections.

OAS. 2005. Informe de la Misión de Observación Electoral en Guatemala Elecciones Generales 2003.
OAS. 2008. *Informe Final de Gestión: Asistencia Técnica al Régimen Electoral Guatemalteco*. Secretaría General de la Organización de los Estados Americanos (OEA)/ Secretaría para Asuntos Políticos (SAP)/Departamento para la Cooperación y Observación Electoral (DECO).
OAS. 2009. Informe de la Misión de Observación Electoral, Elecciones Generales (9 de Septiembre de 2007) y Segunda Vuelta Electoral Presidencial (4 de Noviembre de 2007), República de Guatemala.
Observatorio Legislativo de FUSADES. 2007. Monitoreo Semanal Del 03 al 07 de Diciembre 2007. http://observatoriolegislativo.org.sv/.
El Periódico. 2011. "Unos 17 Mil DPI Aún Manifiestan Problemas." May 19.
Prensa Libre. 2000a. "Clamor por Reforma de la Ley Electoral." January 5.
Prensa Libre. 2000b. "Apoyan Reformas." January 6.
Prensa Libre. 2000c. "Buscarán Reforma Electoral Este Año." February 7.
Prensa Libre. 2000d. "Prudence Bushnell Apoya Reforma de Ley Electoral." February 29.
Prensa Libre. 2000e. "Vuelven al Tapete." March 13.
Prensa Libre. 2000f. "Expertos y Diputados Analizan Enmiendas." August 18.
Prensa Libre. 2000g. "TSE Adversa Reforma Electoral." November 1.
Prensa Libre. 2000h. "Respaldo al TSE por Riesgo en Reformas." November 3.
Prensa Libre. 2000i. "Cambios sin Apoyo." November 8.
Prensa Libre. 2000j. "Apoyan Autonomía Total del TSE." November 23.
Prensa Libre. 2001a. "Reformas Electorales: Demandan Abrir Debate con Sociedad." February 1.
Prensa Libre. 2001b. "FRG Quiere Reforma para Beneficiar a Ríos Montt." June 15.
Prensa Libre. 2001c. "Opisición No Apoya Reformas Electorales." June 16.
Prensa Libre. 2001d. "Se Abre Puerta a Reforma Electoral." June 26.
Prensa Libre. 2001e. "Lunes Pasa al Pleno Ley a Favor de Ríos Montt." July 21.
Prensa Libre. 2001f. "FRG Busca Más Control con Reforma Electoral." August 13.
Prensa Libre. 2001g. "TSE Autoriza Votar en el Lugar de Residencia." December 24.
Prensa Libre. 2002a. "Eferregistas Reactivan Reformas Electorales." September 5.
Prensa Libre. 2002b. "FRG Busca Aprobar Reformas Electorales." September 17.
Prensa Libre. 2004a. "Comienza Segunda Fase de Consenso Político." January 5.
Prensa Libre. 2004b. "Sugieren Retomar las Reformas Electorales." January 6.
Prensa Libre. 2004c. "Seminarios: Socialización de la Agenda Compartida." February 8.
Prensa Libre. 2004d. "Arreglos a la Ley Electoral." February 9.
Prensa Libre. 2004e. "Reformas Aún Necesitan Ser Actualizadas." March 8.
Prensa Libre. 2004f. "TSE Objeta Aprobación de Reformas." March 9.
Prensa Libre. 2004g. "Aprueban Reformas por Artículos." April 1.
Prensa Libre. 2004h. "Reforma a Ley Electoral Pasa con Errores." April 1.
Prensa Libre. 2004i. "Diputados Aprobarán Una Ley Defectuosa." April 5.
Prensa Libre. 2004j. "Aprueban Ley Electoral; TSE Espera Veto." April 22.
Prensa Libre. 2004k. "Deben Esperar Más." June 6.
Prensa Libre. 2004l. "Surgen Dos Propuestas." June 19.
Prensa Libre. 2004m. "Buscan Excluir al TSE del Documento Único." August 17.
Prensa Libre. 2004n. "Breves." September 1.
Prensa Libre. 2004o. "Reformas Electorales Van a Paso de Tortuga." September 20.
Prensa Libre. 2005a. "En Busca del Documento Único." June 5.

Prensa Libre. 2005b. "TSE Quiere Administrar Documento." September 21.

Prensa Libre. 2006a. "Incertidumbre en Proceso Electoral." August 3.

Prensa Libre. 2006b. "Diputados Piden al TSE 689 Sitios de Votación." August 5.

Prensa Libre. 2008. "Congreso Investiga al Renap." May 15.

Prensa Libre. 2009. "Se Quejan de Mala Atención del Renap." October 19.

Prensa Libre. 2010a. "Aumentan Quejas por Mala Atención en Renap." January 26.

Prensa Libre. 2010b. "Guatemaltecos Temen al Fraude." July 15.

Prensa Libre. 2010c. "Renap es Foco de Clientelismo." July 22.

Prensa Libre. 2010d. "Ligan a Proceso a Ex Ministro de Gobernación Jiménez por Anomalías en Caso Renap." July 23.

Prensa Libre. 2010e. "Detienen a Sindicatos por Contrato Ilegal en Renap." July 24.

Prensa Libre. 2010f. "Hacen Negocio con Turnos del Renap." December 8.

Prensa Libre. 2011a. "Información sobre Empadronamiento Será Divulgada en Sedes del Renap." March 25.

Prensa Libre. 2011b. "TSE Llamará al Empadronamiento en Cuatro Idiomas Mayas." May 5.

Prensa Libre. 2011c. "Sugerencias de OEA No Fueron Atendidas." July 2.

Prensa Libre. 2011d. "Padrón Electoral Llega a 7.3 Millones." July 8.

Prensa Libre. 2011e. "Políticos Quieren Bloquear Elección." August 25.

Prensa Libre. 2011f. "Racismo Electoral; Proceso sin Inclusión Indígena." August 26.

Prensa Libre. 2011g. "Tribunal Supremo Electoral Suspende a 50 Electores." September 30.

Prensa Libre. 2011h. "Área Rural es la Más Reñida." November 3.

Sáenz de Tejada, Ricardo. 2005. *Elecciones, Participación Política y Pueblo Maya en Guatemala*. Guatemala City: Universidad Rafael Landívar.

Sánchez, Omar. 2008. "Guatemala's Party Universe: A Case Study in Underinstitutionalization." *Latin American Politics and Society* 50 (1): 123–51.

Sánchez del Valle, Rosa. 2000. *Comités Cívicos: Hacia una Coexistencia de Plataformas Políticas Departmentales?* Guatemala City: Friedrich Ebert Stiftung.

Siglo 21. 2011a. "Renap Hará Llegar el DPI a los Jóvenes." May 12.

Siglo 21. 2011b. "Empadronadas Aumentan 33%." September 6.

Sindicato de Trabajadores del Tribunal Supremo Electoral. 2000 (April 12). [no title].

TSE (Tribunal Supremo Electoral – Guatemala). 1997. Documento Unico de Identitad (D.U.I.). Guatemala. TSE Centro de Documentación, Libro 293.

TSE. 2001a. *Reformas a la Ley Electoral y de Partidos Políticos: Segunda Comparación de Propuestas*.

TSE. 2001b. Acuerdo 390–2001. October 16.

TSE. 2002. Acuerdo 280–2002. November 19.

TSE. 2011a. "Guatemaltecos Contarán con Más de 700 Centros de Información Durante los Comicios de Septiembre." August 16.

TSE. 2011b. "TSE Pone en Marcha Centros de Llamadas y Comienza Envío de Minitelegramas para Divulgar Información sobre Centros de Votación." August 16.

TSE. 2011c. "Director de Informática Presentó Resultados de Mesa Técnica TSE-RENAP." July 21.

TSE. 2012. *Memoria de Elecciones Generales y al Parlamento Centroamericano 2011, Tomo 1*.

TSE. n.d.[a] *Memoria: Elecciones 95–96*.

TSE. n.d.[b]. "Reformas Electorales en 1997 por Diversas Instituciones, Volume 1." TSE Centro de Documentación, Doc. "Ley 547."

TSE. n.d.[c]. *Memoria Elecciones Generales 99*.

USAID (United States Agency for International Development). 2010. "Success Story: Voter Turnout Higher Than Ever." www.usaid.gov/stories/guatemala/ss_gtm_vote.html.

USAID. n.d. "Elections in Guatemala." www.usaid.gov/gt/elections.htm. (Accessed June 3, 2010).

6 Nicaragua

Bringing the ballot to the people, 1984–1996

In the 1980s, Nicaragua established an inclusive and competent election administration system, carrying out two elections free of significant irregularities and significantly more accessible to voters than in neighboring El Salvador or Guatemala. It did so in difficult circumstances, similar to those found in its neighboring countries: a context of armed conflict, political polarization, economic crisis, and generalized poverty and illiteracy. This chapter examines the origins of Nicaragua's inclusive election administration and the beginnings of its unraveling in the mid-1990s.

Background

From 1937 to 1979, Nicaragua was ruled by the Somoza family, first under Anastasio Somoza García and subsequently under his sons. The Somozas at times ruled directly, at other times indirectly through puppet presidents and enjoyed the firm backing of the United States. While elections were held periodically, they lacked even the limited competitiveness found in Guatemala or El Salvador; most Nicaraguan elites were co-opted by the regime and presented no challenge to the Somozas' rule. Opposition to the regime grew in the 1970s in response to rampant corruption and the diversion of foreign relief aid following a devastating 1972 earthquake. A guerrilla insurgency that had been active since the 1960s grew in strength and ultimately led the uprising that toppled Somoza in 1979.

The overthrow of Somoza by the leftist Sandinista Front of National Liberation (FSLN) initiated a revolutionary regime, followed by US efforts to force the Sandinistas from power throughout the 1980s. As the Reagan administration organized and funded the counterrevolutionary forces, the Contras, and waged economic warfare against Nicaragua, the Sandinistas sought economic and diplomatic support from other countries, ultimately including the Soviet Union but also democratic countries in Europe and Latin America. These pressures necessitated the holding of free elections to shore up the revolutionary regime's legitimacy both at home and abroad. As a result, liberal democratic institutions were grafted onto the Sandinistas' vision of a participatory socialist democracy.[1]

To administer elections, a new Supreme Electoral Council (CSE) was established, and new electoral laws were approved prior to the 1984 and 1990 elections. The 1984 law was passed by the Sandinista-dominated Council of State, with input from opposition parties on the Council. As the Sandinista government sought to consolidate domestic and international legitimacy through elections, it was willing to negotiate the rules of the game with the opposition parties to ensure their participation.[2] As a result of such negotiations, the electoral law was amended before the 1984 elections to take opposition concerns into account, including expanding the Supreme Electoral Council from three magistrates – who were thought to be Sandinista supporters – to five (Envío 1984a, 1984b; IHRLG-WOLA 1984, 20; LASA 1984, 11–12).

A new electoral law was drawn up in 1988 in anticipation of elections in 1990, and concessions to the opposition over the contents of the law were even more extensive than in 1984. A number of opposition demands were included in reforms to the law in 1989, although the government refused opposition demands to change the composition of the CSE – which was composed of two Sandinistas, one representative of the opposition UNO coalition, one representative of the opposition party that had obtained the most votes in the previous elections, and one neutral member. The composition of the top level of the CSE was of particular importance because the CSE magistrates named two of the three members of the regional electoral councils (which in turn named the poll workers), so that partisan control at the top could result in partisan control throughout the administrative structure of the CSE. As a result, the FSLN effectively held two of three spots on the regional election councils and the local polling boards (Carter Center 1990a; LASA 1990, 13).

The 1984 and 1990 elections

Despite opposition criticisms over the CSE's composition, Nicaragua's electoral commission proved to be quite competent and was instrumental in establishing a system of election administration that facilitated voter participation. Procedures for voter registration, locating polling stations, and casting a ballot were designed to minimize barriers for voters, while the CSE also conducted extensive voter education campaigns.

Voter registration

For the first elections of the post-Somoza period in 1984, it was necessary to draw up voter lists from scratch. Voter registration was made mandatory because it was to also serve as a census, although voting itself was not compulsory (LASA 1984, 14). Lacking permanent registry offices, the CSE held registration during four consecutive Sundays, with the process taking place at the (widely dispersed) locations to be used as polling stations on election day. Prospective voters were required to show some form of identification (such as a birth certificate or driver's license) or, lacking identification, present two witnesses from the same precinct to verify their identity (Ley Electoral 1984, Art. 70; 1988, Art. 37). Voters would immediately receive a registration card (*libreta cívica*), which would also serve as voter identification on election day, and after each registration day the voter lists were posted publicly so any interested parties could "file complaints about persons who had registered improperly or who did not live within the precinct" (LASA 1984, 14; see Ley Electoral 1984, Art. 75–76). Thus, while registration was only held on four days, the decentralized locations and immediate delivery of registration cards to voters eliminated the need to make multiple trips to faraway registration offices as was the case in Guatemala and El Salvador. Combined with a publicity campaign promoting registration, the voter registration drive produced impressive results, achieving an estimated registration rate of over 93 percent (LASA 1984, 14).

For the next elections in 1990, an ad hoc system of registration was again carried out over four Sundays, with various forms of ID or witnesses used for registration purposes. Voters immediately received their registration cards upon registering, and lists of registered voters were displayed on the doors of polling stations so that interested parties could review them and solicit the CSE to correct errors (IIDH-CAPEL 1990, 22–23; Ley Electoral 1988, Art. 42; ONUVEN 1989a, 6; 1990c, 6, 12). The CSE also distributed the voter lists to the opposition parties so they could review and request corrections (Carter Center 1990b). The voter registration drive was again accompanied by "an intensive and effective publicity campaign to encourage registration" (ONUVEN 1989a, 7), and the process was again widely praised. As the United Nations observer mission noted: "The voter registration process involved a major effort, which was particularly impressive given the lack of financial resources and the inadequacies of transport and communication systems" (ONUVEN 1989a, 27). While estimates of registration coverage are uncertain, the Carter Center reported an 89 percent registration rate (Carter Center 1990a), while the anti-Sandinista newspaper *La Prensa* reported a survey finding of 95 percent of eligible Nicaraguans registered to vote (ONUVEN 1989a, 11).

Despite its successes, there were several limits to the accessibility of voter registration. The most severe shortcoming occurred in several locales (particularly the northern Atlantic region), where poor security conditions prevented registration sites from opening during the October 1989 registration drive. The opposition claimed that the CSE was attempting to keep opposition supporters from registering (ONUVEN 1990a, 5), while international observers generally accepted the government's claims that security conditions did not permit the opening of voter registration sites in areas of Contra activity. In any case, special arrangements were made to open many of the sites in the months leading up to the election, as well as to register demobilized Contras (Carter Center 1990a; ONUVEN 1990a, 4, 31; 1990b, 3).

Another limitation on accessibility was the early deadline for registration for both the 1984 and 1990 elections. For the 1990 elections, the ad hoc registration process ended four months prior to the election. However, for both elections, those turning legal voting age (16 years old in Nicaragua) between the last day of voter registration and election day were allowed (and required) to register to vote (Ley Electoral 1984, Art. 66; 1988, Art. 34). The dates for registration were not fixed in the electoral law, leaving it to the CSE to decide when to carry out voter registration (Ley Electoral 1984, Art. 7; 1988, Art. 4).[3]

Finally, citizens needed to register in the precinct where they permanently resided, even if they were temporarily absent – although exceptions were made for those serving in the armed forces and poll watchers working in other jurisdictions (Ley Electoral 1984, Art. 68; 1988, Art. 35). For some citizens, this may have been an obstacle to registration, although there seemed to have been no reports of disenfranchisement as a result of this requirement.

Getting to the ballot box

While the voter registration process was commended by observers (and drew few criticisms from the otherwise intransigent opposition coalitions), the decentralization of polling sites was also praised by observers. In contrast to Guatemala and El Salvador, polling stations were not limited to municipal capitals. Another key difference was that, in Nicaragua, most precincts were made up of just one polling station (*Junta Receptora de Votos*, or JRVs); thus, rather than concentrating dozens of polling stations in large voting centers, polling stations were dispersed to ensure maximum accessibility.

Almost 4,000 polling sites were used in the 1984 election, and one observer mission noted that

> [i]n large cities, polling sites were located at intervals of three or four blocks. In rural areas, voters seldom had to travel more than three or four kilometers. The number and placement of the polling sites marked a commendable attempt to encourage voter participation.
>
> (IHRLG and WOLA 1984, 38)

In 1990, the number of polling stations increased to 4,394 (CSE 1991, 4; ONUVEN 1989a, 4), with over 46 percent of them located in rural areas (CSE 1991, 5).[4]

The location of polling places was at the CSE's discretion; the electoral law was mostly silent on the issue, simply referring to "a sufficient number" of sites to be established by the CSE (Ley Electoral 1988, Art. 24; see also IFES 1993, 11; Ley Electoral 1984, Art. 64). The CSE could therefore use its own criteria in establishing where voting would take place, and it explicitly used the criteria of voter accessibility in order to facilitate participation, aiming to keep travel for rural voters to a maximum of 5 km and for urban voters to just 300 m, although these goals could not always be met (CSE 1991, 4; Interviews 43, 46; ONUVEN 1989a, 29, note 1). Importantly, this decentralization did not endanger the integrity of the electoral process by facilitating fraud, as was feared in Guatemala and El Salvador. In fact, on this point, inclusive election administration may have served to protect election integrity. As the United Nations observer mission noted, decentralized polling places combined with poll workers and party poll watchers who "are acquainted with the local population" created a "system of 'local control' [which] makes it difficult to carry out fraudulent registrations systematically and on a large scale" (ONUVEN 1989a, 6).[5]

Casting a ballot

In addition to voter registration and polling locations, the voting process itself also posed minimal barriers to participation. While voter identification was required, the registration card to be used as ID had been given to voters just months prior, immediately upon registering. This system avoided problems resulting from delayed delivery of ID cards, which was a significant problem in Guatemala and even more so in El Salvador, and would become a tremendously contentious issue in Nicaragua in later years. In 1984 and 1990, however, there were no reported problems of registered voters lacking identification. With the ad hoc inscriptions on the voter rolls tied directly to the delivery of registration cards, there were also no problems with voters' names not appearing on the voter rolls – another method of disenfranchisement that would become an issue after 2000.

The biggest concern related to the casting of ballots was the potential for long lines of voters. With separate ballots for each election (presidential, congressional, and municipal) in 1990, there were concerns about the time that would be required for the voting, especially because misestimates of the population residing in some areas initially led to many more than the legally prescribed limit of 400 voters assigned to some polling stations (IIDH-CAPEL 1990, 40; ONUVEN 1989a, 10). The CSE took steps to add additional tables to existing JRVs, in order to avoid delays during the voting (IIDH-CAPEL 1990, 40, 48) and, with the exception of the late opening of some polling stations, the voting process proceeded smoothly and quickly, despite a large turnout of 86 percent of registered voters (Carter Center 1990a).

Voter education

Inclusive voter registration, polling locations, and voting procedures were complemented by voter-information campaigns. In 1984, the CSE carried out an extensive voter education campaign prior to election day, explaining the mechanics of the voting process through television, radio, and newspaper ads (IHRLG and WOLA 1984, 38), while on election day the CSE "preempted all programming on all of the country's radio stations. The message 'Your vote is secret, your vote decides' was broadcast continuously, alternating with popular music and explanations of voting procedures" (LASA 1984, 16).

The CSE again carried out a significant voter education campaign leading up to the 1990 elections, with a Publicity and Civic Education division devoted to the task. The first stage of the information campaign explained the procedures for registering, while a later stage encouraged voter participation, explained the necessary steps to vote, and emphasized the secrecy of the vote. The campaign was carried out through diverse media, including radio spots, newspaper ads, fliers, and posters, as well as a frequently run three-minute television advertisement explaining how to vote (CSE 1991, 17; IIDH-CAPEL 1990, 35, 40). The electoral law for both elections put the media at the disposal of the CSE during the 72 hours before election day to disseminate information on "the procedures to exercise the right of suffrage" (Ley Electoral 1984, Art. 41; 1988, Art. 119) and also required the CSE to publicize sample ballots to familiarize voters with them (Ley Electoral 1984, Art. 97; 1988, Art. 133). The UN observer mission evaluated the 1990 information campaign positively (ONUVEN 1990a, 6).

Legal reforms: the Citizen Identification Law and 1995 electoral law

Between the 1990 and 1996 national elections, Nicaragua's electoral system was overhauled by constitutional reforms and two pieces of legislation. Changes began with the civil registry and citizen identification system. Until the early 1990s, Nicaragua did not have a centralized national civil registry, and the CSE had employed an ad hoc system of voter registration for the 1984 and 1990 elections. In 1989, opposition parties had advocated the introduction of a photo ID card for use in the 1990 elections. Lacking time to construct a new civil registry and ID system before the elections, the government pledged to do so following the elections. But after the turnover in power in 1990, when the FSLN was defeated, the issue became less of a priority; the National Assembly did not pass the Citizen Identification Law until 1993 and did not approve the use of the new ID card as voter identification until the electoral law was reformed in December 1995 (Butler et al. 1996).

With the new legislation, the ad hoc system of voter registration gave way to a permanent registry system, based on a new identity card produced and distributed by the CSE. With the CSE managing the civil registry and documentation process, voter registration became automatic – those citizens registering and receiving an ID card would automatically be added to the voter registry.

The other significant legal reform was the drafting of a new electoral law. In 1995, Nicaragua's constitution was amended amid intense conflict between the executive and legislative branches and, after the conflict subsided, the National Assembly finally passed a new electoral law consistent with the constitutional changes (which introduced a presidential run-off and the direct election of mayors). The political paralysis had caused the new electoral law to be approved less than one year before national elections were to be held, and the new law entailed a number of substantial changes to electoral administration, including new rules for the composition of the CSE, changes to the territorial structure of the electoral system, and (related to the citizen identification law) a new system of voter identification and registration.

One of the most significant and contentious elements in the new electoral law was the composition of the Supreme Electoral Council. Despite the heavy

Sandinista influence in the CSE during the 1984 and 1990 elections, international observers were unanimous in their praise of the CSE's impartiality and competence (IHRLG-WOLA 1984, 21; IIDH-CAPEL 1990; LASA 1984, 13; ONUVEN 1989b, 9, 16–17; 1990b, 3, 10). Despite its partisan composition, almost all of the decisions of the CSE magistrates had been unanimous (ONUVEN 1989a, 2; 1989b, 10; 1990a, 5), and the council was highly regarded among the public (Envío 1996a).

But after the FSLN loss in the 1990 elections, non-Sandinista political forces sought to reduce Sandinista influence in the CSE. As CSE president Mariano Fiallos (himself a Sandinista) put it, some in the National Assembly viewed the CSE staff as "contaminated with Sandinismo" (Envío 1996c). Yet, the assembly's plan to reduce Sandinista control of the CSE did not entail making the electoral body non-partisan but, rather, further politicizing it in a new way.

The new electoral law limited the power of the CSE magistrates to name the staff of the departmental electoral councils, requiring that the personnel be chosen from lists provided by political parties (Butler et al. 1996; Walker 1997, 308). In turn, the departmental electoral councils would name the polling station staff. This threatened to deprofessionalize the CSE's administrative structures shortly before an electoral process; furthermore, three new CSE magistrates with no electoral experience had been appointed in June 1995 (Envío 1996e).

At the same time, the new electoral law converted the country's 9 regional zones used for election administration into 17 departmental zones, "implying both greater cost and inexperienced personnel in an election year" (Butler et al. 1996). This administrative and territorial restructuring of the CSE came at a time when the council was frantically trying to distribute new identification cards to voters and compile the new voter registry. The reforms, along with the failure of the government to assign the CSE an adequate budget to finish issuing ID cards, led the highly regarded CSE president Fiallos, who had headed the CSE since its creation, to resign.

The cédula *and voter registration*

Approaching the 1996 elections, the CSE faced the monumental task of registering voters and distributing ID cards. Whereas the opposition UNO coalition had tried to push the Sandinista government to introduce a new ID card before the 1990 elections, the UNO government gave little priority to the creation of the new civil registry after the election. Delays in approving the civil registry legislation, reconciling the electoral law to use the new ID cards for voting, and approving an adequate budget to implement the changes all hampered the process. Ultimately, the CSE began the registration process on its own initiative and drawing on its own operating budget, and it wasn't until 1996 that the government secured $12 million in foreign funding for the project (Butler et al. 1996; Envío 1996b).

In its design, the new registration process was easy enough for citizens, who could use any form of identification or present two witnesses to verify their identity, in addition to providing a birth certificate. The applicant's information would then be checked against the municipal civil registry and the person would return to pick up the ID card when it was ready. The initial ID card was free of charge for citizens (Butler et al. 1996).

But the problems lay in the poor quality of the civil registries and the complexity of the internal CSE handling of ID applications. The CSE decided not to start a new civil registry from scratch, but to compile and computerize the country's existing municipal registries in a central registry office. All ID applications were then sent to the central registry in Managua to be checked against the registry data (IFES 1993, 16, 23). This decision was taken to ensure greater protection against false inscriptions (Interview 43), but it "meant endless checking, rechecking, and hiring of district judges and lawyers to do the legal paperwork required to simultaneously create an accurate Civil Registry and a computerized electoral roll" (Butler et al. 1996).

The biggest challenge for many citizens was the lack of a birth certificate, as some 40–45 percent of the population had never been registered at birth. To obtain an ID, these citizens were required to visit the municipal registrar to receive a document indicating that they lacked a birth certificate and then visit a local judge with two witnesses to request a legal statement that would allow a birth certificate to be issued. Both steps cost money, as both the registrars and judges charged for their services (IFES 1993, 24, 26). The CSE, reportedly unwilling to " 'clash' with the municipalities" over the fees being charged, established a costly parallel system for identification where a registrar, judge, and other staff would work at the municipal level and provide a one-stop service for citizens (IFES 1993, 26–27).

Moreover, many citizens discovered during the registration process that their legal names were different from the names they used (Butler et al. 1996; Envío 1996b). As the news magazine *Envío* (1996b) reported, "Upon registering for their documents, thousands of puzzled and often disgruntled people have discovered that their parents never acknowledged them, that their last name wasn't what they always thought it was, etc.," including one municipality "in which one thousand of its three thousand inhabitants had been registered with the registrar's surname."

With elections approaching in November, it was clear that the CSE would be unable to distribute ID cards to all voters in time, despite its best efforts.[6] As a result, the CSE decided to implement a mixed voter registration system for the 1996 elections, issuing supplementary documents, to be used as voter ID for that year's election only, to those voters who registered but whose *cédulas* would not be ready in time.

The next challenge was distributing *cédulas* and supplementary documents in time for the election. The CSE carried out a massive distribution campaign (*entrega masiva*), which involved sending undelivered ID cards to the corresponding polling stations and opening all of the country's polling places on a staggered basis so that citizens could pick up their cards (OAS 1997, 29). The plan included publicity efforts, such as announcing where voters could retrieve their documents through loudspeakers mounted on circulating vehicles. The process was not without problems, as some voters arrived to pick up their document only to find that it had not yet arrived. The *entrega masiva* ended on September 26 and, by that time, about 75 percent of the ID cards produced had been delivered (Carter Center 1996, 19).

At the same time, the CSE carried out a door-to-door delivery campaign which began in May and continued after the end of the *entrega masiva* campaign (Butler et al. 1996; Carter Center 1996, 18–19; OAS 1997, 29). The CSE received support from the government, as "the Ministry of Education lent teachers and students to help deliver the voter documents until Oct. 19" (Carter Center 1996, 19). Last minute efforts to distribute voter cards involved further door-to-door visits and, in some places, "the operation was accompanied by the music of high-school and municipal bands, who paraded through the streets of the main towns carrying posters and banners urging the people to participate in the October 20 elections" (OAS 1997, 30). Despite these efforts, however, "some undetermined number of voters did not receive documents and thus were prohibited by law from voting" (Carter Center 1996, 19).

Due to the problems encountered during the documentation process, the CSE carried out what would become a regular feature of Nicaraguan electoral processes: voter verification. Beginning in June, over 2,400 verification offices were opened so that voters could check their data on the preliminary voters list and correct any errors that appeared (IFES 1996b, 13). According to the Carter Center (1996, 19), over 70 percent of voters participated. In subsequent electoral processes, the CSE would continue to open polling stations for several weekends before the close of voter registration to allow voters to verify their information and their voting location.

Finally, the CSE carried out an ad hoc registration process in 26 municipalities in former conflict zones, where former army and Contra soldiers were still roaming the countryside, and security conditions (along with financial and logistical obstacles) did not allow for ongoing registration. This process was the same as the ad hoc registration carried out for the previous two elections and, despite some logistical problems (such as outdated census data) and concerns voiced by some political actors and the United States that former supporters of the Contras would be disenfranchised, international observers and political parties ultimately evaluated the process positively. The CSE carried out a house-to-house campaign encouraging registration and opened registration sites on additional weekends with international donor assistance (Butler et al. 1996; Carter Center 1996, 18; NDI 1996; OAS 1997, 18, 31–33). Ultimately, an estimated 90–100 percent of the voting-age population in the affected municipalities registered (NDI 1996, 1).

The results of this mixed registration process were the registration of over 2.4 million Nicaraguans, with about 41 percent receiving a *cédula*, 44 percent receiving supplemental documents, and almost 15 percent receiving a *libreta cívica* from the ad hoc registration (Carter Center 1996, 17; OAS 1997, 24–25). While there remained a number of errors and duplications in the registry data, and some voting credentials had not been picked up by election day, the manner in which voter registration had been conducted was ultimately quite inclusive, involving local registration sites, the use of witnesses for citizens lacking identification, the opening of thousands of local offices for voters to verify their information, and door-to-door delivery of ID cards. *Envío* (1996d) characterized the CSE's registration efforts as "Herculean," while the OAS observer mission concluded that "the CSE made a genuine effort to distribute voting documents to the entire population, and that this effort met with success" (OAS 1997, 31).

Article 41

As the CSE encountered problems carrying out the registration and documentation process, there were concerns about the accuracy of the voter rolls that would result. Concerned about the potential for omissions from the voter rolls, the National Assembly included measures in the 1995 electoral law that would allow any voter with a valid identity card to vote at the polling station pertaining to the address listed on the card, even if the person's name did not appear on the voter roll (Ley Electoral 1995, Arts. 41 and 122). Similarly, voters could cast ballots even if there were minor differences between their name as it appeared on the voter rolls and on their ID card (Ley Electoral 1995, Art. 122), thus giving significant discretion to poll workers.

In supporting the measures, deputies referred vaguely to the possibility of computer errors or other unspecified problems that would result in voters being omitted from the voter rolls (Asamblea Nacional 1995a, 579, 581). Although no similar problems had occurred in previous elections when ad hoc registration had been used, deputies in the assembly were concerned about the accuracy of the new voter registry and wanted to avoid potential problems (Interviews 38, 43) – perhaps worried about partisan manipulation of the voter rolls as well as technical problems. Although the assembly debates over this measure showed few hints of partisanship, the debates over the citizen identification law passed two years earlier evidenced profound distrust of the potential politicization of the documentation and registration process (see Asamblea Nacional 1992, 172–73, 175, 178–79, 260, 265).

One deputy also suggested in later debate that the committee drafting the electoral law was concerned that voters might have errors on their ID card, but because they would be known in their precinct – a presumption made plausible by the country's system of highly decentralized polling stations – it was reasonable to allow them to vote even if there were inconsistencies between their ID card and the voter list (Asamblea Nacional 1995b, 1161). This was thus a case of one inclusive administrative practice – the decentralization of polling locations – alleviating concerns about another inclusive measure that might otherwise be vulnerable to manipulation.

The CSE opposed Article 41 and its provision to allow voters not appearing on the voter list to cast a ballot, fearing that it might give rise to multiple voting (Envío 1996b; Interview 43; OAS 1997, 55), but the assembly was not persuaded: the motion to include the provision in Article 41 passed 65 votes to 0, with no abstentions (Asamblea Nacional 1995a, 582). Political parties' concerns about technical problems and perhaps partisan manipulation of the voter lists led the assembly to include an administrative measure in the electoral law that would help voters avoid being disenfranchised due to problems with the voter rolls. While the measure was controversial after its passage,[7] it also helped ensure that errors in the voter rolls do not prevent registered citizens from voting, as happened in El Salvador and Guatemala.

The 1996 elections

With its mixed voter registration system and a new electoral law passed just the year before, Nicaragua headed into a general election in 1996. As discussed above, the voter registration drive had achieved commendable results. The CSE also carried out a voter-information campaign and, while these efforts were criticized for being insufficient, given the complexity of the voter registration system (IRI 1997, 2, 15; OAS 1997, 37), the OAS concluded "that in some stages of the election process, such as the ad hoc registration, the civic-education campaign was generally effective" (OAS 1997, 37).

But trouble arrived with election day and the subsequent vote count, which saw a number of irregularities, including ballot boxes found abandoned in ditches, accusations of fraud and, ultimately, the nullification of 12 percent of the votes. At least in hindsight, the irregularities were not surprising, considering the recent restructuring of the CSE, the complexities of administering 6 different elections (for the presidency, departmental and national assembly members, mayors, municipal councils, and the Central American Parliament) with the participation of over 20 parties, as well as the doubling of polling places since 1990 due to population growth, postwar repatriation, and expansion of the voter rolls.

An initial problem in the days leading up to the election was the shifting of polling sites. Over 200 polling stations ended up with more than 400 voters and therefore had to be redivided to comply with legal requirements (OAS 1997, 27). Problems resulted from the fact that "the process of subdividing and relocating polling stations continued up to the day before the elections" and "many of the stations that had been divided up were a considerable distance apart, which led to delays and transportation problems, both for the voters and for the poll workers assigned to them" (OAS 1997, 36–37). The problems were particularly severe in Managua, where "[a] majority of voters did not know until some 24 hours before election day where they were supposed to go vote" and where the departmental election council president "decided 48 hours before election day to change the location of many of the JRVs whose presidents were not from his party" (Envío 1996e). This and other methods allowed the Liberal party to disproportionately staff polling stations when the assigned poll workers did not show up for duty (Envío 1996e). Thus, while the ample number of polling stations – 8,955 (IFES 1996a, 3) – was designed to facilitate participation, both logistical disorganization and partisan manipulation at the departmental level of the CSE caused confusion for many voters.

A more extensive obstacle confronting voters on election day was the late opening of polling stations and long lines. Some polling stations also closed before everyone waiting in line was able to vote, although the CSE had instructed voting sites to remain open the full 11 hours even if they opened late (Carter Center 1996, 26–27; OAS 1997, 53). While the late opening of polling stations is common in Nicaragua (and Guatemala and El Salvador), the problem was more severe than usual in 1996, with many stations opening hours late, due largely to the late arrival of voting materials.

As Envío (1996e) reported, "[t]hese generalized delays and irregularities were notably different than the order and punctuality of the 1984 and 1990 elections." The procedural hurdles that voters faced in the form of shifting polling places and long waits resulted, to some extent, from the 1995 electoral reforms that had further politicized the CSE and restructured the election administration bureaucracy. By staffing departmental election councils with partisan appointees, the reforms reduced the technical capacity of the electoral machinery immediately before a complex electoral process, and many problems resulted from poorly trained departmental council members and poll workers (Envío 1996e; IFES 1996a, 3–4). The reforms also provided greater potential for manipulation, and some have blamed the problems during the 1996 election on the fact that the departmental electoral councils in the three most problematic departments where fraud may have occurred were all headed by affiliates of the Constitutional Liberal Party (PLC) (Envío 1996e). It is worth noting that the instances of fraud that may have occurred resulted not from overly inclusive voting practices, but from anomalies during the vote count and transmission of results and the mishandling of ballots and tally sheets, exacerbated by the exhaustion of poll workers (Carter Center 1996, 31–32).

Explaining inclusive election administration

The contrasts between the inclusiveness of Nicaragua's election administration in the 1980s to mid-1990s (summarized in Table 6.1) and that of El Salvador and Guatemala are significant. Whereas the latter two countries concentrated polling places in urban areas, Nicaragua utilized a system of extensive decentralization to minimize voters' travel to the polls. Whereas voter registration processes in El Salvador and Guatemala were onerous and costly for many voters, in Nicaragua the CSE went to great lengths to facilitate registration and deliver voter cards. When a permanent voter registry was created in the mid-1990s, it was accompanied by rules to allow any voter with a valid ID card to vote in their precinct, even if their name did not appear on the voter lists. And the three general elections held during this period were accompanied by extensive voter education campaigns to inform voters of where and how to register and vote. What accounts for Nicaragua's inclusive election administration during this period?

Table 6.1 Election administration inclusiveness, Nicaragua 1984–1996

Dimension	*Description*	*Inclusiveness*
Voter registration		
Extent of state responsibility for registering voters	Voter-initiated, state efforts to distribute voter cards (1984–1990); automatic (after 1993)	Medium/ high
Difficulty of registration process	Decentralized locations; completed in one step prior to 1993, two or more steps after 1993; no cost	High/ medium
Ease of access to ID documents required for registration	Multiple documents or witnesses accepted (1984–1990); birth certificate (often lacking) required after 1993	High/low
Registration closing date	4 months (1989); 90 days after 1993	Low/medium
Residency requirement	None	High
Provisional registration	Those turning 18 between close of registration and election day eligible to register	High
Registry consultation	Voter lists posted at local polling places and distributed to parties; verification exercise in 1996	High
Purging of voter rolls	Voters not purged from the rolls for failure to vote	High
Getting to the ballot box		
Accessibility of polling places	Highly decentralized polling places	High
Assignment of voters to polling places	Residential	High
Convenience voting measures	Not used	Low
Electoral calendar	Voting held on Sunday	High
Casting a ballot		
Voter ID requirement	Voter card required, but voter card delivered to voter upon registration (1984–1990); several ID forms accepted in 1996	Medium
Provisional or tendered ballots	Available only after 1995	Low/high
Voter education		
State efforts to inform voters of where and how to register and vote	Extensive voter education efforts through diverse media	High
Overall inclusiveness		*High*

This section examines the influence of several variables and shows that the origins of Nicaragua's election administration inclusiveness lie in: the different nature of election fraud practiced in pre-democratic Nicaragua compared to Guatemala and El Salvador, and consequently the lesser preoccupation with fraud in Nicaragua in the 1980s; international pressures that prompted a strong desire for high voter turnout, along with international financial and technical assistance that helped Nicaragua implement inclusive election administration measures; and the governing party's confidence that it would be victorious in clean and high-turnout elections.

The specter of election fraud

Like Guatemala and El Salvador in the 1970s, Nicaragua had its share of fraudulent election practices under the Somoza regime. Ballot box stuffing, multiple voting, translucent ballots that violated the secrecy of the vote, and censorship and intimidation were all common (Walker 2003, 140).

Yet these past fraudulent practices did not impact the shape of election administration in the post-Somoza period, as had occurred in Guatemala. The explanation for this difference lies partly in the different nature of those frauds, itself a product of the different roles that elections played in the different regimes. Whereas instances of election fraud in Guatemala had been traumatic events in which presumptive victors in presidential contests had been robbed of victory, in Nicaragua election fraud under the Somozas was simply part of the regime's corrupt business as usual.

These different expectations of and reactions to fraud can be understood by reference to the different role that elections played in the two countries. In Guatemala, while elections were not free – civil liberties were not fully respected and leftist parties were proscribed – and the military retained extensive powers beyond the reach of civilian authorities, elections did exhibit an important degree of competition between officially allowed parties. Within this system of limited competition, it was expected that elections would be conducted fairly.

In Nicaragua, by contrast, electoral competition was a façade, with the understanding that the Somozas would rule directly or through puppet presidents. In some cases, the National Guard (controlled by Somoza) distributed the ballots and counted the votes (Millett 1977, 181; Walter 1993, 92). Nicaragua's Conservative Party played the role of official opposition to Somoza's Liberals, and the Somozas co-opted Conservative party leaders with patronage positions in the government and National Assembly (Walker 2003, 30–31, 140–41; Walter 1993, xviii). As Walker (2003, 28) puts it, "[w]henever possible, the Conservative leadership was bought off," including a pact "in which the Conservative chiefs agreed to put up a candidate to lose in the rigged election of 1951 in return for personal benefits and minority participation in the government." When the Conservatives periodically boycotted elections, Somoza arranged for a token opposition party to run against him. Rather than competitive elections being hijacked on election day or during the vote count, elections under the Somozas were rigged throughout the process and were understood to be façades to provide the Somozas with some veneer of legitimacy, rather than real contests for power in which the outcome was uncertain.

Thus when a new electoral system was established in the 1980s, the legacy of fraudulent elections did not weigh heavily on the minds of legislators and election administrators. The FSLN, after all, had never experienced having an election victory stolen through fraud, as had parties in Guatemala and El Salvador. The Sandinistas also had little to fear from wholesale election fraud, as they held majority control of the electoral management body. There was thus no inclination to centralize voting sites to avoid ballot stuffing or voter manipulation in rural areas or (at least initially) to utilize stringent record checking to prevent potentially fraudulent voter registrations. When asked whether the extensive decentralization of polling places (*voto domiciliario*) caused concern about the possibility of election fraud, a CSE magistrate at the time said this was not a preoccupation and noted the safeguards in place, such as the presence of party poll watchers (Interview 46). As discussed in the following chapter, however, this changed after the 1996 elections. The long-term consequences of the irregularities in that contest would be ominous, as FSLN leaders drew lessons from that election that they would not forget when they would again come to control the country's electoral machinery.

International influences: geopolitical pressures and electoral assistance

While a history of election fraud did not compel the adoption of restrictive election administration measures, a strong force for inclusive administrative practices was international pressure on the Sandinista regime, primarily from the United States. The Reagan administration criticized the regime through the early 1980s for not holding elections, which "seriously eroded international support for the Sandinista government, particularly among the West Europeans on whom the government depend[ed] for most of its foreign economic assistance, as well as among key members of the Democratic Party in the United States" (LASA 1984, 29). As a result of this pressure, the Nicaraguan regime held elections in 1984 rather than the following year, as originally planned. The effect of the elections on international audiences was paramount: as vice president Sergio Ramírez wrote in his memoir of the revolution, "the elections of 1984 were for the United States, as well as for us, part of the mechanism of war. Carrying them out in regal [form], we sought the legitimacy that they, impeding them, wanted to take away" (Ramírez 2007, 152). As both the FSLN and the opposition understood, "foreign sympathy – especially from the Western democracies – was the real object of the electoral contest" (Gilbert 1988, 121).

This meant that Sandinista leaders wanted a high voter turnout to legitimize the elections internationally – not only with the United States but also with Nicaragua's allies – and to demonstrate and enhance their domestic support (Interview 37). As one of the few observation missions to the 1984 elections reported,

> Sandinista officials had stressed the need for a high turnout, to demonstrate the validity of the electoral process and to "send a message to Washington." "Turnout is the most important thing," Comandante Jaime Wheelock told our delegation the day before the election. "It doesn't matter how the vote is divided."
>
> (LASA 1984, 17)

With Reagan just re-elected and his administration's war against Nicaragua expected to intensify, the Sandinistas "hoped that a competitive election with heavy turnout would help to shield Nicaragua against this anticipated onslaught" (LASA 1984, 29).

This pressure intensified up to the 1990 elections, as the United States continued the Contra war and economic embargo throughout the decade. International scrutiny was intense, as the 1990 elections were the most heavily observed elections in history up to that time. The Sandinistas again advanced the date of the elections, as a "shield" against potential aggression from the Bush administration, as one former Sandinista leader put it (Interview 44). Pressure from the United States and other countries also resulted in the government making significant concessions to opposition demands, including permitting foreign campaign donations (LASA 1990, 4–6).[8] International scrutiny and US backing of the opposition coalition competing against the incumbent Sandinistas would have greatly magnified the political costs of any administrative measure that could have been interpreted as an attempt to suppress the opposition vote.

The Sandinistas thus hoped for high turnout, which would legitimate the electoral process and their rule. But international influences on Nicaragua's election administration were not limited to geopolitical pressures. Nicaragua also received large numbers of international election observers and technical and financial assistance in setting up its electoral machinery. Prior to the 1984 elections, Scandinavian countries donated $1.65 million for Nicaragua's elections, representing a small portion of the $25 million cost of the elections, while technical support also came from Swedish experts (IHRLG-WOLA 1984, 17–18; LASA 1984, 29).

Aid greatly increased for the 1990 elections, with a total of $9 million provided to the CSE (CSE 1991, 30). Assistance included technical support for training party poll watchers, assistance from the electoral commissions of Costa Rica and Venezuela, and donated computer equipment to prepare voter lists from Germany and Spain (CSE 1991, 8, 12, 31; ONUVEN 1989a, 11). Financing from Canada, Norway, and Sweden helped overcome shortfalls in funding for the printing of voter education materials (CSE 1991, 17). Also boosting the CSE's budget was a provision in the agreement allowing foreign campaign donations, which included a mandate that half of foreign funds would go to the CSE to cover election costs (ONUVEN 1989b, 5). After 1990, Canada provided computer equipment and technical assistance for generating precinct maps, while European donors provided several million dollars for the civil registry project (IFES 1993, 33–34; 1994, Appendix 3; Interview 43).

For the 1996 elections, the United States provided over $6 million to CAPEL for technical support to the CSE (Envío 1996e), while the International Foundation for Electoral Systems also provided technical support (Butler et al. 1996; IFES 1996a). Foreign donations covered more than half of the 1996 election costs (McCoy 1998, 61) and helped compensate for the fact that the executive branch "dragged its feet in giving the CSE the corresponding funds for both the ID cards and the organization of the elections" (Envío 1996e). As an experienced observer put it, the elections "could not have been held without international assistance" (McCoy 1998, 61).

According to the CSE's executive secretary at the time and president later on, international assistance was critical in establishing decentralized voting, which otherwise would have been impossible to fully implement (Interview 43). A CSE magistrate during this period also noted that technical support from Sweden and Canada was instrumental in developing electoral cartography, among other things (Interview 46).

Foreign funding also made the introduction of the new identity card and civil/voter registry possible. Almost all of the costs associated with this process were covered by foreign donations (Envío 1996b; 1996d). Especially important was support from Spain, which provided most of the materials, equipment, and training (Interviews 38, 43). This support was critical in overcoming domestic resource constraints and, combined with the dedication of the CSE, made it possible to overcome or circumvent the many challenges of constructing a permanent registry in a poor post-conflict country. Nevertheless, foreign donations were limited, so that the CSE only had a few computers and printers with which to produce *cédulas*, while reliance on intermittent and uncoordinated foreign assistance hindered long-range planning for the civil registry project (IFES 1993).

In addition to financial and technical assistance from the international community, Nicaragua also received international election monitors, with over 400 observers present for the 1984 elections (IHRLG-WOLA 1984, 41) and over 2,500 observers in 1990 (ONUVEN 1990c, 7). International observer delegations offered advice throughout the 1990 electoral process, to which Nicaraguan election officials were receptive (IIDH-CAPEL 1990, 39; McConnell 2000, 130). Observers had the most evident impact on administrative inclusiveness in 1996, however. When it became evident that voter cards would not be distributed in time for that year's election, the OAS mission helped devise the plan for issuing supplementary voter cards (OAS 1997, 29). Additionally, the ad hoc registration carried out in 26 municipalities was originally planned for 2 weekends, but the OAS and other observer organizations suggested extending the process when it seemed that there were still many unregistered after the first 2 weekends, a suggestion that the CSE heeded (OAS 1997, 32). Other suggestions were rejected, however, as when the head of the OAS observer mission "suggested that the remaining [voter ID] documents be distributed at the voting tables on election Sunday itself, an idea overruled by the parties, which set a final deadline of noon on Saturday" (Envío 1996f).

International assistance thus made many inclusive administrative practices possible although, without other external pressures and internal political conditions, such assistance would not have guaranteed inclusive election administration. Financial and technical assistance from the international community was thus a necessary but not sufficient condition for producing Nicaragua's inclusive election administration.

Partisan interests

Hoping to gain international legitimacy with high voter turnout, and supplied with the international assistance to put inclusive election administration measures in place, the FSLN government could construct an inclusive system of election administration. A desire for high turnout and the availability of international assistance could only exercise such influence on electoral rules, however, in the absence of countervailing partisan motives. The fact that the Sandinistas fully expected to win both the 1984 and 1990 elections allowed the desire for high turnout to take precedence.

In 1984, both the Sandinistas and the opposition fully expected the FSLN to win fair elections (Gilbert 1988, 121). As opposition leader Arturo Cruz commented, "In fair and free elections, the Sandinistas would possibly win, given that they enjoy considerable popular support" (Envío 1984a). As one CSE magistrate recalled, "there was no doubt" that the FSLN would win in 1984 (Interview 46). Consequently, the FSLN had nothing to fear from high turnout among all segments of voters, confident as the party was in its victory and hoping for high turnout. Thus the FSLN first aimed to achieve a high rate of voter registration. As *Envío* (1984b) reported before the elections, "a high number of voters in November will indicate acceptance of the elections. In this context, Sandinista leaders considered registration the 'first electoral victory…'" Given the desire for high turnout, it was also not surprising that election observers reported that on election day some polling stations stayed open later than prescribed, with "FSLN supporters going into neighborhoods to inform people who had not voted that they could still vote" (IHRLG-WOLA 1984, 43).

Leading up to the 1990 elections, the FSLN again expected to be victorious, and opinion polls consistently showed the party leading the opposition UNO coalition. Top UNO officials even privately conceded to election observer delegations that they expected to lose (Richard and Booth 1995, 214). Expecting victory and seeking legitimacy, the FSLN was willing to negotiate and compromise with opposition parties over the electoral law in 1983–1984 and again in 1988–1989. Prior to the 1984 elections, opposition demands for the most part did not involve election administration measures.[9] But in 1989–1990, opposition demands included introduction of a new identity card, polling stations being limited to 400 voters, delivery of the voter rolls to political parties at least 60 days before the election, and adjustments to the voter registration periods. The government met almost all of these demands (Carter Center 1990a; ONUVEN 1989a, 6–7).[10] Thus, for instance, the CSE had initially planned 2 registration periods of 3 days each, 45 days apart; the opposition demanded 4 Sunday registrations, which "complicated the registration process and added significantly to its cost" (ONUVEN 1989a, 7) but was nevertheless carried out.

Importantly, at least one inclusive measure – the decentralization of polling stations – did not stand to benefit the FSLN electorally. The party enjoyed greater support in urban areas and, as the decade wore on, rural sectors grew increasingly alienated from the party (Interview 44; Orquist 1992, 16–18). As Orquist (1992, 18) notes, "[b]y 1984, the rural vote for the Conservative Democratic Party indicated that the countryside was one of the weakest areas for the FSLN." While over 65 percent of the national vote went to the FSLN, the party garnered 68 percent of the urban vote, and abstention was higher in the countryside than in urban areas in 1984, likely a result of the withdrawal of the main opposition coalition and the greater opposition to the FSLN in the countryside (Castro 1992, 131–32). By the time of the 1990 elections, there were greater signs of FSLN weakness in rural areas, although the party still expected to win nationally (Interview 44). Government policies had driven some rural Nicaraguans to join the Contra forces and many more to lose any goodwill they held toward the Sandinistas. Postelection surveys showed the FSLN winning below 30 percent of the vote in rural areas (Orquist 1992, 18).

Therefore, the FSLN's partisan electoral interest might have been expected to lead to administrative measures to boost urban turnout and depress rural turnout. But countervailing partisan interests prevailed: the FSLN expected to win free and fair elections handily and hoped to maximize voter turnout to legitimize their rule. An additional countervailing factor was ideological: the Sandinistas had attempted to construct a participatory form of socialist democracy during the 1980s. While this vision of participatory democracy, with its focus on mass organizations with ties to the party-state, was generally seen as an alternative to liberal electoral democracy (Gilbert 1988, 34–35), it was only natural that when the Sandinistas grafted competitive elections onto their revolutionary model, they would establish an election administration system that prioritized the participation of voters and sought to eliminate barriers to the ballot.

EMB structure: the Supreme Electoral Council

For the most part, the Supreme Electoral Council was a force for inclusive election administration. In the 1980s, the CSE and its president, Mariano Fiallos, played a central role in designing the system of electoral administration. According to a member of the FSLN's national directorate and a CSE magistrate, the CSE was given carte blanche by the government to design many electoral procedures, including voter registration, the location of polling places, and voter education campaigns (Interviews 44, 46). The CSE had the good fortune to be headed by the widely respected Fiallos, whose recommendations to the National Assembly held great sway (Interview 37).

Enjoying a great deal of discretion in designing election administration procedures, the CSE's initiative and hard work made the decentralization of polling stations possible. The CSE established an electoral cartography division and utilized census maps and topographical photographs to devise a preliminary cartography. The council then organized field visits to update data on population centers and potential locales for polling places (CSE 1991, 4; Interview 43); again in the early 1990s, it sent cartographers out to the field to update precinct maps, in order to disperse new polling places, limit each precinct to 300–350 voters, and minimize travel distances for voters (IFES 1993, 14). While international assistance was essential to the successful implementation of polling-site decentralization, the competence and initiative of the CSE were equally critical in carrying out this technically demanding task.

Thus, the CSE was a case of a nominally partisan electoral management body that acted in a neutral manner to implement inclusive administrative practices. As Booth (1998, 192) puts it, "[a]lthough a majority of its magistrates and staff originally came from the FSLN, the CSE won a strong reputation for technical competence and nonpartisanship during the 1984 and 1990 elections." López-Pintor (1998, 53) similarly notes that the CSE "acted with high standards of neutrality and technical competence" and draws the lesson that "an electoral authority can be party-based and still operate neutrally and independently." Part of the explanation no doubt lies in the fact that the CSE was staffed by militants of a party that expected to win inclusive and fair elections and held a participatory ideology that prioritized inclusion. Another factor undoubtedly was the rectitude of the top CSE leadership.

The CSE's strong reputation and competence also helped ensure the functioning of automatic voter registration in the mid-1990s. There was debate over which institution would be responsible for compiling and maintaining a new civil registry and distributing ID cards, with the executive branch advocating that the Interior Ministry be tasked with the responsibility and the CSE arguing that the registry should be overseen by the electoral body. The confidence that the CSE enjoyed at the time, along with the weakness of the Chamorro administration in imposing its will on the legislature, contributed to the registry and identification process being entrusted to the CSE (Interview 43). While automatic voter registration would still have been possible had another government agency been assigned the responsibility of maintaining the civil registry, assigning the task to the CSE assured that registration would be automatic. It also meant that the institution responsible for getting ID cards in the hands of voters before the 1996 election would be motivated to ensure that all eligible citizens were able to vote.

Yet this began to change after the 1995 electoral reforms, which aimed at reducing Sandinista influence in the CSE by mandating that all three members of departmental councils be named from party lists. As Booth (1998, 192) explains:

> This reform replaced many FSLN sympathizers on the CSE staff with sympathizers of other parties – exactly what most of the mutually suspicious political parties intended. However, this change also transformed the CSE

> staff from a highly experienced and disciplined technical bureaucracy into one penetrated by competing partisans, and it brought in thousands of inexperienced departmental and local JRV personnel at the last minute.

The reforms were passed, over the public opposition of the CSE leadership, which recommended to the legislature that CSE magistrates be prohibited from engaging in partisan activities (IFES 1994, 16). The immediate result of the reforms was an electoral body with diminished capacity, as many departmental election councils and poll workers lacked experience and were insufficiently trained (McCoy 1998, 61; Walker 1997, 308). The consequences in the longer term would be more detrimental, as the following chapter discusses.

Civil society

As was the case in Guatemala in its early years of democratic elections, civil society played no role in the establishment of Nicaragua's election administration. In the 1980s, the most prominent civic and mass organizations were tied to the FSLN and exercised limited autonomy from the party (see, e.g., Gilbert 1988, 72–76). There were no civic groups with a focus on electoral issues until 1996, when the group Ethics and Transparency (*Ética y Transparencia*, or ET) formed with support from the National Democratic Institute to observe the elections that year. ET would become a major actor in domestic election observation in the years ahead. However, when the framework of Nicaragua's election administration was constructed in the 1980s and reformed in the mid-1990s, organized civil society played little role in the choice of electoral procedures. As elsewhere, it was partisans and administrators who crafted the rules of election administration in Nicaragua.

Conclusion

Nicaragua's election administration practices during the country's democratic transition were significantly more inclusive than practices in Guatemala and El Salvador. A number of factors shaped the country's election administration. International political pressures increased the importance of high voter turnout to legitimize the electoral process, while the governing party expected to win the 1984 and 1990 elections and thus sought to facilitate participation even among rural voters, who tended to support the opposition. Headed partly by Sandinistas, the party-based Supreme Electoral Council worked to facilitate participation, and its work was supported by international financial and technical assistance. Unlike in Guatemala, the history of fraudulent elections in Nicaragua under the personalist Somoza regime did not cast a shadow on the new electoral rules, so that concerns about electoral integrity did not crowd out a focus on voter inclusion. By the mid-1990s, the country's election administration system was being reformed; it would go through even more drastic changes in the years to come.

Notes

1 The literature on the revolution and the Sandinistas is immense. For insightful analyses of the Sandinistas' ideology and the interplay between participatory and liberal democracy in revolutionary Nicaragua, see Gilbert 1988 and Vanden and Prevost 1993.
2 Ultimately, the principal opposition coalition withdrew from the elections, with US encouragement, in the face of a certain Sandinista victory.
3 The 1988 election law, however, implied that registration would be carried out several months before election day, since the deadline for soliciting a replacement registration card was 30 days before the election (Art. 49); no such deadline was specified in the 1984 electoral law.
4 Slightly different numbers of polling places are reported in other sources (see Carter Center 1990a; IIDH-CAPEL 1990, 40). The CSE's method of classifying urban and rural areas actually underestimated the number of rural polling places, as all municipal centers (*cabeceras*) and locations with more than 1,000 residents were considered urban (IFES 1993, 14).
5 This point is reiterated in a subsequent ONUVEN report (1990c, 6) and was a prominent theme in discussions of decentralizing polling locations in El Salvador (see Chapter 8).
6 While the long delays in processing ID applications led to concerns about possible partisan bias in excluding voters, the OAS observer mission "conducted a rapid investigation into some of these cases, but found no reasons for the delay other than problems with the checking processes" (OAS 1997, 29). In later years, however, partisan bias in the distribution of ID cards would result in voter disenfranchisement (see Chapter 7).
7 Already during the 1996 electoral process, the OAS observer mission found that while many party representatives expressed support for Article 41, "[s]ome opposed it ... saying that it could contribute to widespread fraud" (OAS 1997, 18).
8 A comment from a Chilean general before the 1988 plebiscite on Pinochet's rule applies equally well to Nicaragua's 1984 and 1990 elections:

> If the government's candidate wins everyone will say it was fraud. If he loses everyone will say it was a fair election. So it is more in our interests than anyone else's to be able to show it was an absolutely fair election.
>
> (Quoted in Hyde 2011, 38–39)

9 Two contentious issues worth noting were the voting age and voting rights of members of the armed forces. The FSLN insisted on a voting age of 16 and voting rights for the military, which the opposition viewed as an attempt to include more FSLN supporters in the electorate (IHRLG-WOLA 1984, 21; LASA 1984, 11–12).
10 UNO also wanted to permit voting for Nicaraguans living abroad, no doubt expecting high levels of support from Nicaraguans who had left the country during the revolution. Ultimately, only registration abroad was allowed, with those registering needing to be in-country on election day to vote.

References

Asamblea Nacional. 1992. Sesión Ordinaria No. 12, Tomo VII, August 18.

Asamblea Nacional. 1995a. Sesión Ordinaria No. 10 de la Onceava Legislatura de la Asamblea Nacional, Tomo IX.

Asamblea Nacional. 1995b. Sesión Ordinaria No. 10, Parte Final, Tomo X.

Booth, John A. 1998. "Electoral Observation and Democratic Transition in Nicaragua." In *Electoral Observation and Democratic Transitions in Latin America*, Kevin Middlebrook, ed. Center for U.S.-Mexican Studies, University of California, San Diego.

Butler, Judy, David R. Dye, and Jack Spence, with George Vickers. 1996. *Democracy and Its Discontents*. Hemisphere Initiatives.

Carter Center. 1990a. Observing Nicaragua's Elections, 1989–1990.

Carter Center. 1990b. Summary Report of Fourth Pre-Election Visit to Nicaragua, January 26–28, 1990.

Carter Center. 1996. The Observation of the 1996 Nicaraguan Elections: A Report of the Council of Freely Elected Heads of Government. Atlanta: Latin American and Caribbean Program, The Carter Center.

Castro, Vanessa. 1992. "Electoral Results in the Rural Sector." In *The 1990 Elections in Nicaragua and Their Aftermath*, Vanessa Castro and Gary Prevost, eds. Lanham, MD: Rowman & Littlefield Publishers.

CSE (Consejo Supremo Electoral). 1991. *Elecciones 1990*. Managua.

Envío. 1984a. "Electoral Process Moves Ahead amid Difficulties." No. 33, March. www.envio.org.ni/articulo/3962.

Envío. 1984b. "The Electoral Process Advances, but Abstention Encourages Intervention." No. 38, August. www.envio.org.ni/articulo/3956.

Envío. 1996a. "Nicaragua Needs a Miracle." No. 175, February. www.envio.org.ni/articulo/1932.

Envío. 1996b. "The Election Labyrinth." No. 177, April. www.envio.org.ni/articulo/1937.

Envío. 1996c. "Mariano Fiallos: I Accepted Because It's a Crucial Election." No. 184, November. www.envio.org.ni/articulo/1984.

Envío. 1996d. "Nicaragua's Elections: The Die Is Cast." No. 184, November. www.envio.org.ni/articulo/1983.

Envío. 1996e. "The Roots of the Electoral Crisis." No. 185, December. www.envio.org.ni/articulo/1988.

Envío. 1996f. "Observing the Observers." No. 185, December. www.envio.org.ni/articulo/1991.

Gilbert, Dennis. 1988. *Sandinistas: The Party and the Revolution*. Cambridge: Basil Blackwell.

Hyde, Susan. 2011. *The Pseudo-Democrat's Dilemma: Why Election Observation Became an International Norm*. Ithaca and London: Cornell University Press.

IFES (International Foundation for Electoral Systems). 1993. Nicaragua Pre-Election Technical Assessment. May 15–June 4.

IFES. 1994. Nicaragua Final Report: International Donor Meeting and Needs Assessment. July 1994.

IFES. 1996a. Nicaragua Election Observation Mission, October 20, 1996. Washington, DC: International Foundation for Electoral Systems.

IFES. 1996b. Nicaragua Misión de Observación: Inscripcion Ad-Hoc y Verificación, Junio 1996.

IHRLG (International Human Rights Law Group) and WOLA (Washington Office on Latin America). 1984. *A Political Opening in Nicaragua: Report on the Nicaraguan Elections of November 4, 1984*. Washington, DC: Washington Office on Latin American and International Human Rights Law Group.

IIDH-CAPEL (Instituto Interamericano de Derechos Humanos – Centro de Asesoria y Promoción Electoral). 1990. Informe de la Misión de Observación, Elecciones Generales Nicaragua, 25 de Febrero de 1990.

IRI (International Republican Institute). 1997. Nicaragua Election Observation Report, October 20, 1996.

LASA (Latin American Studies Association). 1984. The Electoral Process in Nicaragua: Domestic and International Influences. The Report of the Latin American Studies Association Delegation to Observe the Nicaraguan General Election of November 4, 1984.

LASA. 1990. *Electoral Democracy under International Pressure: The Report of the Latin American Studies Association Commission to Observe the 1990 Nicaraguan Election.* Pittsburgh: Latin American Studies Association.

Ley Electoral. 1984. Decreto No. 1413. March 26.

Ley Electoral. 1988. Leyes No. 43 y 56.

Ley Electoral. 1995. Ley No. 221. December 5.

Ley No. 28. Estatuto de Autonomía de las Regiones de la Costa Atlántica de Nicaragua. September 7, 1987.

Ley No. 152. Ley de Identificación Ciudadana. January 27, 1993.

López-Pintor, Rafael. 1998. "Nicaragua's Measured Move to Democracy." In *Postconflict Elections, Democratization, and International Assistance*, Krishna Kumar, ed. Boulder: Lynne Rienner.

McConnell, Shelley A. 2000. "ONUVEN: Electoral Observation as Conflict Resolution." In *Peacemaking and Democratization in the Western Hemisphere*, Tommie Sue Montgomery, ed. Miami: North-South Center Press.

McCoy, Jennifer L. 1998. "Nicaragua's Second Elections." In *Postconflict Elections, Democratization, and International Assistance*, Krishna Kumar, ed. Boulder: Lynne Rienner.

Millett, Richard. 1977. *Guardians of the Dynasty: A History of the U.S.-Created Guardia Nacional de Nicaragua and the Somoza Family*. Maryknoll, NY: Orbis Books.

NDI (National Democratic Institute). 1996. NDI Report: Voter Registration and Domestic Election Observation in Nicaragua.

OAS (Organization of American States, Unit for the Promotion of Democracy). 1997. *Electoral Observation: Nicaragua 1996.*

ONUVEN (United Nations Observer Mission to Verify the Electoral Process). 1989a. Second Report to the Secretary-General by the United Nations Observer Mission to Verify the Electoral Process in Nicaragua. December 7.

ONUVEN. 1989b. Evolution of the Electoral Process in Nicaragua: First Report of the United Nations Observer Mission to Verify the Electoral Process in Nicaragua to the Secretary-General. October 17.

ONUVEN. 1990a. Third Report to the Secretary-General by the United Nations Observer Mission to Verify the Electoral Process in Nicaragua. January 31.

ONUVEN. 1990b. Cuarto Informe al Secretario General de la Misión de Observadores de las Naciones Unidas Encargada de Verificar el Proceso Electoral en Nicaragua. February 22.

ONUVEN. 1990c. Fifth Report to the Secretary-General by the United Nations Observer Mission to Verify the Electoral Process in Nicaragua. March 30.

Oquist, Paul. 1992. "The Sociopolitical Dynamics of the 1990 Nicaraguan Elections." In *The 1990 Elections in Nicaragua and their Aftermath*, Vanessa Castro and Gary Prevost, eds. Lanham, MD: Rowman & Littlefield Publishers.

Ramírez, Sergio. 2007. *Adiós Muchachos*. Madrid: Alfaguara-Santillana Ediciones Generales.

Richard, Patricia Bayer, and John A. Booth. 1995. "Election Observation and Democratization: Reflections on the Nicaraguan Case." In *Elections and Democracy in Central America, Revisited*, Mitchell A. Seligson, and John A. Booth, eds. Chapel Hill and London: University of North Carolina Press.

Vanden, Harry E., and Gary Prevost. 1993. *Democracy and Socialism in Sandinista Nicaragua*. Boulder: Lynne Rienner Publishers.

Walker, Thomas W. 1997. "Epilogue: The 1996 Elections." In *Nicaragua without Illusions: Regime Transition and Structural Adjustment in the 1990s*, Thomas W. Walker, ed. Wilmington, DE: Scholarly Resources Inc.

Walker, Thomas W. 2003. *Nicaragua: Living in the Shadow of the Eagle*. Boulder: Westview Press.

Walter, Knut, 1993. *The Regime of Anastasio Somoza, 1936–1956*. Chapel Hill: University of North Carolina Press.

7 Nicaragua

The slow erosion of inclusiveness, 2000–2012

During the 2000s, Nicaragua saw a slow erosion of its election administration inclusiveness. Many inclusive features of election administration, including highly decentralized polling places, remained in place, and national elections in 2001 and 2006 were carried out in a relatively inclusive manner. But beginning in the mid-2000s, the administrative conduct of the Supreme Electoral Council (CSE), regarding such matters as the issuance of ID cards and the provision of information to voters, made voting more difficult for many voters – particularly those not affiliated with the ruling party. This chapter documents and explains this trend of declining election administration inclusiveness in a country that had been praised for its open and inclusive election system.

Background: the pact and the 2000 electoral reform

Nicaragua approved a new electoral law in 2000, continuing a pattern of approving a new election law shortly before each national election. The new law had its roots in a political pact between the country's two strongest political parties, the Sandinista Front (FSLN) and the Liberal Constitutional Party (PLC) or, more specifically, between the parties' leaders, former president Daniel Ortega of the FSLN and then president Arnoldo Alemán of the PLC. The pact effectively divided positions in state institutions between the two parties, and the electoral reforms that accompanied the pact sought to benefit the two parties and their leaders and exclude potential challengers.

One effect of the new law was to make the formation of new political parties more difficult by imposing strict registration requirements. At the same time, non-party candidacies were eliminated. Since 2000, Nicaragua's party system has been characterized as a cartel system and a two-and-a-half party system,[1] with the major forces being the FSLN and the Liberals, and the latter camp divided between shifting party labels. While a few smaller parties have remained active, the FSLN and the Liberals have been the dominant forces in Nicaragua's party politics.

The electoral reforms also entailed changes to the Supreme Electoral Council that would prove important for voter inclusion. The number of CSE magistrates was increased from five to seven, and municipal electoral councils were established, with the top two positions on the councils to be divided between the top two parties (as with the departmental councils and polling stations) (Envío 1999). The Ortega–Alemán pact also included the early dismissal of the sitting CSE magistrates, a move sought by the FSLN which accused the magistrates of perpetrating fraud against the Sandinistas in the 1996 election (Envío 1998).

While Nicaragua's prior electoral reforms in 1995 had aimed to reduce Sandinista influence in the CSE by politicizing the appointment of departmental electoral councils and poll workers, the 2000 reform politicized the CSE even further, dividing up the council between the top two parties (the FSLN and the PLC) and creating municipal electoral councils that would also be staffed by partisan appointees, thus expanding the patronage positions available to the parties. While

> some Nicaraguans took comfort in the fact that two rival parties … share control of the CSE, such that one may act to check the partisan behavior of the other … others expressed concern that the two parties had allied to disadvantage third parties.
>
> (Carter Center 2000a)

With this bipartisan structure of election administration, Nicaragua held relatively efficient and inclusive national elections in 2001 and 2006. Yet, by the mid-2000s, partisan disputes and jockeying for advantage within the CSE were hampering the council's effectiveness. By 2008, election administration inclusiveness eroded as the CSE's bipartisanship gave way to de facto single-party control. The following sections describe this erosion of inclusiveness and explain how it resulted from a combination of electoral management body structure, political party characteristics, and a permissive international environment.

The erosion of election administration inclusiveness

One of the most inclusive features of Nicaragua's election administration in the 1980s and 1990s was the extensive decentralization of polling places. This administrative feature remains in place, with only slight modification, and is widely considered one of the strengths of the country's electoral system. The number and location of polling places have not been without problems, however. For instance, in order to reduce costs, the CSE reduced the number of polling stations for the 2000 municipal elections compared to 1996, despite a significant increase in the number of voters, creating confusion for some voters about their voting site (Carter Center 2000b, 4; IPADE 2000, 18–19). Since 2001, there has been a slight tendency toward installing additional voting tables within existing voting centers, rather than distributing them in other locations (Carter Center 2001, 2; IRI 2002, 27; OAS 2008, 51). Nevertheless, the system of polling locations continues to be quite accessible for voters.

Other elements of election administration, however, have come to pose significant burdens on prospective voters. The most significant barriers have been related to ID cards and the voter registry and, more recently, the provision of voter education.

Voter registration and ID distribution

Despite few legal changes, the administration of voter registration and the distribution of ID cards has gone from inclusive (if not always efficient) to restrictive. After significant efforts in 1996 to distribute ID cards to voters, voter registration continued to be fairly accessible through the 2001 elections. The CSE made extensive efforts to distribute the cards, including a "backpack" delivery plan (*plan mochilero*) in the final month before election day, involving almost 1,300 citizens delivering ID cards door-to-door in rural areas and at delivery points in cities (Carter Center 2001, 2; 2002, 14; OAS 2002, 5–6). In both the 2001 national elections and the 2002 regional elections on the Atlantic Coast, election observers positively evaluated the CSE's efforts in registering voters (Carter Center 2001, 2; OAS 2002, 5–6, 27).

Nevertheless, the CSE's inability to fully process *cédula* applications in time for each election continued, requiring the issuance of more easily manufactured substitute ID cards, valid only for voting purposes in a single election, to hundreds of thousands of voters for whom the council could not produce *cédulas* in a timely manner (Carter Center 2007, 30; IPADE 2006, 16; OAS 2008, 49).[2] More troubling was the number of ID cards not delivered by election day, often exceeding 100,000.[3] However, it is not clear how many people were disenfranchised as a result, as many undelivered cards pertained to people who had emigrated or were deceased (OAS 2002, 6).

After the 2001 elections, the CSE's efforts to facilitate registration and distribute ID cards began to diminish. Some barriers persisted from previous years. First, civil registry procedures remained antiquated, with births and deaths recorded by hand and manually copied from municipal registries to the central registry. The resulting errors made obtaining an ID card more difficult (EUEOM 2006, 30). Second, applications for *cédulas* are not accepted within 90 days of an election, and *cédulas* are not to be manufactured within 60 days (Ley 152, Art. 37).[4] This early closing date has meant the deadline for registration is prior to the official start of election campaigns.

Other serious obstacles to voter registration were new. One was the closing of municipal registry offices between election periods, ostensibly due to budget restrictions. This required those applying for and picking up an ID card to travel to an office in the departmental capital, which poses a major barrier in time and cost (Carter Center 2007, 20; IPADE 2009, 20; IPADE and NDI 2006, 5; OAS 2008, 19). The closing of municipal offices also resulted in bottlenecks in producing ID cards as the CSE receives a wave of applications before each election.[5]

Additionally, the CSE stopped making efforts to deliver ID cards to voters' homes or notify voters when their cards were ready to be picked up at the registry office (EUEOM 2006, 31). An observer mission reported of the 2006 elections that thousands of cards

> were not picked up by citizens, in part because many citizens did not know whether their ID card had arrived, and did not have the time and resources to make speculative trips to the municipal election office to find out.
>
> (EUEOM 2006, 32)[6]

The burden on voters to make multiple trips to registry offices in the hopes of retrieving their ID cards, common in Guatemala and El Salvador, was now evident in Nicaragua.

The growing difficulties in obtaining an ID card, and thereby being registered to vote, were documented in 2006 by the Nicaraguan NGO Ethics and Transparency in a study tracking over 500 citizens as they applied for identification. The study found an average wait time of 155 days to receive a card after applying, and 11 percent of the sample did not receive a card by election day despite applying months in advance. The study noted that obtaining voter credentials had become more time consuming in Nicaragua than in Guatemala or El Salvador (Ethics and Transparency 2007, 19, 22, 26).

By 2006, the slow delivery of *cédulas* caused suspicions that the two parties in control of the CSE, the FSLN and PLC were "engaged in a parallel distribution of voting documents to their supporters to the detriment of parties lacking representation on the CSE" (Carter Center 2007, 21; see also EUEOM 2006, 6; OAS 2008, 20, 73). These suspicions were allayed somewhat when an independent survey found no partisan pattern among those lacking *cédulas* (Carter Center 2007, 21) and when the CSE published a full list of the *cédulas* that were ready to be picked up (OAS 2008, 19). The OAS observer mission concluded that partisan manipulation of ID card delivery "was isolated … and had a marginal influence on the electoral results" (OAS 2008, 20). But accusations of politicized ID card delivery grew as the FSLN came to dominate the Supreme Electoral Council by 2008.

Leading up to the 2008 municipal elections, observers received complaints that the FSLN-controlled CSE was only distributing *cédulas* to the party's supporters, and polls done among those trying to retrieve their ID card in the final days before the election showed that they were overwhelmingly opposition supporters (IPADE 2009, 20–21; Ethics and Transparency 2008, 3–4; n.d. 4, note 9). Similar reports were received by observers to the 2010 regional elections on the Atlantic Coast (EUEEM 2010, 11).

In 2011, the problem was worse: in two-thirds of municipalities monitored by domestic observers, delivery of ID cards was conducted by political parties – in almost all cases, the FSLN – rather than the CSE (IPADE 2011a, 2; see also EUEOM 2011, 6, 19). Municipal registry offices didn't open until six weeks or less before the registration deadline, and the distribution of *cédulas* at party offices continued even after municipal CSE offices opened (IPADE 2011b, 4, 6). Estimates of the number of people disenfranchised through limited access to ID cards ranged from tens to hundreds of thousands (Ethics and Transparency 2011b, 3; EUEOM 2011, 19). One observer mission reported that "young people were the most commonly affected, and while those without identity cards were not always members of opposition parties, they were always unaffiliated to the FSLN" (EUEOM 2011, 19). As opposition supporters and independent voters struggled to obtain the ID necessary to vote, the CSE distributed newly designed *cédulas* free of charge to government employees, made up largely of FSLN partisans;[7] ordinary citizens were charged approximately $10 for the new ID (Ethics and Transparency 2011a, 1; 2011b, 2; Interviews 31, 33), in violation of the citizen identification law, which requires that *cédulas* be issued free of charge.[8] The failure to process and deliver ID cards caused violent conflicts in a number of municipalities, as citizens protested and, in some cases, occupied local CSE offices demanding their identification (El Nuevo Diario [hereafter END] 2011b; La Prensa 2011b).

One ID card problem was so severe that even FSLN governments had to take some measures to address it: the fact that most Nicaraguans had not renewed their *cédulas*, which were to be valid for only 10 years. Their looming expiration posed the challenge of renewing millions of cards and, as elections approached, the solution was to postpone the challenge by extending the validity of the ID card: first in 2005, again in 2009, and yet again in late 2012. The most recent extension was an FSLN initiative that responded to the fact that less than 15 percent of Nicaraguans had obtained a new ID, for which the CSE was charging $10, while the expiration of existing *cédulas* was only weeks away (END 2012c). These extensions, which have prevented mass disenfranchisement, have been necessary in the face of the enormous challenge of renewing all of the country's ID cards. But other obstacles to obtaining ID cards have not been addressed. Bills introduced in the assembly by opposition deputies sought to make *cédulas* more easily obtainable, by reducing or eliminating their cost and ensuring municipal registry offices remain open permanently, but have not passed the Sandinista-controlled legislature.[9]

It is worth noting that these voter registration obstacles have not coincided with efforts to clean up the voter registry. With deaths and emigrations often unreported, the voter rolls have consistently been inflated (Carter Center 2000b, 4; 2002, 12; EUEOM 2001, 19) – recently by an estimated 20 percent (EUEOM 2011, 6, 18) – and audits have found high rates of inaccuracies in the registry data.[10] However, a 2012 reform requires voters to be purged from the rolls if they do not vote in two consecutive national elections or any intervening local elections (Ley 790). This may help clean the rolls of deadwood, although at the cost of potentially impeding the participation of some voters. Civil society groups opposed the reform, and the measure was unsuccessfully challenged in the courts in 2012 (Asamblea Nacional 2012; END 2012a).

Article 41 and ratón loco

Related to the voter registry is one of the most uniquely inclusive aspects of Nicaraguan election administration: the provision that voters not appearing on the voter rolls can still cast a ballot if their ID card indicates that they live within the polling station's jurisdiction. This provision was maintained in the 2000 electoral law (Arts. 41 and 116), and it was common for a small handful of voters to make use of this provision at each polling station of 400 voters. Although the provision raises some concerns about double voting, most observers supported the measure and noted that problems with double voting generally involve the complicity of poll workers rather than arising from the legal provision itself (Interviews 40, 45, 47).[11]

While generally applied properly (Carter Center 2007, 32–33; IPADE 2000, 9; 2006, 36), there were efforts by the CSE to circumvent Article 41. In the 2004 municipal elections, its application was inconsistent, following mixed signals from CSE magistrates, some of whom had indicated before the election that the measure would not be applied (END 2004a; 2004b; 2004c; IPADE 2004, 19–20).

According to many observers, 2004 was the beginning of efforts by some actors within the CSE to play a game of *ratón loco* ("crazy mouse"), whereby either those with access to the voter lists would relocate some voters to different polling places, or poll workers would redirect voters to different polling places on election day. The result would be that voters would tire of being sent from one polling place to another and would eventually give up without voting. The Liberal Constitutionalist Party (PLC) accused the Sandinistas and the CSE of conducting *ratón loco* in 2004, claiming that tens of thousands had been prevented from voting as a result (La Prensa 2004).[12] There is, in fact, little hard evidence that this practice happened on a significant scale and, to some extent, Article 41 protected voters against this form of disenfranchisement.[13] But renewed signals from the Sandinista magistrates on the CSE that Article 41 would not be applied in the 2006 regional and general elections generated intense controversy. The PLC protested, accusing the FSLN of planning to carry out *ratón loco* to disenfranchise Liberal voters (Carter Center 2007, 17; La Prensa 2006a; 2006b; 2006c), and PLC magistrates on the CSE refused to attend meetings in order to prevent a quorum, threatening to cripple the electoral body (OAS 2008, 22). The CSE ultimately agreed to apply the provision, and some observers estimated that as many as 15 percent of voters in the Atlantic Coast regional elections made use of the provision to cast their ballots (Carter Center 2007, 18; NDI 2006f, 1). Nevertheless, in the 2006 general election and subsequent elections, observers reported that the application of Article 41 was inconsistent across polling places (EUEOM 2006, 56–57; 2011a, 31).

Thus, while Article 41 was a very inclusive legal measure, its implementation by the CSE and poll workers became less consistent after 2004. In 2012, president Daniel Ortega introduced reforms to the electoral law that included the elimination of this provision in Article 41. The package of reforms passed the Sandinista-controlled legislature, although the assembly postponed the modification to Article 41 until 2016. Surprisingly, given the past controversies over this provision, its elimination seems to have garnered little attention from opposition parties, which focused their criticisms on other provisions in the reforms.[14] Once implemented, this revision to Article 41 may raise barriers to voting for those who, whether through intentional disenfranchisement or technical problems with the voter registry, do not appear on their precinct's voters list on election day.

Voter education

Alongside growing registry-related obstacles to voting was a steep decline in the provision of election-related information to voters by the CSE. Observers to the 2006 election characterized voter education activities as limited, as the CSE "only carried out one short media campaign," publicizing the need for voters to pick up their *cédulas* (EUEOM 2006, 48), and "did little to advertise the election date and urge voter participation" (McConnell 2012, 148–49; see also OAS 2008, 62). By 2011, voter education activities had ceased entirely: no efforts were made to inform voters about how to obtain a *cédula* or the mechanics of voting (IPADE 2011a, 6), despite the introduction of a new ballot format that year. While the CSE continued to carry out a registration verification exercise prior to each election, opening polling stations for voters to confirm or update their registration information, efforts to publicize the verification event declined; by 2011, the CSE did nothing to publicize registry verification or any other aspects of the electoral process (Hagamos Democracia 2011, 14; IPADE 2009, 108; 2011b, 9; OAS 2008, 18).

In 2011, the CSE not only eliminated its own voter education activities, it also attempted to prohibit any individual or organization from disseminating information on polling places or voter registry data under threat of prosecution. To justify this limitation on civic education by political parties and non-governmental organizations, the CSE proffered the dubious claim that the voter registry was the CSE's intellectual property (EUEOM 2011, 18–19; Hagamos Democracia 2011, 12, 20; IPADE 2011b, 15). The CSE also made it more difficult for individuals to access information online by making confirmation of one's registration through the CSE website more difficult (Interviews 31, 32, 33; La Prensa 2011c; 2011f). As a result of all of this, it became more difficult for many prospective voters to find out their voter registration status, the location of their polling place, and the type of ballot they would use to cast their vote.

Nicaragua's new election administration

Through partisan distribution of ID cards, the elimination of public voter education, and less reliable protection of voting rights in the face of voter registry errors, Nicaragua's election administration became significantly less inclusive than it had been in the country's early democratic years. Voters also confronted inconveniences such as the chronically late opening, and occasionally the early closing, of polling stations.[15] By 2008, many voters – particularly those without ties to the governing FSLN party – faced substantial obstacles to casting a vote. These obstacles are summarized in Table 7.1.

Less inclusiveness has not been the only change in the country's election administration. Voter suppression has gone hand in hand with other forms of

Table 7.1 Election administration inclusiveness, Nicaragua 2006–2016

Dimension	*Description*	*Inclusiveness*
Voter registration		
Extent of state responsibility for registering voters	Automatic registration upon obtaining ID card	High
Difficulty of registration process	Offices centralized in non-election periods; process obstructed by election officials; no cost before 2010, but monetary cost for some new ID cards after 2010	Low
Ease of access to ID documents required for registration	Birth certificate required, often entailing fees and administrative barriers	Low
Registration closing date	90 days	Medium
Residency requirement	None*	High
Provisional registration	Those turning 16 between close of registration and election day eligible to register	High
Registry consultation	Voter lists posted at local polling places; verification exercise held before elections; publicity of voter rolls diminished over time	High/medium
Purging of voter rolls	Voters not purged from the rolls for failure to vote before 2012; purging instituted by 2012 reform for those not voting in two consecutive national elections or any intervening elections	High/low

Getting to the ballot box		
Accessibility of polling places	Highly decentralized polling places	High
Assignment of voters to polling places	Residential	High
Convenience voting measures	Not used	Low
Electoral calendar	Voting held on Sunday	High
Casting a ballot		
Voter ID requirement	National ID or voter card required	High**
Provisional or tendered ballots	Available before 2016 (anyone with ID pertaining to the precinct eligible to cast valid ballot); not available beginning in 2016	High/low
Voter education		
State efforts to inform voters of where and how to register and vote	No voter education after 2006	Low
Overall inclusiveness		*Medium*

Notes

* There is no residency requirement for most of the country, but to vote for regional councils in the autonomous Atlantic Coast regions, there is a three-month residency requirement for those born in, or with at least one parent from, the Atlantic regions, and a one year residency requirement for everyone else (Ley No. 28, Art. 22).

** Although access to a national ID card is obstructed for many citizens, this represents an obstacle at the stage of voter registration rather than casting a ballot.

electoral manipulation, as the 2008 municipal elections were marked by a range of fraudulent practices on the part of the CSE and poll workers. Irregularities included: the revocation of two opposition parties' registration on questionable grounds; the denial of accreditation to experienced domestic observer groups; the failure to invite international observers; the ejection of many opposition-party poll watchers from polling stations on election day; the failure to post results for many polling stations; and the alteration of vote tallies (Ethics and Transparency n.d., 2, 7; IPADE 2009). The 2011 presidential and legislative elections were again marred by irregularities and a lack of transparency, as well as the unconstitutional candidacy of the incumbent president, who won handily (see EUEOM 2011).

Despite the pathologies of the bipartisan system of control over the electoral management body, as late as 2006 the Carter Center (2007, 39) reported that

> [i]n a country where the election system strives to bring the ballot box into close proximity with the voters, a veteran CSE administration … demonstrated the organizational and logistical capacity necessary to make both the Atlantic Coast and the national elections happen in one year with minimal problems.

Two years later the quality of Nicaragua's election administration had deteriorated, both in terms of inclusiveness and in safeguarding the integrity of the vote. As former CSE president Rosa Marina Zelaya noted, after the advances in electoral cartography and decentralized voting (*voto domiciliario*) that the CSE had achieved in the 1980s and 1990s, the country should be in the "big leagues" by now by implementing such measures as voting by mail and voting abroad (Interview 43). Instead, the conduct of the country's sixth national election since the Sandinista Revolution was worse than the first had been in 1984. The following section turns to explaining this trajectory.

Explaining the erosion of inclusiveness

Why did Nicaragua's election administration, long recognized as being highly inclusive, become more restrictive after the mid-2000s? Why did this change coincide with the return to power of the FSLN, the party that had originally constructed the country's inclusive election system? The changing nature of partisan control over the electoral machinery is central to an explanation, as is the nature of party identification and the more permissive international environment facing the governing party.

Partisan interests and EMB structure

Nicaraguan opposition parties, civil society groups, and international election monitors readily identify the main factor underlying the erosion of election administration inclusiveness: the partisanship of the CSE. Yet, this explanation raises important questions, and closer analysis reveals nuances in the relationship between partisan election administration and inclusiveness.

A partisan electoral body had coincided with inclusiveness during the 1980s and 1990s, and even for a time after 2000 when control over the CSE became bipartisan. The bipartisan division of the CSE extended from the top magistrates – chosen for their partisan loyalties[16] – to the lowest levels. This bipartisan structure had detrimental effects on the CSE's administrative competence and operational coherence. Not only were the national magistrates and positions on departmental and municipal councils divided between Liberals and Sandinistas, but technical staff positions were as well (Carter Center 2002, 11). One observer mission reported "numerous cases of relatively long serving staff being replaced by less qualified political appointees" (EUEOM 2001, 19).[17] Tensions between Sandinistas and Liberals hampered cooperation between different levels of the CSE's organizational structure and between operational divisions (Carter Center 2002, 15; EUEOM 2006, 23–24) and in 2006 resulted in conflicts so severe that CSE magistrates failed to meet the necessary quorum to make decisions for months (Carter Center 2007, 16–17). However, it is important not to overstate the decline in bureaucratic capacity that occurred. As observers to the 2011 elections noted, the CSE has high organizational capacity (EUEOM 2011, 5) and, while some lower-level staff lack adequate training, division directors within the CSE have extensive experience in their positions.[18]

Administrative inclusiveness declined as bipartisan control of the CSE gave way to single-party dominance. In fact, some non-partisan observers viewed the bipartisan control of the CSE as adequately effective and blame subsequent election administration problems on the control exercised by the governing party (Interviews 34, 36, 38). By 2006, the balance between the FSLN and the PLC was tilting toward the Sandinistas, who held four of seven magistrate positions (EUEOM 2006, 23). The FSLN had also come to control more directorates of the operational divisions within the CSE by 2006 (EUEOM 2006, 23; see also Carter Center 2007, 16). According to two non-Sandinistas, the FSLN was more attentive to gaining control of lower-level technical positions, while the PLC was preoccupied with controlling its share of top positions (Interviews 47, 48).

Schisms among the Liberals contributed to FSLN control of the CSE after 2006. In that year's presidential election, PLC dissidents left the party and formed the Nicaraguan Liberal Alliance (ALN). The split among the Liberals allowed FSLN leader Daniel Ortega to win the presidency with 38 percent of the vote, while the ALN candidate came in second – meaning the new party would share control over the CSE with the Sandinistas, leaving the PLC with little representation on the council. Yet the new party, which experienced its own internal schisms after the election, lacked the organizational capacity that the PLC had possessed and was an ineffective counterweight to the FSLN (Ethics and Transparency n.d., 3).

By 2010, observers reported that "political alliances and a divided opposition gave the ruling party a de facto control over the electoral administration" and that "CSE structures from top to bottom have come into the FSLN influence"

(EUEEM 2010, 2, 5). Single-party control was equally evident in the 2011 general election, when the third spots of the three-member departmental and municipal election councils, which are supposed to be divided among the parties not represented in the first two positions, were distributed disproportionately to small parties aligned with the FSLN.[19] Even poll workers supposedly representing opposition parties were in some cases actually from the FSLN or allied parties (EUEOM 2011, 15–16).

The result of single-party control over the electoral council has been a decline in inclusiveness enacted through administrative measures, such as the politicized distribution of ID cards. The puzzle is that the FSLN is the same party (at least in name) that established the inclusive system of election administration in the 1980s. Three factors account for the party's new strategy of restricting access to the vote.

First, there has been a change in the strategic calculations and ideology of the FSLN, as two conditions that contributed to the FSLN's inclusive and transparent election administration practices in the 1984 and 1990 elections – the party's confidence in victory and its participatory ideology – eroded after 1990. The party's unexpected loss in 1990 and awareness of its consistent "ceiling" (*techo*) of electoral support of about 35–40 percent afterward had a strong impact on the party's leadership. Some analysts note that Daniel Ortega and the FSLN feared losing elections despite their favorable standings in the polls, a lesson learned from the 1990 election when the FSLN lost, despite leading in the pre-election polls. The phenomenon of Nicaraguans disguising their political opinions, depending on who is asking, is thought to be so common that it is referred to locally as the "güegüense tradition" (Anderson 1995; Nicaragua Dispatch 2011). According to some, this uncertainty about election outcomes (i.e., a high level of perceived electoral competitiveness) contributes to electoral manipulation (Interview 42). Exacerbating this uncertainty is Ortega's perception that he was cheated out of victory through fraud in the 1996 election (Interview 44; see also Zúñiga 2012). Perceiving a firm upper limit on the party's popular support, distrustful of polls showing the party leading all contenders comfortably, and with lingering resentments against Liberal electoral misconduct, the FSLN employed a wide range of manipulative tactics – including administrative barriers to participation – to increase its chances of maintaining power. According to many observers, further motivation for electoral manipulation in 2011 was provided by the FSLN's desire to win not just the presidency but a supermajority in the National Assembly (see, e.g., La Prensa 2011d). After 2011, the FSLN used this supermajority to push through constitutional reforms that eliminated presidential term limits and replaced the 35 percent vote threshold to win the presidency in the first round of voting with a simple plurality system (BBC News, 2014).

The party is also no longer the revolutionary organization espousing a participatory ideology that it was in the 1980s. Rather, since the 1990s, the party has become the personal vehicle of Daniel Ortega and those closest to him, especially his wife Rosario Murillo (Colburn and Cruz 2012; Martí i Puig 2010). Whatever role the FSLN's commitment to broad popular participation played in the construction of inclusive election administration during the revolutionary period, that commitment seemed abandoned in favor of a less ideological brand of populism.

Second, while these shifts in ideology and perceived electoral competitiveness have provided motive for electoral manipulation, an essential enabling condition is the FSLN's ability to identify its supporters, in contrast to parties in Guatemala that have more ambiguous social bases. As a result, the FSLN can ensure access to ID cards for its supporters, while impeding access for opposition supporters and independent voters. The FSLN is able to identify supporters not so much through indirect indicators of partisan preference, such as social class or ethnicity, but through its highly developed organizational structure that allows the party to identify partisan preferences at the individual level.

The FSLN is the only Nicaraguan political party with a well-developed organizational structure, and "[s]ince 2000, it has been the most powerful party at the local level, maintaining a solid organizational network" (Martí i Puig 2011, 188). As one analyst reported, the FSLN "knows all of Nicaragua block by block" (Interview 36), allowing the party (through the CSE) to impede access to ID cards of non-Sandinistas. Another observer noted the FSLN's superior organizational capacity and reported that the party "knows the neighborhood" (*conoce el barrio*) – in other words, the party's block captains know the political affiliations of everyone in the neighborhood (Interview 37).

This fine-grained disenfranchisement is facilitated by the party's control of the CSE's local administrative structures and mayors' offices (Interview 36), as well as the party-linked Citizens Power Councils (CPCs). The latter were citizen groups created by the Sandinista government in 2007, and thousands of CPCs were organized at the neighborhood level, with coordinating bodies ascending to sub-municipal, municipal, departmental, and national levels. Those participating in the CPCs – an estimated 4.6–6.9 percent of Nicaraguans in 2009 (CEAP 2009, 7) – were overwhelmingly Sandinistas,[20] and the councils were closely tied to FSLN party structures. According to one study of CPCs, they served as quasi-party organizations that aimed to extend and strengthen the social base of the FSLN and, during the 2008 municipal elections, CPCs campaigned on the FSLN's behalf (CEAP 2009, 30, 48). They were also reported to "monitor the political loyalty of members of the community" (Gonzalez-Ocantos et al. 2012, 208, note 24).

This well-organized party machine, which extends downward to the neighborhood level, allows the FSLN to identify its supporters and opposition voters. A more indirect method of identifying and disenfranchising opposition supporters is geographic: for instance, identifying municipalities that are opposition strongholds and impeding access to ID cards in those areas. In 2011, there were accusations that severe obstacles to obtaining an ID card were concentrated in areas where the FSLN's electoral support was weak. As *La Prensa* reported (2011e), in eight of the nine municipalities where disturbances occurred over the CSE's failure to deliver *cédulas*, the FSLN had received fewer votes than other parties in the 2006 election. However, in only six of the municipalities was the

FSLN's 2006 performance below its municipal average, and only in two was its performance more than one standard deviation below its average.[21] In other words, it is not clear that geographic location has been used to target opposition voters with administrative barriers – although geography has been used for other forms of manipulation, such as gerrymandering and annulling votes from precincts in opposition strongholds. Regardless, the FSLN's ability to single out opposition supporters and independent voters – primarily through its highly developed organizational capacity – and the party's control over the CSE have resulted in manipulation of the distribution of ID cards (and therefore voter registration) to the benefit of the ruling party.

Finally, another factor contributing to declining inclusiveness – particularly the disappearance of official voter education efforts – is the fact that the FSLN has a more motivated and mobilized base than other parties and is able to use its resource advantage to provide its supporters with voter education. Many Nicaraguan observers see the decline of voter education as an intentional effort to reduce turnout, which would mostly affect non-Sandinista voters who are less motivated to turn out (Interviews 35, 37, 49). This view finds support in survey data showing that FSLN supporters are more disposed to vote than are other Nicaraguans (Colburn and Cruz 2012, 112). Also, according to a leading domestic election observer, the FSLN is able to use its resource advantage over other parties to provide its supporters with voter education, and so weakening the provision of voter education by the CSE serves the party's interest (Interview 34). Essentially, the provision of voter education has been privatized to the ruling party, rather than carried out by the electoral commission.

Yet, while lower turnout may benefit the FSLN electorally, it also raises questions about the legitimacy of elections, which the Sandinistas sought to gain through high turnout in 1984 and 1990. Legitimacy is perhaps of greater concern to the FSLN, now that its ceiling of support seems to have increased in recent years, and the party firmly controls all branches and levels of government, while the opposition is as weak and divided as ever. The Nicaraguan news magazine *Envío* (2012) noted the tension between turnout and legitimacy in its analysis of the 2012 municipal elections:

> The FSLN benefits from the abstention of opposition voters because its hard-core voters always turn out in droves, but this time abstention could fall below the acceptable limit. The governing party is so sure of winning massively that it would prefer a sizable turnout to provide some legitimacy…

To sum up, at the heart of less inclusive election administration lies the dominance of the electoral management body by a governing party that was not confident in its ability to win fair elections, had shed its participatory ideology of years past and was able to use its organizational capacity and resources to identify and mobilize its supporters. Despite the pathologies entailed by the bipartisan, cartel party model of election administration that prevailed between

2000 and 2006, inclusive practices were not starkly affected, as the dominant parties checked each other's actions and neither was threatened by high turnout (considering their jointly dominant position in the country's party system). Single-party dominance has had more pernicious effects, facilitated by a more permissive international environment, discussed below.

International influences

International pressures and financial and technical assistance contributed significantly to Nicaragua's inclusive election administration in the 1980s and 1990s. Since 2000, the international community has had limited influence, despite consistent engagement by international election observers.

International observers have had a strong presence in Nicaragua, with elections monitored by the Carter Center, the European Union, and the Organization of American States. Observers have recommended measures to make election administration more inclusive, including improved distribution of ID cards and permanent opening of municipal registry offices, streamlining the civil registration process, free issuance of birth certificates, and improving voter education efforts. Observers have also often endorsed the use of Article 41 to prevent disenfranchisement (Carter Center 2006; NDI 2006b, 1), although some EU observer missions have called for the elimination of this measure contingent on improvements in the civil and voter registries (EUEOM 2006, 71; 2010, 27). Beyond these specific proposals have been persistent calls from observers to eliminate or reduce partisan control over the CSE.

Besides election observation, the international community has also supplied financial and technical assistance – which is of special significance in Nicaragua, one of the Western hemisphere's poorest countries. Some assistance has come in the form of financing and advising CSE training sessions related to voter registration (OAS 2008, 56). In 2001, the United States provided funding for a complementary registration plan, which "responded in part to pressure coming from the U.S. Congress in favor of a special effort to guarantee voting documents to 33 outlying municipalities," where former Contra fighters were concentrated (Carter Center 2002, 14). Other assistance supported civil society activities, including voter registration drives, public information campaigns, and voter registry audits (NDI 2006d, 3; 2006e, 3; 2006f, 2; OAS 2008, 60). Another area of assistance has been aimed at opposition-party poll watchers, trained by the National Democratic Institute and the International Republican Institute (NDI 2001, 3; WOLA 2006).

Considering the decline in administrative inclusiveness and overall election quality in recent years, international involvement has clearly had limited effect. Most of the recommendations from election observers – including improving access to ID cards, increasing voter education, and cleaning up the voter rolls – have gone unheeded. As the EU mission to the 2011 elections noted, "[t]he legal framework retains the same flaws which were highlighted by the European Union Election Observation Missions in 2001 and 2006, whose recommendations have not been used as the basis of any reforms" (EUEOM 2011, 9). This accords with the conclusion of Kelley (2012), who notes that "the persistent mistrust and political bias in the Nicaraguan election apparatus has relegated international monitors to serve as validators of election outcomes, rather than as catalysts for reforms" (252).

International financing and technical assistance have also clearly not been sufficient to ensure inclusive election administration. While foreign resources have certainly helped domestic civic groups carry out their work, they have not been sufficient to prompt election authorities to perform their duties more effectively. For instance, when faced with delays in ID card delivery leading up to the 2006 election, the CSE "failed to launch a public information campaign or to carry out a special delivery drive until the last weekend before the elections, *despite having special funds provided by the International Foundation for Election Systems (IFES) for this purpose*" (EUEOM 2006, 33, emphasis added).

The limited impact of international assistance results from the fact that, despite Nicaragua's low level of economic development, resource constraints have not been the primary cause of restrictive election administration measures. Most obviously, the country's severe economic constraints in the 1980s and early 1990s – when the economy was reeling from the aftermath of the revolution, the Contra War and US trade embargo, and mismanagement – did not prevent election administration from being more inclusive than it was following 2006, when the economy was growing. And although budget shortfalls are the reason given by the CSE as to why municipal registry offices are closed between electoral periods (see OAS 2008, 13, 52) – resulting in one of the biggest obstacles to voter registration – the evidence casts doubt on this claim. According to former national and departmental registration directors, when the CSE faced the possibility of closing municipal offices between electoral periods, mayoral offices proposed to fund CSE staff to continue ID card processing at the municipal level. Yet, the CSE rejected the proposal, fearing that mayors would exercise partisan influence in the distribution of ID cards if they funded the CSE's identification operations (Interviews 38, 48). Thus, it was not only budget limitations but also concerns about political advantage that led to municipal registry offices being closed.

More generally, most observers attribute shortcomings in ID card processing, the closing of municipal CSE offices, and the disappearance of voter education to a "lack of will" rather than to budget constraints. Domestic election observation leaders note that the allocation of the CSE's budget is heavily skewed toward funding the salaries of top managerial levels (especially the seven magistrates) rather than funding core operations like ID card processing and voter education (Interviews 33, 40). Many analysts emphasize that it is poor allocation of the budget and corruption within the CSE, and not a lack of resources, that undermine electoral operations (Interviews 30, 36, 45, 48; see also EUEOM 2006, 27). Reports of embezzlement within the CSE lend credence to this interpretation (END 2011a; Ethics and Transparency 2011b, 2).[22]

In short, while limited resources certainly affect the quality of election administration, the causal significance of this factor is cast in doubt by Nicaragua's greater inclusiveness during prior periods of more severe economic hardship, the disproportionate share of CSE resources devoted to the salaries of high-level political appointees, the possible embezzlement of CSE funds, and the unwillingness to accept funding from municipal governments to facilitate voter identification and registration. Thus, the provision of international financial and technical assistance has not had much impact in a context where domestic political forces favor restrictive election administration practices.

If international pressure was influential in prompting inclusive election administration in the 1984 and 1990 elections, what changed after 2006? One shift was declining US interest in Nicaragua following the Sandinista defeat in 1990 and the end of the Cold War. There has been intermittent pressure from the United States Congress related to electoral conduct, especially regarding voter registration among former Contras, and public pronouncements from embassy officials in Nicaragua indicating America's preference for an Ortega defeat (Carter Center 2007, 19). More recently, the erosion of election quality in Nicaragua prompted criticism from the United States, which cancelled $62 million in aid following the 2008 municipal elections and another $3 million following the 2011 elections. European donors have also expressed dissatisfaction and have cut aid to Nicaragua in response to deteriorating election quality (CNN 2009; Nicaragua Dispatch 2012a; Rogers 2012b).

Although these foreign aid cuts are significant, they pale in comparison to the economic and military war waged by the United States against the Sandinista government in the 1980s. American and European pressures were also offset by the flow of money from the Hugo Chávez government in Venezuela to its ally Ortega. Shortly after the United States cut aid in 2009, Chávez offered $50 million to help compensate for the loss (CNN 2009). In 2010, Venezuelan aid to Nicaragua totaled more than $500 million (Spalding 2012, 232), and the US aid cut after the 2011 elections was "equivalent to what Ortega gets every two days from Chavez" (Rogers 2012b). While US and European donors cut hundreds of millions of dollars in aid, Venezuela more than made up the difference, with the additional advantage that Venezuelan aid flows directly to Ortega without entering the government budget and without oversight (Colburn and Cruz 2012, 115; Rogers 2011).

According to one person working at the US embassy, the availability of funds from Venezuela made reductions in US aid ineffective as leverage (Interview 45). Venezuela thus played the role of "black knight" in offering Nicaragua aid without democracy-related conditions attached (cf. Levitsky and Way 2010, 41). With only moderate pressure from American and European donors and flush with money from a foreign patron uninterested in promoting electoral democracy, the FSLN government has not been pressured to administer inclusive and fair elections, as it had been during the revolutionary years. As a result, electoral manipulation, including voter suppression, became less costly.

Civil society

Like international election observation, domestic observation and other civic mobilization efforts have had limited impact on Nicaragua's election administration. Large-scale domestic election observer efforts began in 1996, with Ethics and Transparency mobilizing thousands of observers (NDI 1997). Since then, civic and think-tank groups like the Institute for Development and Democracy (IPADE) and *Hagamos Democracia* (Let's Make Democracy) have taken on election observation, while civic groups like Movement for Nicaragua have engaged in other election-related activities. At times, these groups have directly facilitated voter participation, as when Movement for Nicaragua assisted several thousand Nicaraguans in obtaining birth certificates and completing the voter registration process in 2006 (Carter Center 2007, 21; NDI 2006a, 4). Civic groups have also conducted publicity efforts to promote voter participation (EUEOM 2006, 55; Interviews 31, 32, 33, 39; NDI 2006c, 4), while IPADE and Ethics and Transparency have conducted audits of the voter registry that have been referenced by political parties in their calls for improving the registry and applying Article 41 of the electoral law (NDI 2006c, 4). Many of these activities have been supported by external financing and technical assistance (see, e.g., NDI 2006e, 3; 2006d, 3; OAS 2008, 60).

Civic groups have also actively proposed and advocated for specific electoral measures. They have firmly supported Article 41 (Carter Center 2007, 17; END 2006; Ethics and Transparency 2006a, 27), seeing the measure as necessary, given the low quality of the voter rolls and considering it better to not disenfranchise eligible voters than to add another safeguard against double voting by eliminating the article (Interviews 34, 35). Civil society groups raised the only objections to Article 41's revision in 2012 (Asamblea Nacional 2012). Civic groups have also called for the CSE to keep municipal offices open between election periods to allow citizens access to registration, greater ease of access to ID cards more generally, more extensive voter education efforts, cleaning up the voter registry, and depoliticizing the CSE.[23]

In 2006, an umbrella organization, the Electoral Reform Promotion Group (*Grupo Promotor de Reformas Electorales*, GPRE) was formed. It brought together 14 organizations, including the country's most prominent election observer groups, and the group's proposals were wide-ranging, addressing political party and campaign finance regulations, re-apportionment, gender quotas, and various measures to depoliticize the CSE (GPRE 2008; 2010).

Despite the extensive efforts of civic groups, their influence has been limited. The GPRE presented its proposals to legislators in the hopes that they would use them as a basis to reform the electoral law, and while the legislators expressed agreement with the proposals, no action followed (Interviews 30, 33). When the electoral law was reformed in 2012, the National Assembly invited input from civil society groups and, in response, the GPRE commented on each specific measure in the proposed reform and submitted its own separate proposal. However, as was the case during Guatemala's electoral reform, the proposals from civil society were largely rejected.

According to all accounts, relations between civil society and the CSE, which had been cooperative in the past, soured after the 2006 elections (Interviews 32, 33, 35, 38). An EU observer report in that year noted that "the relations between the domestic observer groups and the CSE were rather tense, as the CSE has always perceived them rather as challengers than as legitimate stakeholders" (EUEOM 2006, 55).

With the limited openness of the CSE and ruling party after 2006, civil society's calls for more inclusive election administration practices have fallen on deaf ears. One exception is a small administrative measure that seems to have resulted from civil society pressure: a 15-day extension of the deadline for ID card applications prior to the 2006 election. This measure was proposed by president Enrique Bolaños and passed unanimously in the National Assembly following pressure from civic groups, especially Movement for Nicaragua, which mobilized protests outside CSE headquarters (NDI 2006b, 1).[24] But civic groups were not united in support of this measure: domestic observer groups joined the CSE in warning "that this move would slow a very tight election calendar, potentially creating further difficulties" (Carter Center 2007, 25). On issues where all civic groups have endorsed inclusive election administration practices, their efforts have been rebuffed. As in Guatemala, crafting the rules and practices of Nicaragua's election administration has been an elite game dominated by politicians and election administrators, with minimal influence exercised by civil society.

Conclusion

The erosion of election administration inclusiveness in Nicaragua after 2000 was marked by the politicization of the distribution of ID cards and the disappearance of voter education efforts. The proximate cause of this trend was the control of the CSE by the FSLN, a party that was not confident of its ability to win fair electoral contests, had shed its revolutionary ideology, and was able to exploit its organizational capacity and strong partisan identification to identify its supporters and single them out for ID cards and partisan voter-information campaigns. These features of partisan identification and organization are marked contrasts with Guatemala and, to a lesser extent, El Salvador. These domestic variables are not sufficiently counteracted by international pressure, as financial aid from Venezuela compensated for the loss of democracy-conditioned aid from US and European donors. Domestic civil society groups were also unable to constrain the electoral practices of the governing party and the partisan-controlled CSE.

Nicaragua's experience shows that the pathologies of partisan election administration can be severe, but they do not result automatically from the partisan composition of the electoral management body. Rather, the effects of partisan election administration are mediated by patterns of party identification, by perceptions of electoral competitiveness, and by pressures from foreign powers.

Notes

1 As Anderson and Dodd (2005, 224) put it, Nicaragua came "to resemble the 'two and a half party systems' that occasionally arise in established democracies," with 30 percent of survey respondents identifying as Sandinistas, 27 percent as Liberals, 7 percent Conservative, and 23 percent independent.

2 For the 2000 municipal elections, about 15 percent of voters received a substitute document rather than a permanent *cédula* (Carter Center 2000a); this figure dropped significantly in subsequent elections, to below 3 percent in 2008 (Carter Center 2002, 17; 2007, 31; IPADE 2009, 21).

3 See Carter Center 2000b, 5; Carter Center 2002, 17; EUEOM 2006, 32; IPADE 2000, 19; IPADE 2004, 21; OAS 2008, 20.

4 For the 2006 elections the National Assembly, at the president's initiative, approved a 15-day extension of the deadline to apply for a *cédula*, while maintaining the deadline for producing *cédulas* (EUEOM 2006, 32; OAS 2008, 20, 47).

5 The early registration closing date might be ameliorated by the fact that voter registration is automatic upon obtaining a national ID card, which is needed for a variety of purposes besides voting; thus, many ID card applications would likely be submitted in between electoral periods. However, the closing of municipal registry offices between electoral periods gives incentive to citizens to wait until an electoral period (when local offices are open) to apply for an ID.

6 The EU mission elaborated: "Simple and helpful measures, such as publicly displaying the list of ID cards that had arrived, reading out the list of names on local radio and TV stations … or delivering that list to all the political parties, were not commonly adopted" by the CSE's municipal offices (EUEOM 2006, 33).

7 After taking office in 2007, the Sandinista government replaced thousands of non-Sandinista public sector workers with employees loyal to the party (Rogers 2012a).

8 See Ley 152, Art. 53 and La Prensa 2011a. Funds for introducing a new *cédula* with more advanced safeguards were donated by Spain in 2005, but the CSE delayed implementation until 2011, when it decided to begin phasing in the new ID cards with state employees (see La Prensa 2010a).

9 These include bills introduced in 2008 and 2010 by non-Sandinista deputies, accessed through the National Assembly's website (www.asamblea.gob.ni).

10 Registry audits in 2006 found that the registry information was incorrect in about 35 percent of cases (Ethics and Transparency 2006a, 20; 2006b, 20). A separate audit in the Atlantic Coast regions found problems of a similar magnitude (IPADE and NDI 2006). Such inaccuracies highlight the importance of the CSE's verification days, when voters can easily update their information in the voter registry, and of Article 41, allowing voters to cast a ballot in the precinct listed on their ID card, even if their name does not appear on the voter roll (Carter Center 2007, 22; Ethics and Transparency 2006a, 22).

11 This provision could lead to double voting if a voter changes his or her address on the voter registry (which does not require obtaining a new *cédula*) and then votes at both the new polling place and the old polling place corresponding to the address listed on the person's ID. As a safeguard against this, polling places check voters' names against a list of voters who have requested a change of residence. In theory, only voters not appearing on this list can cast a ballot. In 2006, observers found that only 0.33 percent of voters could not vote at a polling place because they appeared on the change-of-residence list (IPADE 2006, 36); in this event, these voters are supposed to be directed to the correct polling place.

12 Observers reported that many voters' names did not appear on the voter lists on election day (IPADE 2004, 13–14), although the reasons were not clear.

13 Article 41 only prevents this form of disenfranchisement when a voter is assigned to vote in the precinct that corresponds to the address listed on his or her *cédula*. For

those who have moved to a new precinct and updated their voter registration but have not obtained a new *cédula* listing their new address, Article 41 does not apply.

14 Some of the reforms eliminated antiquated provisions in the law, while other provisions included stronger safeguards for parties to monitor the electoral process, drastic increases in the size of municipal councils, and 50 percent women's quotas for party candidate lists. Most of the opposition deputies voted for the bill, indicating that although the reforms were "cosmetic" and insufficient to guarantee fair elections, they did contain positive elements. Two deputies claimed the reforms were intended to mollify international criticisms (Asamblea Nacional 2012; Navas Corea 2012; Salinas Maldonado 2012).

15 See Carter Center 2002, 21; Consorcio Cívico Electoral n.d., 20, 36; IPADE 2000, 8, 13; 2004, 16; 2006, 34, 56; OAS 2002, 14.

16 As an EU mission noted, the CSE magistrates at the time included "the former FSLN campaign manager, the former chief national party agents of both the FSLN and the PLC, and two former PLC Interior Ministers" (EUEOM 2006, 23, note 17).

17 Electoral reform in 1995 had begun to fill the CSE with more partisan appointees, especially at the departmental level. As this happened, CSE president Rosa Marina Zelaya "preserved the professional staff by putting them in charge of the ID card process and urged them to provide all possible technical and logistical support to the new CSE offices" (Butler et al. 1996). The 2000 electoral reform extended the politicization of the CSE even further.

18 This is the view of the former director of the civil registry (see END 2010 and La Prensa 2010b) and was also shared by another neutral observer (Interview 36).

19 See Ethics and Transparency 2011c, 3; EUEOM 2011, 5; Hagamos Democracia 2011; IPADE 2011b.

20 A 2009 study found that 81 percent of CPC members identified themselves as Sandinistas, while 15 percent identified as independents and 3.6 percent identified with opposition parties (CEAP 2009, 8, 41).

21 Based on author's calculations using municipal-level results of the 2006 presidential election.

22 CSE president Roberto Rivas is believed to have amassed a large personal fortune during his tenure (see Nicaragua Dispatch 2012b).

23 See Ethics and Transparency 2011d, 3; EUEOM 2006, 48; IPADE 2000, 21; IPADE 2006, 21, 58; IPADE 2011a, 7–8; IPADE and NDI 2006, 20; OAS 2008, 14.

24 The deadline was extended by 15 days again prior to the 2012 municipal elections, although it is unclear if this extension responded to outside pressure (see END 2012b).

References

Anderson, Leslie. 1995. "Elections and Public Opinion in the Development of Nicaraguan Democracy." In *Elections and Democracy in Central America, Revisited*, Mitchell A. Seligson and John A. Booth, eds. Chapel Hill and London: University of North Carolina Press.

Anderson, Leslie, and Lawrence C. Dodd. 2005. *Learning Democracy: Citizen Engagement and Electoral Choice in Nicaragua, 1990–2001*. Chicago: The University of Chicago Press.

Asamblea Nacional. 2012. Debate de Leyes, May 15. www.asamblea.gob.ni/trabajo-legislativo/diario-de-debates/.

BBC News. 2014. "Nicaragua's New Constitution Becomes Law." February 11.

Butler, Judy, David R. Dye, and Jack Spence, with George Vickers. 1996. *Democracy and Its Discontents*. Hemisphere Initiatives.

Carter Center. 2000a. Pre-Election Statement on Nicaragua Elections. October 25. www.cartercenter.org/news/documents/doc256.html.

Carter Center. 2000b. Second Report, The Carter Center Mission to Evaluate Electoral Conditions in Nicaragua. November 1–8. www.cartercenter.org/documents/288.pdf.

Carter Center. 2001. Statement of the Second Pre-Electoral Delegation of the Carter Center. Managua, Nicaragua. October 3. www.cartercenter.org/documents/289.pdf.

Carter Center. 2002. Observing the 2001 Nicaraguan Elections. www.cartercenter.org/documents/1027.pdf.

Carter Center. 2006. Statement by Former U.S. President Jimmy Carter on Nicaragua's Pre-Election Climate. July 6. www.cartercenter.org/news/documents/doc2398.html.

Carter Center. 2007. Observing the 2006 Nicaragua Elections. www.cartercenter.org/documents/nicaragua_election_final06.pdf.

CEAP (Centro de Estudios y Análisis Político). 2009. Consejos del Poder Ciudadano y Gestión Pública en Nicaragua. Managua.

CNN. 2009. "Venezuela to Help Nicaragua after U.S. Rebuff." June 14. http://edition.cnn.com/2009/WORLD/americas/06/14/nicaragua.venezuela/.

Colburn, Forrest D., and Arturo S. Cruz. 2012. "Personalism and Populism in Nicaragua." *Journal of Democracy* 23 (2): 104–18.

Consorcio Cívico Electoral. n.d. Nicaragua Elecciones 2001.

El Nuevo Diario. 2004a. "Miles No Votarán Mañana." November 6.

El Nuevo Diario. 2004b. "EyT No Acreditó a Observadores." November 7.

El Nuevo Diario. 2004c. "OEA Avala Elecciones." November 9.

El Nuevo Diario. 2006. "Advierten Riesgo en Padrón Electoral." May 24.

El Nuevo Diario. 2010. "Dionisio Palacios: 'Cambiar CSE de Raíz.'" April 11.

El Nuevo Diario. 2011a. "Roberto Courtney: 'El CSE Tiene Suficiente Plata.'" May 28.

El Nuevo Diario. 2011b. "Tregua en Ciudad Antigua Pero Reclamo por Cédula Sigue." October 12.

El Nuevo Diario. 2012a. "Bendaña Recurre de Inconstitucionalidad Contra Reformas Electorales." July 4.

El Nuevo Diario. 2012b. "Prorrogan el Plazo para Obtener Cédula." August 9.

El Nuevo Diario. 2012c. "Extienden Vigencia de Cédulas Hasta 2014." November 30.

Envío. 1998. "Re-election: Centerpiece of the Pact." No. 205 (August). www.envio.org.ni/articulo/1380.

Envío. 1999. "Is the Game All Sewn Up? Questions and Contradictions." No. 218 (September). www.envio.org.ni/articulo/2268.

Envío. 2012. "The Path to the Polls." No. 375 (October). www.envio.org.ni/articulo/4603.

Ethics and Transparency (Grupo Cívico Ética y Transparencia). n.d. Informe Final Elecciones Municipales 2008.

Ethics and Transparency. 2006a. Study of the Voter Register Audit, National Elections, 2006.

Ethics and Transparency. 2006b. Second Study of the Voter Register Audit, National Elections, 2006.

Ethics and Transparency. 2007. National Identification Card Assessment 2006–2007.

Ethics and Transparency. 2008. Valoración Preliminar de Problemas Encontrados, Elecciones Municipales. November 12. Managua.

Ethics and Transparency. 2011a. Primer Informe Mensual Elecciones Nacionales 2011. April 14.

Ethics and Transparency. 2011b. Valoración Técnica Preliminar. November 6.

Ethics and Transparency. 2011c. 4to. Informe Mensual de Observación Elecciones 2011.

Ethics and Transparency. 2011d. Informe Preliminar Elecciones 2011. March 2.

EUEEM (European Union Election Expert Mission, Republic of Nicaragua – Regional Elections). 2010. Final Report.

EUEOM (European Union Election Observation Mission). 2001. European Union Election Observation Mission to Nicaragua, Final Report.

EUEOM. 2006. Final Report: Presidential and Parliamentary Elections, Nicaragua 2006.

EUEOM. 2011. Nicaragua Final Report, General Elections and PARLACEN Elections 2011.

Gonzalez-Ocantos, Ezequiel, Chad Kiewiet de Jonge, Carlos Meléndez, Javier Osorio, and David W. Nickerson. 2012. "Vote Buying and Social Desirability Bias: Experimental Evidence from Nicaragua." *American Journal of Political Science* 56 (1): 202–17.

GPRE (Grupo Promotor de Reformas Electorales). 2008. "Problemas y Propuestas: Reformas a la Ley Electoral."

GPRE. 2010. "Propuesta Desde la Sociedad Civil Para Restaurar la Confianza en el Sistema Electoral."

Hagamos Democracia. 2011. Observatorio Electoral 2011: La Precampaña. Managua.

IPADE (Instituto Para el Desarrollo y la Democracia). 2000. Observación Electoral en Nicaragua: Elecciones Municipales 2000.

IPADE. 2004. Monitoreo y Observación Electoral de las Elecciones Municipales 2004.

IPADE. 2006. Informe de Observación Electoral: Elecciones Nacionales 2006.

IPADE. 2009. Elecciones Municipales, 2008/2009: Informe Final. Nicaragua: IPADE.

IPADE. 2011a. Primer Informe de Observación Electoral de IPADE, Enero-Abril, 2011.

IPADE. 2011b. Segundo Informe de Observación Electoral, Mayo – Julio 2011.

IPADE and NDI. 2006. Verificación Técnica de Dos Vías del Padrón Electoral de las Regiones Autónomas de la Costa Caribe Nicaragüense.

IRI (International Republican Institute). 2002. Nicaragua: Election Observation Report, November 4, 2001.

Kelley, Judith G. 2012. *Monitoring Democracy: When International Election Observation Works, and Why It Often Fails*. Princeton: Princeton University Press.

Levitsky, Steven, and Lucan A. Way. 2010. *Competitive Authoritarianism: Hybrid Regimes after the Cold War*. New York: Cambridge University Press.

Ley No. 152. Ley de Identificación Ciudadana. January 27, 1993.

Martí i Puig, Salvador. 2010. "The Adaptation of the FSLN: Daniel Ortega's Leadership and Democracy in Nicaragua." *Latin American Politics and Society* 52 (4): 79–106.

Martí i Puig, Salvador. 2011. "Nicaragua: Chapiolla Democracy." In *The Quality of Democracy in Latin America*, Daniel H. Levine, and José E. Molina, eds. Boulder, CO: Lynne Rienner Publishers.

McConnell, Shelley A. 2012. "The Uncertain Evolution of the Electoral System." In *The Sandinistas and Nicaragua since* 1979, David Close, Salvador Martí i Puig, and Shelley A. McConnell, eds. Boulder and London: Lynne Rienner Publishers.

Navas Corea, Camilo. 2012. "Reforma Electoral No Generará Confianza." *Confidencial*, May 11. www.confidencial.com.ni/articulo/6539/reforma-electoral-no-generara-confianza.

NDI (National Democratic Institute). 1997. "Nicaraguans Embrace Domestic Election Observers." NDI Reports (Winter). www.ndi.org/files/1246_ww_ndireports_123197_0.pdf.

NDI. 2001. "Peaceful Elections, Yet Significant Challenges Ahead." NDI Reports, No. 3. www.ndi.org/files/1328_ww_newdemocs1101_0.pdf.

NDI. 2006a. NDI Bulletin: Nicaragua, September 30, 2006. www.ndi.org/files/2085_ni_bulletin_093006_0.pdf.

NDI. 2006b. NDI Bulletin: Nicaragua, July 31. www.ndi.org/files/2083_ni_bulletin_073106_0.pdf.

NDI. 2006c. NDI Bulletin: Nicaragua, June 1–30. www.ndi.org/files/2082_ni_bulletin_063006_0.pdf.

NDI. 2006d. NDI Bulletin: Nicaragua, May 31. www.ndi.org/files/2081_ni_bulletin_053106.pdf.

NDI. 2006e. NDI Bulletin: Nicaragua, April 30. www.ndi.org/files/2080_ni_bulletin_043006_0.pdf.

NDI. 2006f. NDI Bulletin: Nicaragua, March 31. www.ndi.org/files/2079_ni_bulletin_033106_0.pdf.

Nicaragua Dispatch. 2011. "Can Ortega Overcome the 'Gueguence Factor'?" October 31. www.nicaraguadispatch.com/news/2011/10/can-ortega-overcome-%E2%80%98gueguense-factor%E2%80%99/1057.

Nicaragua Dispatch. 2012a. "Germany Cuts Aid over Concerns for Democracy." January 19. www.nicaraguadispatch.com/news/2012/01/germany-cuts-aid-over-concerns-for-democracy/1919/1919.

Nicaragua Dispatch. 2012b. "Narco-Magistrate Scandal Rocks Nicaragua." May 30. www.nicaraguadispatch.com/news/2012/05/narco-magistrate-scandal-rocks-nicaragua/4113.

OAS (Organization of American States). 2002. Report of the Electoral Observation Mission, National General Elections, Regional Elections in Costa Atlántica, Nicaragua, 2001–2002.

OAS. 2008. Informe de la Misión de Observación Electoral, Elecciones Generales de la República de Nicaragua, 5 de Noviembre de 2006.

La Prensa. 2004. "PLC Evade 'Mea Culpa.'" November 14.

La Prensa. 2006a. "Elecciones Agitan el Atlántico Sur." January 24.

La Prensa. 2006b. "Pleito de CSE Pasa a Corte." February 2.

La Prensa. 2006c. "La Crisis del Consejo Supremo Electoral." February 2.

La Prensa. 2010a. "Cédulas Atrasadas 5 Años." May 11.

La Prensa. 2010b. "Urge Depurar el Padrón Electoral, Dice Palacios." October 7.

La Prensa. 2011a. "Gente del FSLN de los Barrios Llega a Retirar Cédulas al CSE." February 15.

La Prensa. 2011b. "Descontento por Cédulas Se Extiende." October 11.

La Prensa. 2011c. "No Hay Manera de Consultar 'On Line' Padrón." October 11.

La Prensa. 2011d. "FSLN Busca Mayoría en Asamblea con Fraude." October 19.

La Prensa. 2011e. "FSLN Anula a Oposición." October 19.

La Prensa. 2011f. "CSE Crea Confusión entre Los Electores." November 2.

Rogers, Tim. 2011. "Venezuela's Chávez Bankrolled Nicaragua with $1.6 Billion since 2007." *Christian Science Monitor*, April 7. www.csmonitor.com/World/Americas/2011/0407/Venezuela-s-Chavez-bankrolled-Nicaragua-with-1.6-billion-since-2007.

Rogers, Tim. 2012a. "In Nicaragua, Sandinista Membership a Prerequisite for Government Work." *Global Post*, June 7. www.globalpost.com/dispatch/news/regions/americas/120606/nicaragua-workers-sandinista-membership.

Rogers, Tim. 2012b. "US Cuts Aid to Its Poor Old Foe." *Global Post*, June 21. www.globalpost.com/dispatch/news/regions/americas/120621/nicaragua-us-aid-ortega-chavez-clinton-sandinistas.

Salinas Maldonado, Carlos. 2012. "Maquillaje Electoral Pasó Sin Oposición." *Confidencial*, May 20. www.confidencial.com.ni/articulo/6719/maquillaje-electoral-paso-sin-oposicion.

Spalding, Rose J. 2012. "Poverty Politics." In *The Sandinistas and Nicaragua since* 1979, David Close, Salvador Martí I Puig, and Shelley A. McConnell, eds. Boulder and London: Lynne Rienner Publishers.

WOLA (Washington Office on Latin America). 2006. Memo on Nicaraguan Elections, October 30. www.wola.org/publications/memo_on_nicaraguan_elections.

Zúñiga, Mauricio. 2012. "How We Got to These 'Low Intensity' Elections." *Envío*, 376 (November). www.envio.org.ni/articulo/4620.

8 El Salvador

From voter exclusion to halting reform

During its transition to democracy, El Salvador adopted administrative barriers to voting similar to those in Guatemala, such as centralized voting sites, the assignment of voters to polling places based on alphabetical order rather than proximity, and onerous voter registration requirements. And, like Guatemala, El Salvador's administrative practices became more inclusive over time, although the sequencing of reform differed from the Guatemalan case, with voter registration simplified first and polling decentralization subsequently implemented gradually.

This chapter shows that El Salvador's restrictive administrative measures were adopted in the country's pre-democratic period, in response to the security conditions during the country's civil war and the desire to eradicate the election fraud that had been common in prior elections. These restrictions continued long after these initial conditions had changed, due to both institutional inertia and partisan calculations about the likely effects of expanding the electorate through more inclusive election procedures. Ultimately, pressure from the left, civil society, and international election observers and experts led to halting reforms, while calculations of partisan interests dictated the sequence and shape of reform. Voter registration reform was less contentious because it was expected to provide greater protection against electoral manipulation without adversely affecting partisan interests, while making polling stations more accessible was repeatedly delayed because the perceived risks to partisan interests were greater, particularly on the right, while the benefits for deterring election fraud were more limited.

The first section of this chapter provides brief background on El Salvador's democratic transition, while the second section overviews the establishment of restrictive election administration practices in the 1980s and the continuation of restrictive practices through the 1994 general election. I then explain the initial adoption of election administration practices during this transition period in the third section. Section four describes the election administration reforms undertaken since 1994, while the fifth explains the factors that influenced those reforms.

Background

El Salvador's full transition to democracy is commonly marked by the 1994 elections, the country's first elections held after the country's civil war that included the participation of the FMLN guerillas-turned-political party. Prior to this transition, the country's military regimes had held periodic elections, with those of the 1970s marked by blatant fraud. This began with fraudulent National Assembly elections in 1970, followed by a presidential election in 1972 in which the Christian Democratic Party (PDC) candidate José Napoleón Duarte appeared to be winning handily, before the official candidate Arturo Molina was suddenly declared ahead by some 100,000 votes. The fraudulent outcome helped prompt a group of military officers to unsuccessfully attempt a coup (Anderson 1988, 77). Subsequent mayoral and legislative elections in 1974, 1976, and 1978 were patently fraudulent, involving "*tamales* – stuffed ballot boxes – transported in military vehicles," as well as a broader climate of repression (Baloyra 1982, 55). As a result, many opposition parties boycotted the contests (Anderson 1988, 78; Webre 1979, 194).

The 1977 presidential election was rigged by the ruling PCN (Partido de Conciliación Nacional) party, as it faced an opposition coalition that included the Christian Democrats. Although the opposition most likely won the balloting, the official results gave victory to the PCN candidate (Anderson 1988, 79; Baloyra 1982, 73). Opposition poll watchers were prevented from monitoring the polls in many locations, and "[b]allot boxes in some areas were reported already filled when the polls opened" (Webre 1979, 197). As Anderson (1988, 79) reports, PCN headquarters communicated with polling stations on election day, and "[a]s the contest progressed, cryptic messages emanating from the PCN offices urged backers to 'put more sugar in the urn than coffee,' meaning, of course, to stuff the ballot boxes for [PCN candidate] General Romero."

Elections in the early to mid-1980s were held under conditions of civil war and severe human rights abuses on the part of the military and paramilitary death squads. The conditions for democratic elections improved in the late 1980s, and a turnover of civilian parties took place when the right-wing ARENA (Republican Nationalist Alliance) won the 1989 presidential election, defeating the Christian Democratics. That election also saw the first participation of leftist parties under the Democratic Convergence coalition.

By the beginning of the 1990s, the government and FMLN guerrillas were engaged in peace talks. During these negotiations, the latter sought constitutional and electoral reforms, and in 1991 both sides agreed to replace the electoral management body – the Central Elections Council (CCE) – with a Supreme Electoral Tribunal. The CCE had been composed of one representative of each branch of government until 1983, when it became party-based with magistrates nominated by the top parties in the previous presidential election and approved by the Legislative Assembly. After a 1991 constitutional reform that replaced the CCE with the TSE, two additional non-partisan magistrates were added, to be named from lists put forward by the Supreme Court and chosen by two-thirds vote in the assembly.

Since the TSE's creation, it has been pervaded by partisanship at all levels, with staff in the technical directorates, departmental and municipal election councils, and polling stations appointed by a party quota system (Baloyra 1998, 21; EUEOM 2009a; IFES 1994, 10). Despite the legal requirement that they be nonpartisan, observers sometimes note the partisan behavior of the court-nominated magistrates (CIS 2004; 2006, 9) and the political influence in the composition of the court itself (Artiga-González 2008a, 529). Conservative parties, led by ARENA, held majority control of the TSE until 2009 (EUEOM 2009a).

The 1992 peace accords also created an electoral sub-commission within the National Commission for the Consolidation of Peace (COPAZ). This subcommission, with representation of all political parties, drafted a new electoral code, which was unanimously approved by the Legislative Assembly (IFES 1994, 9; Spence and Vickers 1994, 9). The electoral code increased party participation in the administration of all aspects of the electoral process, including a multiparty oversight body, the *Junta de Vigilancia* (JVE), to monitor the work of the TSE (Spence and Vickers 1994, 9).[1]

Establishing restrictive election procedures: 1982–1994

Despite the significance of El Salvador's 1994 elections, the origins of many features of the country's election administration lie in the 1982–1991 period. Thus, while the country's elections during this period have been variously characterized as "demonstration elections" and "electoral authoritarianism" (Montgomery 1995, 156–57, 185), several administrative practices that lasted long into the postwar period originated during these electoral processes.

In the early 1980s, the Salvadoran regime sought to hold acceptable elections in order to maintain American support. To this end, steps were taken to boost voter turnout to legitimize the elections. Voting was compulsory for the 1982 constituent assembly election, and a change in the electoral law allowed people to vote in any municipality, not just where their *cédula* had been issued (Baloyra 1982, 213, note 16). A similar system of absentee balloting was used in 1984 (Baloyra 1995, 49; García 1989, 76). Also, prior to 1985 the voter rolls were taken directly from the country's civil registries, so no additional registration steps were required for voters with the ID card (Baloyra 1993, 8–11).

Given the *cédula*'s lack of safeguards, and following serious problems with the quality of the voter lists in the 1982 and 1984 elections, several changes were made. Absentee polling places were eliminated after 1984, a move that may have disenfranchised several hundred thousand displaced persons (Baloyra 1995, 51). Even more importantly, a separate electoral registry was created in 1985, and in 1988 a new voter ID card (the *carnet electoral*) was used for the first time (Baloyra 1993, 8–9; Consorcio 2000, 22; IFES 1994, Annex II). This introduced an extra step to register to vote: a citizen would present identification or two witnesses at a registration office, and the applicant's information was then sent to the central CCE office to be verified and, if approved, a voter card would be issued (Freedom House 1989, 39; NDI 1989, 11–12).

A deadline of 30 days before the election for delivering voter cards was set by an amendment to the electoral code pushed by the ARENA party.[2] Other parties "charged that this reform would deprive many otherwise qualified citizens of exercising their right to vote" (NDI 1989, 8; see also Freedom House 1989, 39). But ARENA justified the measure to prevent manipulation of the voter rolls and ID cards, claiming that in previous elections PDC members within the CCE had printed fraudulent voting cards.

> The earlier deadline for voting card delivery would presumably reduce the opportunity for such activity by allowing a more thorough scrutiny of the process ... In defending this reform, ARENA members insisted that "it is better to maintain the quality, than the quantity of voting cards."
>
> (NDI 1989, 7–8)

The elections of 1989 and 1991 were marked by administrative problems in processing registration applications and delivering voter cards, along with accusations between political parties "about local functionaries preventing people from registering by misplacing forms or not accepting valid ID, or removing names from the CCE database" (NDI 1989, 12). As a result, several hundred thousand people who had registered prior to the 1989 and 1991 elections did not receive their voter cards in time to vote (Baloyra 1993, 15; Freedom House 1989, 40; NDI 1989, 13–14). These problems were compounded by inconsistencies between information on voter cards and the voter rolls, including the omission of many registered voters from the rolls (IFES 1994, Annex II; Montgomery 1995, 222–23; 1998, 118–19).

The 1980s also saw the centralization of polling stations in municipal centers, with most municipalities having just one voting center. Additionally, in the larger urban municipalities that had more than one voting center, voters were assigned to a polling place alphabetically, rather than to the site closest to their residence. As a result, voters in both rural and urban areas often had to travel significant distances to reach their polling place.

After the end of the country's civil war in 1992, El Salvador headed into what were dubbed the "elections of the century." The elections were the first in which the FMLN participated, and presidential, legislative, and municipal elections were all held concurrently, which only occurs once every 15 years in El Salvador's election calendar. The country headed into the elections with a new electoral management body and electoral law, but with restrictive election administration practices still in place.

The most significant impediment to participation was voter registration. Underlying voter registration was a decentralized civil registry system run by municipalities, as in Guatemala. Despite the mechanisms put in place in the 1980s, registry data was unreliable, due to uneven record keeping practices, the destruction of registry offices during the war, and the displacement or emigration of large numbers of Salvadorans (IFES 1994, 11; Spence and Vickers 1994, 15).

To register to vote, citizens applied at a registration office in their municipal center, presenting a birth certificate or ID card or, lacking those, two witnesses. The application would then be sent to the TSE office in San Salvador to be checked against the TSE's archives of birth certificates, which led to many applications being delayed or denied.[3] If the application was approved, the applicant would be added to the voter registry and a notification card (*ficha*) sent to the office where the person applied. The citizen would then need to return to the registry office to have a picture taken and the *carnet electoral* issued. However, the registry offices did not notify voters when their applications had been approved, and the processing of applications took weeks or months. "[A]s a result, people often had to return to the town hall three, four, or five times looking for their *fichas*. Many tired of fruitless journeys and simply never came back" (Montgomery 2000, 148; see also Spence and Vickers 1994, 15). As Montgomery (1998, 126) summarizes: "[i]n a country with 60 percent illiteracy, the TSE devised a Byzantine voter registration process that would have cowed even a well-educated voter."

Compounding the obstacles posed by the application process was the slow delivery of voter ID cards, and surveys showed that nearly 30 percent of voting-age citizens were unregistered and lacked voter cards (Córdova Macías 1996, 39; IFES 1994, 12; Montgomery 2000, 162, note 29). The problems with registration and pressure from the international community led the TSE to carry out a registration plan, with US and UN financing, consisting of "a publicity campaign, mobile registration units, extension of the local Tribunal office hours, and an extension of the deadline for handing out the *carnets*" (IFES 1994, 12). Another plan to facilitate voter registration came from the UN observer mission directly and involved well-publicized one-day registration events (*megajornadas*). As Montgomery (2000, 149) explains, UN election observers "assumed responsibility for the logistical support for voter registration, including traveling to municipalities in order to find individual birth certificates required for registration, a task originally intended for the TSE and mayoral offices."

With these efforts, delivery of voter ID cards improved over time (Córdova Macías 1996, 39–40). However, some 300,000 voter ID cards had not been retrieved by election day, and an additional 75–80,000 registration applications had not been approved due to birth certificates not being on file, leaving the applicants unable to vote (IFES 1994, 13; Lehoucq 1995, 181). Many unretrieved voter cards may have been duplicates or belonged to people who had left the country since registering,[4] but likely tens of thousands of registered voters were unable to vote because they did not receive their voter card.[5]

Other problems with the voter registry occurred on election day, when many voters arrived at their polling table to find that their names were not on the voters list or the number of their ID card did not match the numbers of their polling table. The UN observer mission estimated 25,000 voters were disenfranchised due to these problems; other estimates were 87,000 voters or more (IFES 1994, 2; Lehoucq 1995, 181; Spence et al. 1997). In sum, a complex registration process, slow delivery of voter cards, and errors in the voter lists on election day combined to make voting difficult or impossible for many Salvadorans.

Getting to the ballot box presented further obstacles for many voters. In the 1994 elections and afterwards, El Salvador continued to employ a system of polling locations and assignment of voters to polling sites that imposed barriers to participation similar to those in Guatemala. Voting centers were concentrated in municipal centers, with about 80 percent of municipalities having only one voting center (Consorcio 2000, 74). They frequently contained dozens or hundreds of individual polling tables (JRVs). For instance, in the 1994 elections, only 350 voting centers were used in the entire country, containing 6,970 polling tables (IFES 1994, 11).[6] While this increased to 384 voting centers in 1999, the number of centers decreased in the next 2 elections, even as the number of voters and polling tables increased (TSE-ES 1999, 11, 17; 2000, 49; 2003, 25). Voters also continued to be assigned to voting centers alphabetically, rather than by distance from their residence. This meant that many urban voters had to travel across town to vote, and often family members would be assigned to different voting locations (Spence, Lanchin, and Thale 2001, 6; Ulloa et al. 2000, 31).

Polling-site location and alphabetical voter assignment presented two obstacles for voters: transportation and overcrowding. The limited number of voting centers necessitated long travel for some voters, which was compounded by the limited public transportation available (IFES 1994, 2; Manca 1997). One consequence of distant voting centers, as in Guatemala, was the use of transportation by political parties to mobilize their supporters. The limited number of centers also resulted in overcrowding, particularly in large urban areas, "making it very difficult for citizens to locate (and access) their JRV and names on the electoral registry" (IFES 1994, 2). The resulting confusion and long lines led some people to leave their center without voting (IFES 1994, 20, 22–23; Lehoucq 1995, 181).

Explaining the origins of restrictive election administration practices

A number of restrictive election administration measures were adopted in the 1980s, including an additional step for voter registration, an early cutoff date for distributing voter cards, and centralized voting centers to which voters were assigned alphabetically. Many of these measures lasted through the 1990s (see Table 8.1).

As in Guatemala, the desire to prevent election fraud was a central motive behind some voting procedures put in place in the 1980s. Election fraud throughout the 1970s involved ballot box stuffing, intimidation of voters, and altered vote counts. These experiences, which had contributed to the erosion of middle-class support for the military regime (García 1989, 64), shaped subsequent election administration practices.

In the early 1980s, permissive voter registration and absentee balloting rules were adopted to boost voter turnout, but concerns about fraud led to more restrictive practices later in the decade. The 1980s elections were marked by mutual accusations of fraud, much of them centered on voter registration. The issuance

Table 8.1 Election administration inclusiveness, El Salvador 1994–2000

Dimension	*Description*	*Inclusiveness*
Voter registration		
Extent of state responsibility for registering voters	Voter-initiated, inconsistent state efforts to register citizens	Low
Difficulty of registration process	Complex process involving multiple trips to centralized offices	Low
Ease of access to ID documents required for registration	Multiple ID forms or witnesses accepted; birth certificate required to be on file at central registry	Medium
Registration closing date	60–120 days	Medium/low
Residency requirement	None	High
Provisional registration	None	Low
Registry consultation	Voter lists distributed to political parties and posted in public places	High
Purging of voter rolls	Voters not purged from the rolls for failure to vote	High
Getting to the ballot box		
Accessibility of polling places	Polling places centralized in municipal centers; limited public transportation	Low
Assignment of voters to polling places	Alphabetical (not based on residence)	Low
Convenience voting measures	Not used	Low
Electoral calendar	Voting held on Sunday	High
Casting a ballot		
Voter ID requirement	*Carnét* required; many *carnét*s not received by registered voters by election day	Low
Provisional or tendered ballots	Not used	Low
Voter education		
State efforts to inform voters of where and how to register and vote	Modest voter education campaigns, increasing in scope over time	Medium
Overall inclusiveness		*Low*

of *cédulas* was under the authority of mayors, many of whom were from the PCN and ARENA parties; thus, the Christian Democrats, who were governing by the mid-1980s and who had been victims of election fraud in the 1970s, had reason to oppose basing the voter lists on ID cards distributed by their opponents. A 1984 bill supported by ARENA to require only a *cédula* to vote, without any use of voter lists, drew opposition from the Christian Democrats, “alleging that this opened the door to large-scale fraud" (Baloyra 1993, 12); the bill was ultimately vetoed by the president (Baloyra 1995, 49). At the same time, the other parties "feared being victimized by the very tactics that they had masterminded in the past" (Baloyra 1993, 8) and, in fact, ARENA leaders believed they had been cheated out of victory in the 1984 presidential election (WOLA 1991, 4).

The requirement for voters to obtain a separate voter ID card (the *carnet*) and the cumbersome system of verifying voters' data were thus intended to ensure greater control over the registry and prevent fraud (Artiga-González 2004, 200–201; Consorcio 2000, 12; WOLA 1991, 7). During this checking process, many registration applications were rejected, due to minor discrepancies between the name on the application and the name in the municipal records, which apparently was caused in part by a computer program used by the CCE to prevent multiple registrations (IHRLG 1989, 62). The early cutoff date for distributing voter cards was apparently also an attempt to prevent manipulation of the voter rolls.

While voter registration procedures were aimed at preventing fraud, the connection between centralized polling places and fraud prevention is less clear, in contrast to Guatemala. Sources offer several reasons for the centralization of polling places, including preventing electoral manipulation. Baloyra (1993, 9) suggests that concentrating polling sites may have been intended to make multiple voting difficult by causing long lines for voters. He more broadly suggests a link between restrictive practices and the goal of preventing fraud and the intimidation of rural voters, noting that parties like the Christian Democrats "had bitter recollections of the outcomes of the 1972 and 1977 elections" and "worried about *tamaleo* (ballot stuffing) attempts and girded themselves to counteract the onslaught of clientele voting and intimidation by rightist *jefes civiles* and military officers in rural areas" (Baloyra 1993, 8).

This argument is consistent with the view that polling centralization was intended to ensure the secrecy of the vote (EUEOM 2009a) and that rural voters were subjected to influence by local elites. Describing elections prior to the 1970s, Webre (1979, 168) writes:

> … in small towns and rural areas *oficialista* interference, imposition, intimidation, and ballot-box stuffing continued unhindered. … In a world view defined by personal relationships, the *campesino* often regarded his vote as simply part of the tribute owed his *patrón*. Rural voters, more so than urban, were willing to accept "guidance" in their civic duty from local authority figures, and the local authority figures – landlords, *alcaldes*, Guard commanders – tended in the vast majority to be *oficialistas*.

Concentrating voting in municipal centers thus might have been a means of reducing the social control exercised by rural elites over campesinos as they cast their ballots. Others suggest a different motive for the centralization of polling sites: the desire to generate large crowds of voters that would give the appearance of massive participation, thus legitimizing the elections in the media

(Consorcio 2000, 73; ISD 2009; 2011a, 2). In this view, long lines of voters were considered useful not as a way of making it difficult for someone to vote more than once, but as a tool to influence media coverage. At least for the 1982 elections, national and international media reports did indeed stress the high voter turnout, which "became a political weapon against the guerrillas" (García 1989, 72).

While all of these considerations might have influenced the centralization of polling places, an explanation that enjoys more support is that the centralization of voting centers was intended to ensure security in the context of guerrilla insurgency (EUEOM 2009a; UN 2009, 4). In fact, the FMLN was able to prevent voting in many parts of the country in the 1980s. They attempted to disrupt the 1982 constituent assembly election, and voting did not take place in one departmental capital because of fighting between guerrillas and the military (Baloyra 1982, 173). In 1984, voting was not held in 58 municipalities where the FMLN presence was strongest, including 2 in which guerrillas destroyed the ballot boxes (CIDAI 1984, 212–13; see also Ratliff and Perry 1984, 12–13). Again in 1988, the guerrillas did not permit voting in areas under their control, where "[t]hey seized and burned voting cards in several villages" and in one case "publicly executed two civilians after finding out they had applied for and received voter registration cards" (García 1989, 80).

More generally, the state was unable to ensure security in many areas, as the FMLN executed a number of local officials and issued death threats to many others who were elected in areas they controlled, causing at least 50 mayors to resign in the late 1980s (IHRLG 1989, 112). In such a context, it almost certainly would have been impossible to guarantee the government's control over polling in all corners of the country, making it necessary to concentrate voting in more easily secured areas.

Thus in 1982, "[i]n an effort to manage the security problem the CCE kept the number of *puestos de votación* (polling stations) small, so that the army, the national guard, and the police would not have to spread themselves too thin" (Baloyra 1982, 173). The electoral code also allowed the CCE to not install voting sites in some municipalities, instead locating polling stations for citizens in those areas in nearby municipalities (Electoral Code 1988, Art. 278; IHRLG 1989, 49).

While it is difficult to know the exact mix of motivations, it appears that security was the primary reason for centralizing voting centers, with the goal of preventing various types of manipulation (ballot stuffing, coercion of rural voters) as a possible secondary motive.[7] Security concerns also played a role in Guatemala and Nicaragua, where relatively free elections preceded the termination of civil conflict. But security played a larger role in El Salvador, given the fact that the FMLN guerrillas were a much more formidable military force capable of holding significant territory than were the URNG guerrillas in Guatemala or the Contra forces in Nicaragua.

Aside from polling centralization was the alphabetical assignment of voters to voting centers in the larger municipalities. As in Guatemala, there appears to have been no substantive reason for adopting this method in El Salvador. As later TSE president Eugenio Chicas explained, this method was administratively simpler for those conducting the elections (Interview 55) and was apparently adopted for this reason. In a context of less-than-free elections held during civil conflict and administered by an election council with low technical capacity, and where the method of assigning voters to polling sites was only relevant in the few municipalities with more than one voting center, the CCE opted to shift the burden onto urban voters to reach their polling site, rather than undertake the work necessary to assign voters geographically.

For the 1994 elections, the immense obstacles to participation presented by the voter registration system resulted from several factors, although it is difficult to assign relative weight to each. First was simple inertia, as the complicated registration process was largely a holdover from previous elections, which in turn were driven by a desire to prevent fraud. The complicated system of verifying each application against birth certificate archives, as well as an early closing date to allow time for parties to review the rolls, reflected the continuing distrust between the parties and concerns about election rigging. New registration procedures were considered at the time, including introducing a new identity document and conducting an ad hoc voter registration (Martel 2010, 16–17; UN 1992, 16). Ultimately, it was decided that there was not enough time or money to introduce a new ID card by 1994, a decision supported by a recommendation from the UN electoral mission to maintain and update the existing registry rather than construct a new voter list (Montgomery 2000, 144).

Second, partisanship affected how voter registration procedures were carried out. Because of the decentralization of civil registries in local municipal offices, mayors could obstruct voter registration in attempts to exclude opposition supporters from the electorate, even if not directed to do so by their political party. Mayors of the governing ARENA party in particular were accused of obstructing citizen efforts to obtain birth certificates and voting cards, and this may have cost the FMLN several tightly contested local races (Lehoucq 1995, 181; Montgomery 1995, 265; 2000, 149–50). Stahler-Sholk (1994, 29) argues that the more burdensome postwar registration requirements in El Salvador compared to Nicaragua reflected the fact that supporters of the FMLN (which had not previously contested elections) tended to be unregistered, and thus "[o]bstructing registration was a way of keeping the pool of voters similar to those who had returned ARENA majorities in the last two elections." This sentiment was widespread on the left, while the UN observer mission concluded that registration problems were due largely to the limited technical capacity of the TSE, rather than an effort to disenfranchise some voters (UN 1993, 3). A UNDP survey on voter registration also "found that the large majority of those affected by the deficiency of the system … could not be identified as members of any party" (Manca 1997). While the evidence regarding partisan manipulation is unclear, at the very least some of the bottlenecks in processing voter registration applications appeared to result from some mayors failing to send applicants' birth certificates to the TSE so that their registration could be processed.

Finally, some of the registration obstacles resulted from TSE incompetence and logistical difficulties, as the UN concluded. The TSE had been created only two years prior to the elections and was administering a general election in difficult postwar circumstances, in which civil registries had been destroyed and over one-fourth of the population had been displaced (Spence, Lanchin, and Thale 2001, 2). The TSE's partisan, rather than technocratic, staffing likely didn't help in this regard.

Like the voter registration system, the system of locating polling places used in 1994 was a holdover from previous elections. Despite the fact that security concerns had disappeared with the end of the war, the decentralization of polling locations seems not to have been considered for the 1994 elections although, as election day approached, the necessity for such a reform was recognized. Short on time and resources, and with its hands full with voter registration, the TSE stuck with the established method of concentrating polling sites in municipal centers and assigning voters to polling places alphabetically.

In sum, restrictive election administration procedures in El Salvador were initially a result of efforts to ensure security during the civil war and prevent election fraud and, once in place, those procedures persisted due to a combination of institutional inertia, partisan machinations, and the limited technical capacity and competence of the country's new electoral management body.

Election administration after 1994: halting steps toward greater access

While the milestone 1994 elections were marred by procedural hurdles that made voting difficult for many Salvadorans, many administrative barriers persisted in subsequent elections. But the TSE undertook some administrative measures after 1994 that sought to improve voter access, while major legal reforms after 2000 significantly increased inclusiveness.

Administrative measures to increase voter access

Voter registration requirements were largely unchanged until 2003, and again in the 1997 elections the number of voter cards retrieved by voters fell well short of the number of new registration applications (TSE-ES 1997, 11–12).[8] However, with the support of the international community, the TSE made extra efforts to register voters and deliver voter cards for the 1997 elections, carrying out *mega-jornadas* on the weekends to promote registration, conducting house-to-house visits, sending telegrams to voters, and extending registration office hours (TSE-ES 1997, 11–12; UN 1997, 2).[9] Another restrictive aspect of voter registration was the early closing date, with new applications ending 120 days before election day (Electoral Code 1992, Art. 31). This meant that voter registration closed two to three months before the legal start of the campaign season. Thus, the TSE had taken steps in 1997 to facilitate voter registration, but significant barriers remained.

Greater efforts were also made to ensure the availability of public transportation on election day. The TSE began to contract buses to provide free transportation for voters by 1999 and, although it was limited to major urban areas, the covered areas accounted for just over half of voters by 2003 (TSE-ES 1999, 29; 2003, 32). A subsequent amendment to the electoral code required the TSE to contract free public transportation "to the extent of its economic possibilities" and "with the objective of facilitating citizen participation" (Art. 347, amended by Decreto 228), although many voters continued to depend on political parties for transportation to distant voting centers, with the attendant concerns about pressure placed on voters to vote for the party providing the ride (CIS 2003, 2004; OAS 2009a, 30).

The scope of the TSE's voter-information campaigns also gradually expanded after 1994. In that year, the TSE had carried out a campaign to inform voters about registration requirements and the voting process, which was complemented by a more extensive campaign by civic groups with USAID funding (IFES 1994, 17). However, observers evaluated the voter education efforts to be inadequate and noted that many voters did not understand the registration process (IFES 1994, 2, 23, 28–29).

By 2000, voter-information efforts came to include new methods for voters to check their registration status and voting location, such as information kiosks installed in commercial centers and parks, a telephone hotline, and a website (TSE-ES 2000, 38). Efforts intensified in 2004 with the first use of a new voter ID document and registry system (see below), with 1.5 million telegrams containing voter registration information sent to residents in urban areas, television and radio ads, and billboards (TSE-ES 2004, 43, 74). The TSE continued to use these different tools in its extensive information campaigns in subsequent elections (TSE-ES 2006, 40, 85; 2009, 40), allowing voters a number of ways to check their registration status before the closing of the electoral register, confirm their voting location, and find out about public transportation routes on election day. The 2009 observer mission from the European Union, one of the most critical election observer organizations, called the TSE's voter education campaign "massive and well designed" (EUEOM 2009b, 6). Voter-information efforts in 2012 were also evaluated positively and involved house-to-house visits in many urban areas to inform voters where they were assigned to vote (Interviews 51, 58; ISD 2011a, 13, note 18).

Finally, the act of casting a ballot became more accessible for some voters, although improvements in election day procedures were halting. After 1994, many voters continued to find that their name was not on the local voter roll or that there were inconsistencies between the data on the voter roll and on their ID card (CIS 2000; 2003; Ramos 1997). There have been such cases even after the creation of a new electoral registry and identity card (Martel 2010, 31–32; NDI 2009, 3; OAS 2009a, 16), but the problem has diminished considerably. The TSE has also taken greater steps to orient voters in crowded voting centers by posting signs and recruiting volunteers to work in the centers,[10] although overcrowded polling places have remained a problem, as has the frequency with which polling places open late.[11]

Legal reforms

While administrative measures taken by the TSE after the 1994 elections tended toward more inclusiveness, the most important changes to El Salvador's election administration came from a series of legal reforms. The need for electoral reform was already evident in 1994, when the top two presidential contenders agreed to pursue reform after the elections, including the introduction of a new identity and voting document, a more professional TSE, and residential voting. The major political parties and civil society groups publicly supported these reforms (Baloyra 1998, 33; IFES 1994, 4, 26; IFES 1997). In 1995, a presidential commission with representation from all political parties was formed to study and make recommendations on electoral reforms. But despite regular amendments to the electoral code prior to electoral processes,[12] the key reforms were slow in coming. The most important election administration reforms involved voter registration and identification, and residential voting.

The new civil registry and unique identity document

One of El Salvador's most important electoral reforms has been the introduction of a new identity document and associated creation of a new civil and electoral registry. The reform replaced the voter ID card (*carnet*) and personal ID card (*cédula*) with a single identity card. As the TSE had shown leading up to the 1994 elections that it lacked the capacity to efficiently issue identity cards, the legislature opted to create a new agency, the National Registry of Natural Persons (RNPN) to manage the national civil registry and distribute ID cards (Mena and Rodríguez 2005, 68).

Legally established in 1995, the RNPN was slow to begin operations, but the distribution of the new Unique Identity Document (*Documento Único de Identidad*, or DUI) began in late 2001 and was first used as voter ID in 2004 (Artiga-González 2008b, 19). The significance of the DUI for inclusiveness is that voter registration became automatic with its introduction: when a citizen applies for an ID card – which is needed for a wide range of common transactions – his or her information is automatically sent to the TSE to be added to the electoral registry.

The process of obtaining a DUI consists of a visit to a registry office, most of which are located in departmental capitals, with a recently issued birth certificate from the municipal office where one was born; the ID card is given to the voter that day, eliminating the waiting period involved with the *carnet*. First-time registrations are free, but renewals, replacements, and modifications cost \$10.31 (EUEOM 2009a; Mena and Rodríguez 2005, 73; RNPN 2011). When a person moves to a new residence, they are supposed to obtain a new DUI with their updated address but, since this implies paying the modification fee, many people choose not to do so. As there is no way to update one's residence for voting purposes apart from modifying one's DUI, this presents a challenge in assigning voters to polling stations and also means some voters travel to a municipality where they no longer reside to vote.

Thus, the process of acquiring a DUI can present some obstacles, given the travel and potential costs involved. But some steps have been taken to ensure inclusiveness. While most DUIs were set to expire before the 2009 general election,[13] the Legislative Assembly extended their validity through 2009 so that citizens would not be faced with the costs of renewal in order to vote (EUEOM 2009a). When most of the country's DUIs expired in 2010, the state issued free renewals in the country's 32 poorest municipalities. The assembly also approved free renewals in December 2011 and January 2012 with the March 2012 elections on the horizon (FUSADES 2011, 13). Other measures have been taken to facilitate first-time registrations of young people.[14]

The result has been an inclusive voter registry, with an estimated 95 percent of eligible Salvadorans having a DUI and thus being registered to vote (UN 2009, 7).[15] At the same time, the DUI includes better safeguards than did the *carnet* and *cédula*, making it more difficult to forge, although many concerns remain over the lack of control at the municipal level over the issuance of birth certificates, which can result in falsely obtained DUIs (EUEOM 2009a; 2009b, 6; 2009c, 7–8; Interview 53). The construction of a new electoral registry based on the DUI also allowed the deceased and emigrated on the old registry to be purged, although the registry quickly became bloated again due to the emigration of registered voters and a lack of standardization in municipal reporting of deaths to the central registry.[16] Finally, the DUI also made possible the use of photographic voter lists on election day, which not only helps prevent voter impersonation but can also help prevent illiterate voters from being told (falsely) by poll workers or party poll watchers that they are not on the voter list (Mena and Rodríguez 2005, 69; see also Peña 2003, 8).

Closing date: the low profile reform

While the introduction of the new identity card and electoral register was a highly visible reform, a registration-related reform to the electoral code in 2007 received much less attention. The closing date for new inscriptions in the electoral registry was extended from 100 days to 180 days before the election.[17] On top of that, a stringent residency requirement was added, prohibiting changes of municipal residence on the voter registry in the year prior to election day.[18] This reform was introduced by the ARENA party, with the stated purpose of preventing pre-electoral registration fraud (the illegal movement of voters across jurisdictions, or *traslados*). As an ARENA official said in regard to the reform, "[w]e are looking to have clean and transparent elections" (EDH 2007m).[19] An advisor to the legislative committee on electoral reforms concurred that the reform was aimed at eliminating this type of fraud (Interview 57), and the reform was accompanied by stiff penalties for registration fraud added to the penal code.[20] At least initially, an FMLN official expressed opposition, alluding to the impediment to voting that the measure would represent (EDH 2007m). At the same time, the FMLN has accused ARENA of orchestrating the movements of voters across municipal lines that the measure sought to prevent (EDH 2008a).

Ultimately, the reform passed, with FMLN legislators voting against the bill.[21] However, the bill also contained a number of other reforms to the electoral code and, according to several people involved, there was consensus across parties on the earlier registration closing dates (Interviews 55, 57, 61). As the FMLN's head of electoral issues indicated, the party was in agreement with the earlier closing date but wanted to see enforcement of penalties for falsifying residence for electoral purposes, as well as mechanisms for allowing voters to change their voting residence with the TSE without needing to obtain a new identity card (Interview 61).

The FMLN's magistrate on the TSE characterized the earlier cutoff for residency changes as useful and indicated that it diminishes the *traslado* problem. Interestingly, this is not because it allows more time for election officials to verify voters' residences to detect illegal registrations: the TSE, in fact, has no mechanism for verifying voters' residency (Interview 55; UN 2009, 22). Rather, according to the magistrate, the early cutoff for residency changes occurs before political parties select their mayoral candidates, and it is these candidates that sometimes organize and pay for the illegal shifting of voters across jurisdictions (Interview 55).

The 180-day closing date for new registrations most affects young people who are not yet registered. While those people who will turn 18 years old by election day can pre-register before the closing date, few do so. For example, of 58,000 Salvadorans coming of age in the 6 months prior to the 2012 elections, only 14,000 had applied for their DUI (and thus for voter registration) before the closing date (FUSADES 2011, 13, note 21), despite a TSE publicity campaign targeting this population. The early cutoff for residency changes can result in another problem: those who change their residence from one municipality to another on their DUI during the year between the residency cutoff date and election day may encounter problems trying to vote, when the municipality on their ID card doesn't match the municipality where they are registered to vote. There have been isolated cases of people being denied the vote because of this (JVE 2009, 40).

Residential voting

The other major election administration reform in El Salvador was the gradual implementation of residential voting. As used in El Salvador, the term "residential voting" refers to both decentralizing polling sites and assigning voters to the voting center nearest their residence. Whereas in Guatemala the assignment of voters to voting centers was reformed prior to the decentralization of voting sites outside of municipal capitals, in El Salvador the two have always been considered as one issue.[22]

The desirability of residential voting had been recognized by major political actors and international observers since the 1994 elections. It was one of the priorities agreed to by the top two presidential candidates in that year's election, while four UN missions to study electoral reforms in the 1990s proposed a variety of ways of implementing it. Plans for residential voting in the mid-1990s included a proposal sent to the Legislative Assembly in September 1995 from a special presidential commission, which was revised by the assembly's electoral committee by August 1996 but not passed, as the upcoming 1997 elections made major electoral reforms impossible (CIS 2009, 32; ISD 2009). Several studies were also conducted by the TSE, including a plan for an electoral census that would have re-registered all voters and served to collect cartographic information for residential voting. However, this plan and others didn't get off the ground (ISD 2009; UN 1997, 14–17).

El Salvador came closer to realizing residential voting with a plan developed by the TSE in the late 1990s to begin implementing it in 120 municipalities for the 2000 elections, based on recommendations from a UN electoral mission. The plan involved an enlistment of voters over a 3-week period at 730 locations, which would later serve as voting centers. Some 341,000 voters were enlisted to participate at a cost of over $2 million. But this plan was scrapped by the TSE magistrates who took office in August 1999, with little explanation (Consorcio 2000, 77; Cuéllar 2009, 975; ISD 2009; UN 2009, 9). The TSE magistrates from the conservative parties were in favor of rejecting the plan altogether, while the FMLN magistrate in the TSE wanted to press ahead (Consorcio 2000, 77–78; Martel 2010, 26); ultimately, the opposition of the two conservative magistrates was sufficient to block implementation (UN 2009, 9, note 15).

In 2001, the Legislative Assembly approved, with the support of all parties, a law mandating the implementation of residential voting, beginning in 2003 (Decreto 293). The following year, however, the assembly postponed implementation until 2004 (Decreto 834) and then, in 2003, postponed it once again until 2006 (Decreto 133). Finally, the assembly determined in 2005 that residential voting would only be carried out through a small pilot program in 2006 and gradually expanded thereafter at the discretion of the TSE (Decreto 842).

The 2002 bill postponing residential voting until 2004 was sponsored by 3 ARENA and 3 FMLN deputies and passed with a large majority of 73 votes (of 84 deputies).[23] The 2003 decision to postpone residential voting came from the conservative ARENA and PCN parties and was more contentious. The conservative magistrates on the TSE argued that the tribunal lacked the technical preparation to carry out residential voting; the other magistrates disagreed. ARENA deputies on the Legislative Assembly's electoral commission pointed to the lack of unanimity among the TSE magistrates as the reason to delay implementation, while the FMLN opposed the postponement and accused ARENA and PCN of basing their positions on political calculations (EDH 2003a; 2003b; 2003c; 2003d). The measure passed in the assembly with a bare majority of 43 votes.

After these delays, a very small residential-voting pilot plan was carried out in 2006 that covered approximately 40,000 voters in 7 municipalities, involving an increase from 7 to 24 voting centers (OAS 2008, 3; TSE-ES n.d.[a], 1; 2009, 69). The plan involved subdividing each municipality into voting sectors, each corresponding to one voting center. Unlike in Guatemala, there was no attempt by the assembly to mandate a polling place in each population center of a given size; rather, the TSE was free to choose appropriate locations (UN 2009, 15).

The following year, an interparty commission was formed to discuss a range of electoral reforms, with residential voting being one of the most prominent. The key debate centered on how far to extend residential voting for the 2009 elections. Most parties wanted it extended to most or all of the country, while ARENA advocated a more gradual approach. The ARENA magistrate on the TSE took the position that technical obstacles and financial limitations could not be overcome to extend it nationally; the FMLN magistrate disagreed on both counts (EDH 2007c). The FMLN hoped to push through a bill to require the TSE to extend residential voting nationally, but this prospect faded when the PCN and PDC parties withdrew their support from this position (EDH 2007d; 2007e; 2007j).

The interparty sub-commission working on the issue ultimately proposed residential voting be extended to half of the country's 262 municipalities, with ARENA being the only 1 of the 6 parties that opposed this position, citing technical considerations (EDH 2007k; 2007l). President Saca of the ARENA party noted that his party had always supported residential voting, "but in order," and even suggested that ARENA would win more local elections in greater San Salvador with residential voting (EDH 2007h; 2008b). The interparty commission's recommendation came to naught, however, and the TSE was left to determine the extent to which residential voting would be used in 2009.

Thus, in 2009, residential voting was expanded to a total of only 23 municipalities, involving 73 voting centers and covering less than 5 percent of the country's voters. In the department of Cuscatlán, where residential voting was implemented, the number of voting centers increased fourfold.

Debate then resumed over how far to extend residential voting for the 2012 elections. This debate centered on the TSE's capacity to implement it nationwide. After the 2009 elections, the EU observer mission reported that the TSE had the technical capacity to do so (EUEOM 2009c, 6). A UN mission also analyzed the prospects for extending residential voting to the entire country, and the TSE adopted its recommendations, which involved creating a catalog of voting centers from which citizens would choose their voting center (within their municipality) when renewing their DUI, most of which were set to expire in 2010 (UN 2009, 18–24). The plan would have covered the entire country and had a low cost by exploiting the renewal process for ID cards (UN 2009, 22), and the UN also offered technical and financial support to implement the program (La Prensa Gráfica 2009b [hereafter LPG]). When the TSE failed to get the catalog of voting centers prepared in time, it sought ways to systematize voters' addresses for the purpose of assigning voting centers (EDH 2009d; 2009e).

At this point, costs became a decisive factor. The TSE's new plan to extend residential voting to the entire country would cost $12–14 million, but president Funes of the FMLN indicated that he had other priorities for his budget and would not fully fund the TSE plan. Funes and the president of the TSE, also from the FMLN, briefly clashed over the issue (EDH 2009c; 2010; LPG 2009c). After the conflict over funding, and with the TSE's technical preparations proceeding slowly, a more limited expansion was planned for 2012. Residential voting was extended to 185 municipalities covering 47 percent of the country's registered voters (TSE-ES n.d.[b], 2–3).

Residential voting was finally extended to the entire country for the 2014 presidential election, 20 years after being recognized as a necessary reform. Whereas the country had 399 voting centers in 2006, the number jumped to 1,148 in 2012 and 1,591 in 2014 (EDH 2012; TSE-ES 2006, 42; 2014a).

Explaining El Salvador's election administration reforms

El Salvador undertook major election administration reforms from the mid-1990s onward that increased inclusiveness, particularly the streamlining of voter registration and the gradual implementation of a more accessible system of polling locations. These measures are summarized in Table 8.2. This section discusses the factors that contributed to the substance and timing of these reforms.

Fraud, partisanship, and voter registration reform

The trajectory of voter registration rules in El Salvador and the sequencing of election administration reforms responded to the lingering specter of election fraud. While concerns about fraud initially led to the adoption of restrictive registration procedures, these measures did little to ensure a reliable voter list. The registration system thus represented the worst of both worlds: it was neither accessible to citizens nor particularly secure against manipulation. And voter registration problems had been so severe in 1994 that they threatened the legitimacy of the election's outcome.

Due to the widespread lack of confidence in the electoral registry, registration reform became a high priority. A UN electoral mission to the country in the 1990s noted that the lack of confidence in the registry was "a constant theme in Salvadoran political-electoral debate and the motivation of the better part of the [electoral reform] projects under discussion," and reported that the main interest of instituting a new identity card was the opportunity it offered to clean up the voter rolls (UN 1997, 9). Thus, the process of registration reform began the year after the 1994 elections (although years would pass before changes were fully implemented) and addressed both accessibility and election integrity.

Thus, while concerns about voter fraud had contributed to imposing strict voter registration practices in the 1980s and early 1990s, similar concerns subsequently led to more inclusive practices that sought not only to facilitate voter access but also to clean up the voter rolls. The introduction of the DUI allowed for better (though still imperfect) control over the issuance of identity cards and the use of photographic voter lists, which make double voting and voter impersonation more difficult.[24] At the same time, it also made voter registration automatic, eliminating a major hurdle for potential voters. At least initially, El Salvador's voter registration reform successfully pursued both voter access and electoral integrity simultaneously.

Table 8.2 Election administration inclusiveness, El Salvador 2004–2014

Dimension	*Description*	*Inclusiveness*
Voter registration		
Extent of state responsibility for registering voters	Automatic registration upon obtaining ID card	High
Difficulty of registration process	One trip to centralized office; free first-time ID, $10.31 for renewals	Medium
Ease of access to ID documents required for registration	Birth certificate required, but sometimes lacking	Medium
Registration closing date	90–180 days	Low
Residency requirement	1 year (since 2007); new ID card listing new address required	Low
Provisional registration	Those turning 18 between the close of registration and election day eligible to register	High
Registry consultation	Voter lists distributed to political parties and posted in public places; consultation on TSE website	High
Purging of voter rolls	Voters not purged from the rolls for failure to vote	High
Getting to the ballot box		
Accessibility of polling places	Fully decentralized by 2014; moderately accessible public transportation	Low/high
Assignment of voters to polling places	Fully residential by 2012	Low/high
Convenience voting measures	Not used	Low
Electoral calendar	Voting held on Sunday	High
Casting a ballot		
Voter ID requirement	DUI required (no additional burden beyond registration)	High
Provisional or tendered ballots	Not used	Low
Voter education		
State efforts to inform voters of where and how to register and vote	Extensive information campaigns through diverse media	High
Overall inclusiveness		*Medium*

But while concerns about wholesale election rigging subsided, Salvadoran political actors remained concerned about registration fraud and the shipping of voters across municipal (or even national) lines by local candidates to vote on election day (CIS 2000, 2003; 2009, 12; EUEOM 2009b, 2; OAS 2009a, 18, 22).[25] These preoccupations have led many actors to favor more restrictive registration rules, reflected in the early closing dates for registration and residency changes aimed at preventing the transfer of voters across municipalities.

Partisan interests played less of a role in shaping voter registration rules. While some thought that the political left was disadvantaged the most by registration obstacles, there was general concern among all political actors about registration fraud and the unreliability of the voter rolls (see, e.g., UN 1997, 11). The reforms enjoyed widespread support: when the DUI was introduced to replace the *carnet* as voter identification, all parties – including the right-wing ARENA – supported the measure, and there was consensus among political parties to make voter registration automatic (EDH 2003c; Interviews 51, 54, 55, 57). It appears that no political parties felt threatened by these reforms, and the UN electoral mission at the time suggested that the new civil registry and ID card would not benefit some parties over others (UN 1997, 31). If any parties had hoped to benefit from restrictive voter registration practices in previous elections, by 1995 (when the RNPN law was passed) and certainly by 2004 (when the use of the DUI as voter identification began) this had changed.

Despite agreement on the major changes, there were some partisan differences over the details of voter registration. ARENA advocated early cutoff dates for registration and residency changes, but such measures drew only mild opposition from the FMLN. On the issue of whether or not to subsidize ID cards, the left and the right have shifted positions. ARENA initially opposed the free first-time distribution of cards, while other parties were in favor of the measure. In typical fashion, some attributed partisan motives to ARENA's stance: "Only ARENA would give its sympathizers the 90 *colones* so that they can go vote," said one opposition politician (EDH 2001). Yet when the issue arose again in 2009, it was ARENA advocating free renewals of DUIs and the governing FMLN reluctant to devote the necessary funds (LPG 2009a). Despite the controversies surrounding voter registration in the 1994 elections, jockeying for partisan advantage explains little of the evolution of El Salvador's voter registration rules in subsequent years.

Explaining the course of residential voting

Partisan interests were more influential in the torturous course of implementing residential voting, with financial and technical obstacles also contributing to the long delay after it had been endorsed by the major political forces in 1994. Publicly, all parties consistently supported residential voting, and decisions to delay it always involved technical or economic justifications (Interview 57; Martel 2010, 29). And, in fact, residential voting presented a major technical challenge for the TSE. These challenges included imprecise residence information in the electoral registry (due to such problems as the lack of uniformity in the country's address system), which made assigning voters to polling stations difficult (FUSADES 2011, 10–11; Interviews 55, 60; UN 2009, 13). Another challenge was funding, given the costs of developing the necessary electoral cartography and conducting voting in more polling places on election day.

So in 2007, for example, when the extension of residential voting was being debated, ARENA and others could point to technical challenges such as the fact that some 16 percent of identity cards did not include an exact address (EDH 2007i; see also UN 2009, 14). They could also point to a report of two Panamanian technical advisors who in 2007 recommended a gradual extension of residential voting and an overhaul of the system for coding voters' addresses (EDH 2007f). But as TSE magistrate Eduardo Urquilla noted, these challenges were not insurmountable (EDH 2007i). One member of the centrist CD party accused the ARENA and PDC parties of using the recommendations from the Panamanian advisors to cover their political motives for not wanting to extend residential voting (EDH 2007g).

Indeed, while these technical challenges were significant, they do not account for why residential voting was delayed for so long. In fact, much technical preparation and financial investment were wasted by decisions to delay residential voting. According to one FMLN official, the necessary cartography and funding was available in 2000, and the decision to abandon the residential-voting plan that the TSE had been developing was the result of a lack of "political will" (Interview 58). Again in 2003, when the assembly postponed residential voting, the TSE was prepared with the logistical plan and already had the funding to implement it for the 2004 election (Interview 60; TSE-ES 2004, 24).[26] According to one TSE magistrate at the time, when the parties realized how prepared the TSE was to implement residential voting on a large scale, they were nervous about how it would affect them electorally. Ultimately, two magistrates on the TSE – one from ARENA, another from the Supreme Court – opposed going ahead with the plan (Interview 60), and an ARENA-backed bill postponing implementation passed through the assembly. Although the financial cost was a consideration, it was not what caused the repeated postponements of implementing residential voting; in fact, funding constraints were more important after 2009 than when residential voting was delayed during the mid-2000s (Interview 59).

Instead of technical or financial impediments, it was primarily electoral calculations that delayed residential voting. Despite all parties' public statements of support, according to many sources the major impediment was uncertainty about who would benefit electorally from the reform. According to some observers, this fear was generalized among the major political parties (Interviews 51, 52, 59). Others believe it was conservative parties that feared the consequences of residential voting, as the prevailing idea at the time was that it would benefit the left. This view was commonly expressed by those from the FMLN (Interviews 53, 55, 58, 61, 63), but it comes from other sources as well. An official with the CD party and a former TSE magistrate indicated that the decision in 1999 to abandon residential voting plans came from ARENA and that the 2003 decision to postpone residential voting (which was also backed by ARENA) was ultimately political, rather than based on technical considerations (Interview 60). An advisor to the Legislative Assembly's committee on electoral reform also reported that parties on the right were privately reluctant about the possible electoral consequences of residential voting, and that the technical capacity to carry out residential voting existed long before it actually was implemented (Interview 57). Other sources also suggest that reluctance about residential voting came primarily from the right (Dalton 2010; ISD 2011a, 5–6, note 10), although ARENA officials deny that electoral concerns played a role (Interview 54).

The fact that the implementation of residential voting was delayed for so long while the Legislative Assembly and presidency were controlled by the right offers some indication that reluctance by these parties was critical (the FMLN never had enough seats in the assembly to pass legislation on its own; see Holiday 2010, 4). More direct evidence comes from the parties' positions at key decision points. As noted above, all parties supported the initial bill mandating residential voting and the first postponement of implementation for one year. In 2003, however, it was the conservative ARENA and PCN parties that pushed for the postponement of residential voting. The decision in 2005 to gradually implement residential voting was endorsed by all parties, with the bill receiving 80 votes in the assembly; the bill itself was sponsored by deputies from the ARENA, PCN, and PDC parties. But, according to the FMLN's secretary of electoral matters, ARENA had wanted to rescind the existing residential-voting bills altogether, and it was the FMLN's magistrate on the TSE that intervened to secure an agreement on gradual implementation (Interview 61).[27]

The basis for the idea that residential voting would benefit the left was that low-income voters would most benefit, and this would supposedly redound to the left's advantage. More generally, it had long been suggested that the ARENA party hoped to benefit from low turnout, particularly among low-income voters who would tend to support the leftist opposition (Freedom House 1989, 48–49; Montgomery 2000, 158). The social bases of the FMLN and ARENA parties didn't bear this out, however. While both parties are sometimes characterized as catch-all parties (Artiga-González 2004, 80–83; Ulloa et al. 2000, 40–41), the FMLN has been stronger in urban than rural areas (Artiga-González 2004, 76; Colindres 1997, 19; Spence, Lanchin, and Thale 2001, 5; Ulloa, Ramos, and Cruz 1997, 139) and does better among more educated voters of higher socioeconomic status (Artiga-González 2004, 82; Nevitte 2009, 117). ARENA, on the other hand, is stronger in rural areas (Ulloa, Ramos, and Cruz 1997, 138–39).[28] ARENA's rural and lower-income base suggests that the party would stand to benefit from decentralization of polling locations (Interviews 52, 54). However, the dual nature of residential voting, including not just decentralization to rural areas but also residence-based assignment of voters to polling stations, meant that it would facilitate the participation of urban voters as well.

In any case, the uncertainty about the electoral consequences of residential voting not only caused its delay but also led to the assembly's decision to implement residential voting through small pilot programs rather than all at once (Interviews 52, 53, 55, 58). The small pilot programs allowed the parties to gauge the effects of residential voting without risking significant electoral outcomes. One of the lessons of the pilot programs was that residential voting didn't seem to favor any particular parties over others (Dalton 2010; Interviews 53, 55, 58, 59; ISD 2011a, 5). It also appeared to have had limited impact on voter turnout. In 2006, average turnout in the 7 municipalities with residential voting was some 13 percentage points higher than the national average, and increased significantly (between 7.5 and 18.8 points) in each municipality, compared to the previous legislative and municipal elections in 2003 (CIS 2006, 23; TSE-ES 2006, 76). But in 2009, although turnout in municipalities with residential voting surpassed the national average, it was lower than turnout in the previous presidential election in 2004 (ISD 2009; TSE-ES n.d.[a], 2; 2009, 88). When residential voting was fully implemented nationwide in the 2014 presidential election, turnout was only 53 percent of registered voters. Despite any modest effect that it may have had on turnout, reluctance about extending residential voting dissipated, as its implementation seemed to have no effect on the electoral fortunes of the political parties.[29]

Thus the greatest resistance to making polling places more accessible came from the right, although at times there seems to have been reluctance on the left as well. The contrast with Guatemala, where there was no partisan opposition to decentralizing voting sites, can be understood as a consequence of differences in the two countries' party systems. In contrast to Guatemala's personalist and ephemeral parties, El Salvador's major parties are highly institutionalized, and levels of party identification are higher.[30] These parties have a core vote (*voto duro*), and residential voting presented the prospect of drawing new voters into the electorate that were not part of the parties' core base.[31] While the right, which was already in power, had more to fear from unpredictable new voters entering the electorate, the left also couldn't be certain that it would benefit from higher turnout. These partisan calculations were crucial in postponing residential voting and determining the nature of its implementation.

EMB structure: the Supreme Electoral Tribunal

While partisan interests and the specter of election fraud help explain the dynamics of El Salvador's election administration reforms, an understanding of those reforms is incomplete without considering the Supreme Electoral Tribunal. The partisan composition of the TSE, born of the distrust between the main protagonists of the peace accords, is frequently blamed for a number of ills. Critics argue that election officials function more as party representatives than neutral administrators (EUEOM 2009b, 3–5; OAS 2008, 6) and, although many of the decisions taken by the TSE magistrates are unanimous (Interview 59), on at least one crucial issue – residential voting – the positions of TSE magistrates have often coincided with the positions taken by their political parties. In cases such as this, the lack of a non-partisan electoral body that could act as an independent force is a notable contrast to Guatemala, where the electoral tribunal has been an important agent in prompting electoral law reforms. In El Salvador, the TSE lacks the authority to directly introduce legislation in the assembly (Artiga-González 2008a, 558) and, although it submits proposals to the assembly's electoral committee, there is little institutionalized collaboration between the TSE and the committee (Interviews 57, 59) – perhaps because the largest parties prefer to deal with the TSE through their magistrates.

The composition of the TSE not only hampers its ability to be an independent advocate for reform, it has also generated distrust over the implementation of reforms like residential voting. While at least some parties were concerned about the electoral consequences of residential voting in general, parties have also been preoccupied with the potential for partisan implementation – namely, that decisions about where to place voting centers would be based on the support that parties enjoy in a particular locale, rather than on objective criteria. These concerns were evident in the preoccupation over which party controls the TSE divisions responsible for putting residential voting into practice (Interview 60). These concerns, which contributed to the long delay in making polling places more accessible to voters, would likely have been less prevalent if the electoral body were non-partisan.

The partisan composition of the TSE also has implications for its technical capacity. At the top level, the magistrates named by political parties are not required to be specialists in electoral matters (Artiga-González 2008a, 558, note 33), while the directors and staff of the operational divisions are partisan appointees who may or may not be qualified. This certainly played a role in the voter registration problems in years past and has contributed to the slow progress in implementing residential voting – though, in this case, technical capacity was secondary to partisan motivations. At lower levels, observers have repeatedly documented the poor training of poll workers, who are named by political parties and are not always qualified. Many do not receive training from the TSE but instead are trained by political parties or not at all (CIS 2004; Colindres 1997, 87; Consorcio 2000, 20; OAS 2009a, 24). According to the TSE, for instance, only half of poll workers attended the TSE's training sessions prior to the 1999 elections (TSE-ES 1999, 15). Additionally, the sale of poll-worker credentials between parties is thought to be common (CIS 2009, 31), with obvious consequences for the capacity and suitability of some people working the voting booths. Aside from the myriad problems that poor training can cause with vote counting, preventing voter fraud, and the handling of election materials, it can also make voting more difficult if poll workers are not trained to direct voters to the appropriate voting table, open polling tables late due to confusion over procedures, or lack a clear understanding of the conditions under which a prospective voter can be turned away.

The TSE has improved its technical capacity over the years and has been proactive in areas such as expanding voter education. It is no longer the "cauldron[] of incompetence" (Montgomery 2000, 142) that it was characterized to be in its first years. But its partisan composition has, over the years, obstructed more inclusive election administration in several ways: by depriving the country of an independent authoritative force for electoral reform, by magnifying partisan uncertainties over residential voting, and by producing a corps of lower-level staff that is not as professional or capable as it might be.

International influences

While partisan interests, concerns about election fraud, and the composition of the Supreme Electoral Tribunal at times worked in favor of restrictive election administration practices, international influences (in the form of international election observers, technical and financial assistance, and other types of democracy promotion) pushed in the direction of greater inclusiveness. El Salvador has seen wide variation in the presence of international election observers. The 1994 elections were heavily observed, with over 2,500 observers including the massive 900-plus member UN mission (IFES 1994, 18; TSE-ES 1994, 31). A large observer presence was not seen again until the 2009 elections that saw the presidential victory of the FMLN. The largest impact of election observation certainly occurred in the 1994 elections, when the UN's observer mission (ONUSAL) exceeded its mandate in the face of massive problems with voter registration: it directly assisted with surveys to identify bottlenecks in the registration process (the results of which prompted additional voter registration efforts by the TSE) and provided direct support in registering voters, with financial support from UNDP and USAID (Baloyra 1998, 19; Manca 1997; Montgomery 1995, 247, 251). Beyond that direct activity, however, "international observation had a limited impact on the way in which Salvadorean electoral officials chose to discharge their duties," according to one analyst closely involved (Montgomery 2000, 142).

Since then, the impacts of election observation on longer term structural reforms have been limited, but not negligible. Observer reports have overwhelmingly endorsed more inclusive election administration measures, including residential voting, simplifying voter registration procedures, and improving voter education efforts (see Appendix). And observer organizations have enjoyed close relations with the TSE and seen their recommendations taken up on the agenda of the Legislative Assembly's electoral reform committee (CIS 2004; Interview 53, 62). The slowness with which reforms such as residential voting have been implemented points to the limited influence of such recommendations, however, and according to an advisor to the electoral committee, the decisions taken by the parties are not strongly affected by observer recommendations (Interview 57). Kelley (2012, 225–26) likewise concludes that the country largely neglected observer recommendations as the international community focused on consolidating the peace process and did not pressure particularly hard for electoral improvements. But the intermittent pressure that observers have applied, along with consistent pressure from domestic civil society groups, have at least made it more difficult for political parties to indefinitely delay reforms that are seen as indispensable for a modern democracy.

This form of international influence – living up to international standards of election administration – is worth noting. Studies of residential voting, TSE publications, and media reports frequently made reference to the fact that El Salvador was the only country in the region without residential voting, and there was a clear sense of being behind other countries in the modernization of election administration as a result (FUSADES 2011, 1; Martel 2010, 5, 22; TSE-ES n.d.[c]; UN 2009, 8, note 12). Some TSE magistrates, in advocating a more rapid extension of residential voting, pointed out in the media that countries less developed than El Salvador had residential voting (EDH 2007g; 2008c; 2009a; 2009b). It's not clear that this gap between domestic practice and international standards exercised much influence in prompting residential voting or other reforms, but the fact that it was invoked in debates points to a potential influence on election administration practices.

Aside from election observation, El Salvador has also received significant international financial and technical support for election administration. Funds totaling $20 million came from a variety of donors to support all aspects of the 1994 electoral process (Baloyra 1998, 19; TSE-ES 1994, 23–24). After 1994, international financial support was especially aimed at supporting the introduction of the new ID card and registry, audits of the electoral registry performed by the OAS, and technical assistance on residential voting provided by Panama's electoral tribunal and the UN (TSE-ES 2004, 73; 2006, 14; 2009, 9; UN 2009). Especially in the case of residential voting, El Salvador has looked to the experiences of other countries, such as Panama and Costa Rica, for models (EDH 2007a; 2007b). Implementation of residential voting was also supported financially by the European Union, which provided over a million dollars for its extension in 2014 (TSE-ES 2014b).

While international funding has been important, even more critical has been technical assistance in implementing reforms. Such assistance has been critical in putting residential voting into practice (Interview 55). But, as in Guatemala and Nicaragua, this assistance has been a necessary but insufficient condition for enacting reforms to facilitate voter participation. Domestic politics have largely determined the nature and pace of reforms, while international technical assistance has helped put them into practice.

Civil society

As in Guatemala and Nicaragua, civil society has had little impact on the shape of election administration in El Salvador. Election-related civil society groups have included individual organizations, as well as umbrella groups uniting diverse organizations. In the 1990s, the Consortium of Civic Education NGOs of El Salvador predominated in monitoring elections and advocating reforms. Subsequently, individual organizations such as the Independent Movement for Electoral Reform (MIRE) and umbrella groups such as the Coalition for Political and Electoral Reform (CREE) emerged, while Central American University's Institute of Public Opinion (IUDOP) has undertaken election monitoring. Civil society groups frequently criticized restrictive election administration features and advocated for reforms such as residential voting (e.g., Consorcio 2000, 2001; ISD 2011b; Martel 2010). For instance, in 2010 three non-governmental groups endorsed TSE president Eugenio Chicas' plan to extend residential voting to the entire country for the 2012 elections and proposed making voter registration procedures simpler for citizens (such as simplifying forms and increasing the number of locations where DUIs are distributed) (Martel 2010, 30–31, 36–37).

As was the case in Guatemala's reform process, Salvadoran civic groups are formally consulted on electoral issues. Civic groups submit proposals to the Legislative Assembly and are often granted an audience in its electoral reform committee; they generally enjoy good relations with the TSE (Interviews 50, 52, 55, 57). Yet, proposals emanating from civil society are rarely taken into consideration when electoral reforms are drafted, according to an advisor to the electoral reform committee and others (Interviews 57, 60; Martel 2010, 16, 20). The civil society groups working on electoral issues in El Salvador are small and have little capacity to mobilize large numbers of people and, as a result, their impact has been limited (Interview 60). Despite the advocacy efforts of civil society groups, election administration in El Salvador, as elsewhere, has been an elite affair played primarily by the major political parties and their representatives in the electoral management body.

Conclusion

El Salvador's election administration slowly shifted from large-scale barriers to voting to more inclusive practices. A number of factors contributed both to the establishment of the country's election administration practices and to their evolution over time.

El Salvador's restrictive administrative measures were adopted in the country's pre-democratic period in response to the security conditions during the country's civil war and the desire to eradicate the election fraud that had been common in prior elections. These restrictions continued long after these initial conditions had changed, due to both institutional inertia and partisan calculations about the likely effects of expanding the electorate. Ultimately, intermittent pressure from the left, reinforced by pressure from domestic civil society and (more importantly) international election observers and experts, led to halting reforms. However, calculations of partisan interests, the composition of the country's electoral management body, and lingering concerns about voter registration fraud dictated the sequence and shape of reform.

Notes

1 With its budget set by the TSE and with the major parties already controlling the TSE, the JVE's influence has been limited.

2 Decreto 170, January 25, 1989, amending Art. 40 of the 1988 Electoral Code. ARENA wanted a 45-day cutoff, but agreed to a shorter 30-day cutoff for the 1989

elections at the behest of the Christian Democrat party (IHRLG 1989, 60–61). Another reform in 1990 allowed *carnets* to be delivered up to eight days before the election (WOLA 1991, 7).

3 If the central archives did not have a copy of an applicant's birth certificate on file, the applicant would need to provide a copy or request the mayoral office of the municipality in which they were born to send a copy to the TSE. This was made difficult by some mayors who failed to deliver copies of birth certificates to the TSE or charged exorbitant fees (IFES 1994, 12; Lehoucq 1995, 181; Montgomery 2000, 149; Spence and Vickers 1994, 15).

4 The TSE estimated that the effective voter register (excluding deceased, emigrants, and duplicates) was 2.2 million voters, and the UN observer mission estimated that 300–400,000 people on the voter register were deceased (IFES 1994, 13).

5 The electoral law was revised to allow the distribution of voter ID cards between the first and second rounds of voting for the presidential election, resulting in 10,000 new additions for voters whose birth certificates had been found (IFES 1994, 3, 13).

6 An additional 35 voting centers were added for the second round of presidential voting (IFES 1994, 3).

7 The centralization of voting sites was not specified in the electoral code but rather a decision of the CCE and later the TSE, thus leaving no legislative record. However, several political actors of different partisan persuasions agreed that polling centralization was due to security concerns (Interviews 51, 54, 63).

8 The TSE reported that 325,119 registrants had not been delivered their voter cards, but the number of these that had emigrated or were deceased is unknown (TSE-ES 1997, 12). By the 2000 elections, the number dropped to 234,003 (Consorcio 2000, 14, note 4), and by 2003 to 50,000 (CIS 2003).

9 These efforts seemed to have declined in the three subsequent elections, however, as TSE post-election reports of those elections make no mention of such registration activities.

10 See TSE-ES 1997, 24, 29; TSE-ES 2000, 47; TSE-ES 2004, 45–51; and TSE-ES 2006, 80.

11 On overcrowded voting centers, see CIS 2000, 2003, 2004; OAS 2008, 10; OAS 2009b, 21, 23. On polling places opening late, see CIS 2003; CIS 2006, 26; CIS 2009, 30; EUEOM 2009b, 11; OAS 2008, 6; OAS 2009b, 21.

12 The Electoral Code has seen some 200 amendments since 1994, most of which have been minor changes made in pre-election periods. For analysis of the reforms until 2007, see Artiga-González 2008b.

13 DUIs were valid for five years and are now valid for eight.

14 Recognizing that many young Salvadorans turning 18 by election day had not applied for their DUI in part due to lack of a birth certificate, the Legislative Assembly in 2011 passed a temporary measure waiving the requirement for a birth certificate for first-time registrations if a record of the birth certificate was on file with the RNPN (Decreto 826).

15 This compares to a high estimate of voter registration coverage of 78.6 percent in 1990 (UN 2009, 7).

16 The electoral registry for the 2004 elections included 3.31 million people, down from 3.53 million previously (Artiga-González 2008b, 21, note 16), reflecting not a less inclusive registry but a less bloated one. But, by 2009, it was estimated that the electoral registry of 4.2 million exceeded the number of voting age Salvadorans residing in the country by 500–750,000 (EUEOM 2009b, 6; OAS 2009a, 7, 31).

17 The closing date had been 120 days and was reduced to 90 days with the introduction of the DUI and new electoral registry. In 2005, the closing date was increased to 100 days at the prompting of the TSE, for the purpose of allowing more time for voters to consult the provisional voter rolls and correct any errors (El Diario de Hoy 2005 [hereafter EDH]; TSE-ES 2006, 16).

18 Decreto 502 (December 6, 2007), amending Article 30 of the Electoral Code. Prior to this reform, the electoral code made no distinction between the deadline date for changes of residence and the deadline for new voter registration applications.
19 The motivations for the reform expressed in the bill itself included "eliminat[ing] any legal loophole that results in improper practices such as the transfer of voters…" (Decreto 502).
20 A 4–6 year prison term was specified for those who falsely change their residence on their registration, and 7–10 years for public officials involved in the practice (TSE-ES 2009, 11).
21 A report on the bill's vote indicates that the parties on the right voted in favor, while parties on the left (presumably the FMLN and CD) voted against (Observatorio Legislativo de FUSADES 2007, 9–10).
22 The terminology used in each country can cause confusion, as in El Salvador the centralization of, and alphabetical assignment of voters to, voting centers is referred to as *voto domiciliario* (domicile voting), in the sense that "domicile" signifies one's municipality and not one's specific address (see UN 2009, 12). The same term in Guatemala generally signifies the assignment of voters to the nearest voting center, and in Nicaragua it signifies both decentralization and voter assignment based on residence.
23 Data on assembly votes prior to 2007 come from a public information request made by the author to the Legislative Assembly. Only the number of votes in favor of bills is available; the number of votes against or abstentions is not available, nor are the names or party affiliations of those voting in favor.
24 While cases of voter impersonation and the use of fake ID cards have been reported by observers, such irregularities are thought to be isolated (NDI 2009, 4; OAS 2009a, 21).
25 Some people suggest that the "traslados" problem is relatively isolated (Interviews 54, 56, 58), and certainly detection and prosecution of the problem is rare (UN 2009, 12). The introduction of the DUI, the costs of changing one's residence in the registry, and an early closing date for residence changes have no doubt made this form of manipulation difficult. However, other sources suggest the practice of *traslados* is routine (Arauz 2006), and in 2012 elections in three municipalities were cancelled due to concerns about a large number of *traslados* (Misión de Expertos Electorales de la Unión Europea 2012, 17).
26 The TSE in fact returned excess funds after the elections (Interview 60; see also EDH 2003c; 2009a).
27 I was unable to find corroborating evidence on this point.
28 In 2009, only 57.6 percent of ARENA sympathizers lived in urban areas, compared to 72.8 percent of FMLN sympathizers (Nevitte 2009, 118).
29 For a more in-depth analysis of residential voting's electoral impact, see FUSADES 2012.
30 For 3 years for which data are available (2006, 2008, and 2010), party identification levels were 31 percent, 41 percent, and 34 percent, respectively (LAPOP n.d.).
31 For a similar analysis, see El Diario de Hoy 2007i.

References

Anderson, Thomas P. 1988. *Politics in Central America: Guatemala, El Salvador, Honduras, and Nicaragua*. Westport, CT: Praeger Publishers.

Arauz, Sergio. 2006. "El Arte de Trucar el Padrón." *El Faro*, February 20. http://archivo.elfaro.net/secciones/noticias/20060220/noticias1_20060220.asp.

Artiga-González, Álvaro. 2004. *Elitismo Competitivo: Dos Décadas de Elecciones en El Salvador*. San Salvador: UCA Editores.

Artiga-González, Álvaro. 2008a. "Reforma Política en El Salvador." In *Reforma Política y Electoral en América Latina, 1978–2007*, Daniel Zovatto, and J. Jesús Orozco Henríquez, eds. International Institute for Democracy and Electoral Assistance/Universidad Nacional Autónoma de México.

Artiga-González, Álvaro. 2008b. *Las Reformas a la Legislación Electoral Salvadoreña (1993–2007)*. San Salvador: FundaUngo.

Baloyra, Enrique A. 1982. *El Salvador in Transition*. Chapel Hill and London: University of North Carolina Press.

Baloyra, Enrique A. 1993. "The Salvadoran Elections of 1982–1991." *Studies in Comparative International Development* 28 (3): 3–30.

Baloyra, Enrique A. 1995. "Elections, Civil War, and Transition in El Salvador, 1982–1994: A Preliminary Evaluation." In *Elections and Democracy in Central America, Revisited*, Mitchell A. Seligson, and John A. Booth, eds. Chapel Hill and London: University of North Carolina Press.

Baloyra, Enrique A. 1998. "El Salvador: From Reactionary Despotism to *Partidocracia*." In *Postconflict Elections, Democratization, and International Assistance*, Krishna Kumar, ed. Boulder, CO: Lynne Rienner.

CIDAI (Centro de Información, Documentación y Apoyo a la Investigación). 1984. "Destapando la 'Caja Negra': Condicionamientos Técnicos del Proceso Electoral 1984." *Estudios Centroamericanos* 39 (426–27): 197–218.

CIS (Centro de Intercambio y Solidaridad). 2000. Final Report, Elections 2000, El Salvador, Mission of Electoral Observers.

CIS. 2003. Final Report – Legislative and Municipal Election, El Salvador, International Observer Mission.

CIS. 2004. Final Report 2004, Presidential Election, El Salvador, International Observer Mission.

CIS. 2006. 7a Misión Internacional de Observadores Electorales, Elecciones Legislativas y Municipales, El Salvador, Marzo de 2006, Informe Final. San Salvador.

CIS. 2009. Informe Final: Octava Misión de Observadores Electorales. San Salvador: CIS.

Colindres, Eduardo. 1997. *El Sube y Baja de los Partidos Políticos: Resultados y Consecuencias de las Elecciones de 1997 en El Salvador*. San Salvador: Konrad Adenauer Stiftung and FUCAD.

Consorcio de ONG's de Educación Cívica de El Salvador. 2000. Diagnóstico Sistema Electoral Salvadoreño 2000. San Salvador.

Consorcio de ONG's de Educación Cívica de El Salvador. 2001. Plataforma Ciudadana para la Reforma Electoral en El Salvador. San Salvador.

Córdova Macías, Ricardo. 1996. "El Salvador: Transition from Civil War." In *Constructing Democratic Governance: Mexico, Central America, and the Caribbean in the 1990s*, Jorge I. Domínguez, and Abraham F. Lownethal, eds. Baltimore and London: The Johns Hopkins University Press.

Cuéllar, Benjamín. 2009. "Derechos Humanos, Pactos y Elecciones: Análisis Jurídico-Histórico." *Estudios Centroamericanos* 62 (709–10): 971–85.

Dalton, Juan José. 2010. "Eugenio Chicas: Es un Falso Mito que el Voto Residencial Beneficie a un Solo Partido." *Contrapunto*, October 21.

Decreto 133. September 18, 2003. Disposiciones Especiales para la Emisión del Voto Residencial.

Decreto 170. January 25, 1989.

Decreto 228. December 11, 2003.

Decreto 293. February 12, 2001. Disposiciones Especiales para la Emisión del Voto Residencial.
Decreto 314. March 24, 2010. Reformas a la Ley Especial Reguladora de la Emisión del Documento Único de Identidad.
Decreto 502. December 6, 2007. Disposición Transitoria, que se Refiere a la Suspención de la Modificación de Residencia de Ciudadanos que Establece el Art. 30, para los Eventos Electorales del Año 2009, se Realizará el uno de Marzo del Año 2008.
Decreto 552. December 21, 1995. Ley Orgánica del Registro Nacional de las Personas Naturales.
Decreto 581. October 18, 2001. Ley Especial Reguladora de la Emisión del Documento Único de Identidad.
Decreto 755. December 15, 1993.
Decreto 826. September 1, 2011.
Decreto 834. May 9, 2002.
Decreto 842. October 13, 2005.
Decreto 853. October 17, 1996.
El Diario de Hoy. 2001. "Documento Único de Identidad Será Gratuito." February 2.
El Diario de Hoy. 2003a. "En Duda Voto Residencial." September 17.
El Diario de Hoy. 2003b. "Contradicción en el TSE." September 19.
El Diario de Hoy. 2003c. "Desecharon el Voto Residencial." September 19.
El Diario de Hoy. 2003d. "Candidato de ARENA Da Espaldarazo a Derogación." September 19.
El Diario de Hoy. 2003e. "Facilitarán el DUI para Nuevos Votantes." September 20.
El Diario de Hoy. 2005. "Centralizan Poder en TSE." October 14.
El Diario de Hoy. 2007a. "México y Panamá Son los Modelos de Ley Electoral." January 22.
El Diario de Hoy. 2007b. "En Busca de Acuerdo por Voto Residencial." March 9.
El Diario de Hoy. 2007c. "Pleito en TSE por el Voto Residencial." April 24.
El Diario de Hoy. 2007d. "Aval a Voto Residencial con Posturas Divididas." May 18.
El Diario de Hoy. 2007e. "Diferencias Imperan en la Mesa Electoral." May 20.
El Diario de Hoy. 2007f. "Sugieren Ampliar Voto Residencial Hasta 2010." June 8.
El Diario de Hoy. 2007g. "Discrepancia en TSE por voto residencial." June 9.
El Diario de Hoy. 2007h. "Saca: ARENA Siempre Ha Apoyado el Voto Residencial." June 13.
El Diario de Hoy. 2007i. "Divergencias por Aplicación del Voto Residencial." June 15.
El Diario de Hoy. 2007j. "FMLN Impulsará Decreto por Voto Residencial." June 16.
El Diario de Hoy. 2007k. "Subcomisión Pide Acercar Más Urnas." July 25.
El Diario de Hoy. 2007l. "Presionan por Voto Residencial." September 5.
El Diario de Hoy. 2007m. "Piden Poner Candado a Migración de Votantes." October 16.
El Diario de Hoy. 2008a. "Pleito en la Asamblea por una Reforma al Código Electoral." February 28.
El Diario de Hoy. 2008b. "En Cabañas Deben Viajar Casi 70 km para Votar." June 29.
El Diario de Hoy. 2008c. " 'Voto Residencial Generaría Confianza.' " October 9.
El Diario de Hoy. 2009a. "Un Largo Camino, Pero con Pocos Avances." August 29.
El Diario de Hoy. 2009b. "Implementar el Voto Residencial Costaría $2 Millones, Según TSE." October 27.
El Diario de Hoy. 2009c. "Sin Avance por el Voto Residencial." November 20.
El Diario de Hoy. 2009d. "Superan el Escollo para Acercar Urnas." December 10.

El Diario de Hoy. 2009e. "Cartografía de Centros de Votación Continúa en los Planes del TSE." December 25.

El Diario de Hoy. 2010. "TSE Define Mapa para Voto Residencial." September 29.

El Diario de Hoy. 2011. "Piden a TSE Hacer Campaña para los Nuevos Votantes." January 20.

El Diario de Hoy. 2012. "Los Centros de Votación, Más Cerca de su Casa." March 10.

Electoral Code of El Salvador. 1988. Decreto 863. January 8.

Electoral Code of El Salvador. 1992. Decreto 417. December 14.

EUEOM (European Union Election Observation Mission, El Salvador 2009). 2009a. Final Report on the General Elections.

EUEOM. 2009b. "Preliminary Statement." Legislative, Municipal, and PARLACEN Elections. January 20.

EUEOM. 2009c. "Preliminary Statement." Presidential Elections. March 17.

Freedom House. 1989. Mission to El Salvador. Freedom House Special Report. May 1. New York: Freedom House.

FUSADES (Fundación Salvadoreña para el Desarrollo Económico y Social). 2011. "Desafíos del Voto Residencial en El Salvador: Acercamiento de Urnas al Domicilio o Voto Residencial?" Boletín No. 8 (November/December).

FUSADES. 2012. "Impacto de la Reforma Electoral de 2012: El Voto por Persona y el Voto Residencial."

García, José Z. 1989. "El Salvador: Recent Elections in Historical Perspective." In *Elections and Democracy in Central America,* John A. Booth, and Mitchell A. Seligson, eds. Chapel Hill and London: University of North Carolina Press.

Holiday, David. 2010. "El Salvador." Freedom House, Countries at the Crossroads.

IFES (International Foundation for Electoral Systems). 1994. El Salvador Election Observation: March 20, 1994 – April 24, 1994. Washington DC: International Foundation for Electoral Systems.

IFES. 1997. Encuentro Salvadoreño Post-Electoral. San Salvador: IFES.

IHRLG (International Human Rights Law Group). 1989. Report on the 1989 Salvadoran Electoral Process. Washington, DC: International Human Rights Law Group.

ISD. 2009. "La Larga Historia del Voto Residencial." http://isd.org.sv/isddocs/documentos-y-articulos-electorales/Lalargahistoriadelvotoresidencial.pdf.

ISD. 2011a. Primer Monitoreo Sobre Voto Residencial 2012. San Salvador.

ISD. 2011b. "Agenda Ciudadana Nacional para la Reforma Democrática del Sistema Electoral 2011–2016." San Salvador: ISD.

JVE (Junta de Vigilancia Electoral). 2009. *Informe Elecciones 2009*. San Salvador.

Kelley, Judith G. 2012. *Monitoring Democracy: When International Election Observation Works, and Why It Often Fails*. Princeton: Princeton University Press.

LAPOP (Latin American Public Opinion Project). n.d. Americas Barometer Online Data Analysis. http://lapop.ccp.ucr.ac.cr/Lapop_English.html.

Lehoucq, Fabrice Edouard. 1995. "The Election of 1994 in El Salvador." *Electoral Studies* 14 (2): 179–83.

Manca, Francesco. 1997. "The UN and the Observation of the Electoral Process in El Salvador." Paper presented at the Electoral Observation and Democratic Transition in Latin America conference, Center for US-Mexican Studies at the University of California, San Diego, January 24–25. www.studiperlapace.it/documentazione/manca.html.

Martel, Juan José. 2010. *Fundamentos para la Modernización del Sistema Político Electoral Salvadoreño: Una Propuesta desde la Sociedad Civil*. San Salvador: Friedrich Ebert Stiftung.

Mena, José Sergio, and Jorge Ernesto Rodríguez. 2005. "Registro Civil y Documento de Identidad Ciudadana: La Experiencia de El Salvador." In *Encuentro Internacional: La Gestión de Registro Civil y la Emisión de Documentos de Identidad Ciudadana en Centro América*, Tribunal Supremo Electoral (Guatemala). Guatemala: Organization of American States.

Misión de Expertos Electorales de la Unión Europea en El Salvador. 2012. Elecciones Legislativas y Municipales, 11 de Marzo 2012.

Montgomery, Tommie Sue. 1995. *Revolution in El Salvador: From Civil Strife to Civil Peace*. Boulder: Westview Press.

Montgomery, Tommie Sue. 1998. "International Missions, Observing Elections, and the Democratic Transition in El Salvador." In *Electoral Observation and Democratic Transitions in Latin America*, Kevin Middlebrook, ed. Center for U.S.-Mexican Studies, University of California, San Diego.

Montgomery, Tommie Sue. 2000. "The Good, the Bad, and the Ugly: Observing Elections in El Salvador." In *Peacemaking and Democratization in the Western Hemisphere*, Tommie Sue Montgomery, ed. Miami: North-South Center Press.

NDI (National Democratic Institute for International Affairs). 1989. The 1989 Salvadoran Election: Challenges and Opportunities. A Pre-Election Survey Report, February 18–23, 1989. National Democratic Institute for International Affairs.

NDI. 2009. "El Salvador Election Bulletin." February 19. www.ndi.org/files/NDI%20El%20Salvador%20Election%20Bulletin-2009Feb.pdf.

Nevitte, Neil. 2009. El Salvador 2009 Benchmark Democracy Survey: Initial Findings. National Democratic Institute for International Affairs.

OAS (Organization of American States). 2008. Informe de la Misión de Observación Electoral sobre las Elecciones Legislativas, Municipales y de Parlamento Centroamericano de la República de El Salvador, 12 de Marzo de 2006.

OAS. 2009a. Informe de la Misión de Observación Electoral, Elección de Presidente y Vicepresidente del 15 de Marzo de 2009 en la República de El Salvador.

OAS. 2009b. Informe de la Misión de Observación Electoral, Elecciones de Diputados al Parlamento Centroamericano, Asamblea Legislativa y Consejos Municipales del 18 de Enero de 2009 en la República de El Salvador.

Observatorio Legislativo de FUSADES. 2007. Monitoreo Semanal Del 03 al 07 de Diciembre 2007. www.observatoriolegislativo.org.sv/.

Peña, Ramiro. 2003. "Informe y Diagnóstico sobre Abstencionismo y Participación: El Caso de El Salvador." XVII Conferencia Protocolo de Tikal, San José, Costa Rica, September 25–26. Informe Nacional.

La Prensa Gráfica. 2009a. "A Discusión Subsidio de Gratuidad de DUI." August 18.

La Prensa Gráfica. 2009b. "ONU Sugiere que Electores Escojan Centro de Votación." August 28.

La Prensa Gráfica. 2009c. "Voto Residencial no es Prioridad para Funes." December 23.

Ramos, Carlos G. 1997. "A Trial by Fire with Good Results." *Envío* 190 (May). www.envio.org.ni/articulo/2012.

Ratliff, William E., and William Perry. 1984. *El Salvador Election Project: Background and Outlook Report*. Washington, DC: Center for Strategic & International Studies.

RNPN (Registro Nacional de las Personas Naturales). 2011. "Tipos de Trámites a Realizarse." www.rnpn.gob.sv/.

Spence, Jack, and George Vickers. 1994. Toward a Level Playing Field? A Report on the Post-War Salvadoran Peace Process. Cambridge, MA: Hemisphere Initiatives.

Spence, Jack, Mike Lanchin, and Geoff Thale. 2001. *From Elections to Earthquakes: Reform and Participation in Post-War El Salvador*. Cambridge, MA: Hemisphere Initiatives.

Spence, Jack, David R. Dye, Mike Lanchin, and Geoff Thale, with George Vickers. 1997. *Chapúltepec Five Years Later*. Hemisphere Initiatives.

Stahler-Sholk, Richard. 1994. "El Salvador's Negotiated Transition: From Low-Intensity Conflict to Low-Intensity Democracy." *Journal of Interamerican Studies and World Affairs* 36 (4): 1–59.

TSE-ES (Tribunal Supremo Electoral – El Salvador). 1994. *Memoria Anual de Labores Correspondiente a 1994 y Memoria de Labores de las Elecciones de 1994*. San Salvador.

TSE-ES. 1997. *Memoria Especial: Elecciones 97*.

TSE-ES. 1999. *Memoria Especial: Eleccion 99*.

TSE-ES. 2000. *Memoria Especial: Elecciones 2000*. San Salvador.

TSE-ES. 2003. *Memoria Especial: Elecciones 2003, 16 de Marzo*. San Salvador.

TSE-ES. 2004. *Memoria Especial: Eleccion Presidencial 2004*. San Salvador.

TSE-ES. 2006. *Memoria Especial Elecciones 2006*.

TSE-ES. 2009. *Memoria Especial Elecciones 2009*. San Salvador.

TSE-ES. 2014a. Revista Digital: Datos Estatísticos. www.tse.gob.sv/revistadigital/index.php/institucion-3/datos-estadisticos.

TSE-ES. 2014b. Revista Digital: El Voto Residencial en Todo el País. www.tse.gob.sv/revistadigital/index.php/institucion-3/nuevo-modelo-de-votacion.

TSE-ES. n.d.[a]. "Antecedentes del Voto Residencial en El Salvador." www.tse.gob.sv/documentos/documentosvarios/antecedentesdelvotoresidencial.pdf.

TSE-ES. n.d.[b]. "El Voto Residencial." www.tse.gob.sv/documentos/documentosvarios/conceptosvotoresidencial.pdf.

TSE-ES. n.d.[c]. "Impactos del Voto Residencial." www.tse.gob.sv/documentos/documentosvarios/impactosdelvotoresidencial.pdf.

Ulloa, Felix, Carlos Guillermo Ramos, and José Miguel Cruz. 1997. *El Salvador: Elecciones 1997*. San Salvador: Fundación Dr. Guillermo Manuel Ungo.

Ulloa, Felix, Alberto Arene, Beatriz Barraz Diaz, and Álvaro Artiga Gonzalez. 2000. Country Report – República de El Salvador. International Institute for Democracy and Electoral Assistance.

UN (United Nations). 1992. Report of the Secretary-General on the United Nations Observer Mission in El Salvador, S/24833, November 23.

UN. 1993. Report of the Secretary-General on the United Nations Observer Mission in El Salvador, S/26606, October 20.

UN. 1997. Informe Preliminar de las Misión de las Naciones Unidas en Materia Electoral, 1997, El Salvador. November 17. TSE (Guatemala) Centro de Documentación doc. #RV648.

UN (United Nations Misión de Evaluación de Necesidades). 2009. Implementación del Voto Residencial en El Salvador.

Webre, Stephen. 1979. *José Napoleón Duarte and the Christian Democratic Party in Salvadoran Politics, 1960–1972*. Baton Rouge and London: Louisiana State University Press.

WOLA (Washington Office on Latin America). 1991. A Step toward Peace? The March 1991 Elections in El Salvador. Washington, DC: Washington Office on Latin America.

9 Conclusion

Countries holding competitive elections vary significantly in the extent to which the administrative conduct of elections – the voter registration process, the location of polling places, the manner in which voters cast ballots, and so on – facilitates or impedes voter participation. Some countries strive to bring the ballot box to the people, minimizing the procedural hurdles that citizens confront in exercising their right to vote. In other countries, the administrative barriers to participation can be so onerous as to call into question the legitimacy of the election results.

This book has put forward the concept of election administration inclusiveness to encapsulate the various features of electoral administration that bear on voter access to the ballot. It has also described the many facets of election administration that at various times have made voting easier or more difficult in Central American countries since their transitions to electoral democracy and investigated the reasons why those election administration practices were put in place. This chapter summarizes the book's main arguments, beginning with a brief synopsis of the three primary cases, followed by discussion of the causal factors outlined in Chapter 2. The chapter concludes with a discussion of avenues for future research that are suggested by my findings.

Case summaries

Guatemala

Chapter 4 documented and explained the origins of Guatemala's highly restrictive election administration practices, which posed significant obstacles to participation for many voters, particularly women and indigenous citizens in rural areas. In particular, onerous voter registration procedures and the strict prohibition against locating polling stations outside of municipal centers required many voters to negotiate significant procedural and logistical obstacles to voting. These procedural barriers were the consequence of efforts to overcome the country's history of election fraud in the 1970s and early 1980s. In order to inoculate the electoral system against several types of fraud, the act of voting was, in many ways, made more difficult. To deter ballot stuffing and manipulation of rural voters by landlords or political bosses, polling places were limited to municipal centers where election officials and party poll watchers could exercise greater oversight. To protect against voter registration fraud, a system of registry checks was put in place that resulted in a complex process of voter registration. And in the focus on rooting out election fraud, other tasks such as informing voters of procedural requisites through voter education campaigns received low priority from election officials. While other factors also influenced election administration, such as financial constraints, the evidence suggests that it was concerns about election fraud – and not partisan interests in excluding certain segments of voters – that had the biggest impact on electoral procedures.

Chapter 5 examined the process of electoral reform in Guatemala, which resulted in the elimination or reduction of several procedural barriers to participation that had been put in place in the early years of electoral democracy. These reforms included the decentralization of polling stations to facilitate the vote of rural citizens and significant improvements in the provision of voter education. I argued that a confluence of factors came together to produce these reforms. One permissive condition was the nature of the party system, consisting of weakly institutionalized personalist parties that lacked clearly identifiable constituencies which competing parties might hope to exclude from the electorate. As a result, although leftist guerrillas pushed for inclusive election administration reforms to be included in the country's peace agreements, political parties across the spectrum supported administrative reforms that were expected to have little effect on the parties' electoral competitiveness, while (in the case of polling-place decentralization) reducing their costs of voter mobilization.

While partisan interests did not prevent electoral reform, the non-partisan Supreme Electoral Tribunal actively sought to boost the legitimacy of the electoral regime by cautiously increasing voter access, while maintaining the integrity of the election process that it had safeguarded since the mid-1980s. As time went on, confidence in the TSE and in the electoral process grew, and concerns about election fraud abated somewhat, making polling decentralization possible. International actors also played a crucial role in providing the financing and technical expertise to implement electoral reform, although it was domestic actors who set the reform agenda.

While several factors facilitated reform, some events impeded the trend toward greater inclusiveness. This was the case when Congress, motivated by the desire to control patronage resources and wary of strengthening the TSE, created a new civil registry agency rather than giving authority over the civil registry to the electoral tribunal. This decision inadvertently derailed the possibility for automatic voter registration. Thus, while Guatemala's election administration became significantly more inclusive from the mid-1990s onward, some attempts at increasing voter access were frustrated.

Nicaragua

Chapter 6 addressed the puzzle of why Nicaragua exceeded its Central American neighbors in inclusiveness, despite having a partisan electoral management body and facing severe economic crisis. Nicaragua's election administration practices from the mid-1980s to 2000 included voter registration processes that were relatively easy to negotiate (with significant efforts by the state to register voters and distribute voter ID cards), highly decentralized polling locations that minimized travel to the polls, and significant voter education efforts. These practices were later complemented by other measures not found in neighboring countries, such as accepting ballots from registered voters whose names did not appear on the voter rolls on election day.

Several crucial differences from the other cases help explain this outcome. First, the election fraud that marked the pre-democratic period in Nicaragua was of a different type than that which occurred in Guatemala and El Salvador, which in turn was a product of the different authoritarian regime types across the three countries (personalist in Nicaragua and military in Guatemala, El Salvador, and Honduras). As a result, the overriding preoccupation of those designing the electoral system after the fall of the Somoza regime was not preventing ballot stuffing or double voting but ensuring high voter turnout. The goal of high turnout was driven especially by international political pressures, as the revolutionary regime sought high-turnout elections to appease its European supporters, mollify or fend off hostility from the United States, and consolidate political legitimacy at home. Importantly, the governing FSLN party did not feel threatened by inclusive measures that would facilitate voter turnout, as it was confident it would win fair elections with massive participation. The party could thus afford to facilitate the vote even of rural sectors, where the party's support was weak. Aside from international pressures, the technical and financial assistance offered by international actors was a necessary but not sufficient condition to implement some inclusive election administration measures.

Chapter 7 documented the slow erosion of inclusiveness in Nicaragua's election administration after 2000. This erosion was marked by the politicization of the distribution of ID cards, which are needed to vote, as well as the disappearance of voter education efforts on the part of the electoral management body. I argued that the proximate cause of this change has been the dominance of one political party in the electoral management body. However, the puzzle is that the party in control of the electoral machinery now, the FSLN, is the same party (in name) that created the inclusive system in the 1980s. This raised the question of what has changed to make this party now want to restrict access to the vote. I argued that the explanation lies in the party's perceptions of electoral competitiveness, the nature of partisan identification and party organization, and the lessening of external pressures. I further argued that the FSLN was no longer confident of its ability to win in fair electoral contests, despite arguably being objectively stronger than it was in 1990. Equally important is strong partisan identification and the FSLN's organizational capacity, which allows the party to identify its supporters and thus single them out for ID cards and partisan voter-information campaigns. These features of partisan identification and organization are marked contrasts with the other cases, especially Guatemala. Finally, these domestic factors were not sufficiently counteracted by international pressure, as US interest waned and financial aid from new actors (mainly Venezuela) compensated for the loss of democracy-conditioned aid from US and European donors.

The Nicaragua case shows that the pathologies of partisan election administration can be severe, but they do not result automatically from the partisan composition of the electoral management body. Rather, the case shows that the effects of partisan election administration are mediated by patterns of party identification, by perceptions of electoral competitiveness, and by pressures from foreign powers.

El Salvador

Chapter 8 examined the slow transformation of El Salvador's election administration from large-scale exclusion to more inclusive practices. In the 1980s, election administration practices were put in place that presented severe barriers to voter participation, such as onerous voter registration processes, the centralization of polling locations, and the assignment of voters to municipal polling locations in alphabetical order rather than according to residence. Following the transitional 1994 elections, El Salvador undertook a slow process of electoral reform that instituted automatic voter registration and gradually put in place a system of residential voting, whereby polling places were decentralized and voters were assigned to polling sites based on residence.

El Salvador's restrictive administrative measures were initially adopted in the 1980s in response to the security conditions during the country's civil war and the desire to eradicate the election fraud that had been common in the elections of the 1970s. I argued that these restrictions continued long after these initial conditions had changed, due to both institutional inertia and partisan calculations about the likely effects of expanding the electorate. Ultimately, intermittent pressure from the left, reinforced by persistent pressure from domestic civil society and international election observers and experts, led to halting reforms. However, it was calculations of partisan interests that dictated the sequence and shape of reform, especially in the case of residential voting. While the technical and financial challenges of implementing residential voting were significant, uncertainty about the electoral consequences led the major parties (and, at times, especially the conservative ARENA party) to delay the reform and then carry it out through small pilot programs to gauge its effects. The partisan control of the Supreme Electoral Tribunal also played a part, exacerbating parties' uncertainties over the implementation of residential voting. Only once it appeared to have no impact on election outcomes was residential voting rapidly expanded. In contrast, voter registration reform was less contentious because it was expected to provide greater protection against electoral manipulation without adversely affecting partisan interests. This, in combination with the severity of voter registry problems in the 1980s to mid-1990s, helps explain why El Salvador took on voter registration reform before residential voting, while the reverse was true in Guatemala.

The determinants of election administration inclusiveness

With the preceding case summaries as background, this section offers a more systematic evaluation of the influence of the hypothesized causal factors outlined in Chapter 2: partisan interests, EMB structure, the specter of election fraud, domestic civil society, and international influences.

Partisan interests

Given the potential for election administration rules to shape the electorate and thereby influence election results, the natural place to seek explanations of those rules is in the interests of political parties. Indeed, the case studies revealed such partisan interests at work at certain times. After 2006 in Nicaragua, the governing party manipulated the distribution of ID cards and eliminated voter education in order to depress turnout of opposition supporters. Some evidence suggested that the governing party in El Salvador in earlier years also manipulated voter registration to its benefit.

But when will partisan interests play a predominant role in choosing election administration practices? When should we expect parties to use restrictive measures for their own electoral advantage? One condition suggested by the case studies is the competitiveness of elections. As discussed in Chapter 2, higher levels of competitiveness are more likely to result in electoral manipulation, including the use of administrative measures to make voting more difficult. This is consistent with the evidence from the case studies. In Nicaragua's 1984 and 1990 elections, the governing party's confidence in victory coincided with inclusiveness, while in later years the same party had motives to manipulate electoral rules in part because of the party's perception of competitiveness (including the party's traditionally firm upper limit of support).[1] In El Salvador, elections have been highly competitive between the two largest parties, which have therefore been very attentive to the potential electoral effects of election administration reforms. In contrast, parties in Guatemala tend to be so fluid and short-lived that electoral competition has not resulted in efforts by governing parties to restrict the participation of opposition supporters.

While highly competitive elections pose an electoral threat to incumbent parties, a second factor that allows partisan motives to influence election administration inclusiveness is the knowledge of voter loyalties. Such knowledge enabled the FSLN in Nicaragua to restrict access of voters who are not supporters of the party, while singling out the party faithful for voter credentials and voter information. The lack of knowledge of voters' sympathies facilitated inclusive reform in Guatemala, as parties – and importantly in the Guatemalan context, party leaders – had no reason to expect that greater access (and resultant higher levels of participation) would affect their electoral prospects. El Salvador represents an intermediate case in which parties are more institutionalized, and partisan identification is stronger than in Guatemala, but the major parties do not have the capacity to single out opposition supporters to the extent that the FSLN does in Nicaragua. Thus, while parties did not single out opposition supporters to target for voter suppression, uncertainty about each party's social base and how those bases would be affected by residential voting delayed reform, as the ARENA and FMLN parties were fearful that expansion of the electorate might benefit the other party.

Thus some knowledge of voter preferences – either direct individual-level knowledge or indirect group-level correlations – appears to be a necessary condition for the intentional use of administrative measures to disenfranchise voters (or of voter suppression). This is consistent with other forms of manipulation, such as vote buying and gerrymandering, which require information about voter preferences (Katz 1997, 173; Lehoucq 2007, 39; Schaffer 2008, 121). It also implies that party systems characterized by low levels of party identification and personalist or catch-all parties that are not linked to social cleavages may be more conducive to election administration inclusiveness than institutionalized parties with clear social bases.

A third, and related, consideration regarding partisan motives relates to the social base of individual parties. Because administrative obstacles to voting most affect citizens of lower income and education, it was suggested in Chapter 2 that parties with strong lower-class support would tend to support inclusive rules, while parties with upper-class support might tend to favor administrative restrictions that would burden poorer voters more than well-to-do voters. The evidence from the case studies is only partly consistent with this hypothesis. In Nicaragua, the leftist FSLN put inclusive measures in place in the 1980s but in later years used restrictive practices to exclude opposition supporters. Despite enjoying strong support from the urban poor, the party's individual-level knowledge of voter preferences allows it to target administrative barriers at individual voters, rather than putting in place blunt measures that have disproportionate impacts on entire segments of voters (such as low-income, young, or geographically segregated groups). In El Salvador, the leftist FMLN generally endorsed lowering barriers to voting, while the right-wing ARENA was more reluctant about instituting residential voting. Yet here, class cleavages did not neatly coincide with partisan divisions, as the leftist FMLN had a strong middle-class base, and the right-wing ARENA party enjoyed strong support among low-income rural voters. In Guatemala, the absence of a strong left was associated with restrictive election administration measures, and the leftist URNG pushed for inclusive practices in the country's peace accords. But this push from the left was not decisive, as the URNG and allied parties were too small to push reforms through the legislature. Ultimately, the country's moderate and conservative parties, most of which lack an identifiable or stable social base, also supported inclusive reforms such as polling decentralization and voter registration reform.

EMB structure

Intersecting with partisan interests is the issue of partisan control of the electoral machinery. One hypothesis raised in Chapter 2 was that non-partisan electoral management bodies tend to adopt more inclusive measures than partisan EMBs, and quantitative data presented in Chapter 3 provided modest support to this claim. The case studies showed that the relationship between EMB partisanship and inclusiveness is more complex than this, however. Simple bivariate analysis across the three cases shows that in the early democratic period, non-partisan electoral administration coincided with restrictive practices in Guatemala, while partisan electoral administration coincided with restrictive practices in El Salvador and inclusive practices in Nicaragua. In later periods, Guatemala's non-partisan EMB was associated with more inclusive practices, while the partisan EMBs in the other two cases were again associated with both restrictive (Nicaragua) and more inclusive (El Salvador) practices. Such simple comparisons show that non-partisan election administration is neither a necessary nor sufficient condition for inclusive electoral procedures.

Yet, within-case analysis revealed greater support for the hypothesis linking non-partisan EMBs to inclusiveness than the correlational analysis would suggest. If we consider whether partisanship and inclusiveness were causally linked, we find that in Guatemela during its early democratic period restrictions resulted only partly from the non-partisan EMB's administrative decisions; major restrictions (especially the centralization of polling places) were included in the country's electoral law and therefore outside the authority of the EMB. In El Salvador during its democratic transition, partisanship in the EMB contributed to restrictions, although it was not the only cause. We find the clearest causal link in Nicaragua after 2006, where election administration restrictions resulted directly from the behavior of the single-party-dominated EMB.

The case studies also showed that independent, non-partisan EMBs can promote inclusive rules by playing an active role in electoral reform. A significant finding was that where non-partisan electoral management bodies contribute to inclusiveness, they often do so not just by neutrally applying electoral rules but through lobbying for legal reforms and developing bureaucratic capacity. The central role of an independent EMB in the electoral reform process was most evident in Guatemala, where the Supreme Electoral Tribunal actively shaped the reform agenda and influenced Congress by providing information to legislators and publicly opposing some Congressional decisions. This contrasts with El Salvador, where even though there were no legal impediments to implementing residential voting, the party-based TSE did not push ahead and put the reform into practice, instead deferring to the Legislative Assembly to decide on the pace and scope of implementation. The El Salvador case also suggested that partisanship can inhibit the development of bureaucratic capacity within the EMB. This is consistent with the suggestion of Hartlyn, McCoy, and Mustillo (2008, 90) that EMB partisanship can potentially lead to "lower technical competence" than that found in non-partisan electoral bodies.

The case of Nicaragua also suggests two additional lessons that are relevant for inclusiveness and election administration more broadly. First, it is not only partisanship or non-partisanship of an electoral management body that is important. Rather, the nature of partisanship also matters. Nicaragua's CSE has always been partisan, but the nature of its partisanship changed over time, going from FSLN-led with opposition representation to an explicitly bipartisan structure dominated by cartel parties to once again being FSLN-controlled with no effective opposition counterweight. These shifts in the nature of partisanship have had important implications for inclusiveness and the effective functioning of the electoral body, suggesting the appropriateness of measurements of EMB partisan autonomy that distinguish between single-party and multiparty structures (see Hartlyn, McCoy, and Mustillo 2008).

Second, the experience of Nicaragua shows that the political independence and neutrality of an electoral management body can be undone. This challenges the view that "once such independence has taken root, it tends to replicate itself over time and even survive assaults by authoritarian rulers" (International IDEA 2012, 9). While independence and professionalism may be durable in many cases, the Nicaraguan case shows that even countries that have built a highly professional election administration may be subject to successful efforts to undermine the institutional independence and neutrality of the electoral body (see Middlebrook 1998, 21–22).

Access versus integrity: the specter of election fraud

While a highly competitive election environment presents incumbent parties with one form of electoral threat, another threat is posed by the possibility of election fraud. I have argued that a history of election fraud often leads democratizing countries to adopt strict safeguards against fraud, which in turn impose procedural barriers to voting. In El Salvador and Guatemala, very restrictive practices were adopted at least in part to prevent particular types of electoral manipulation, such as multiple voting, voter impersonation, voter intimidation, and ballot stuffing. Restrictive measures responded to the major episodes of election fraud that occurred in the pre-democratic period, in which apparently victorious opposition parties were cheated of their victory. In short, historical legacies strongly influenced institutional choices during democratic transitions: legislators and election administrators sought first and foremost to curb the ills that had afflicted previous elections, "[i]llustrating the principle that people tend to rate most highly those values in the shortest supply," as Katz (1997, 301) puts it in his discussion of electoral reform in a different context.

Although concerns about fraud led to restrictive election administration practices, the relationship between voter inclusion and preventing election fraud is more nuanced than is often presumed in popular debates over voting procedures. Some restrictive measures were ineffective at preventing fraud, while in some instances making voting easier can make some types of election fraud more difficult. For instance, while it is impossible to know whether the centralization of polling places prevented fraud in Guatemala and El Salvador, subsequent decentralization appears not to have resulted in more fraud in either country. The decentralization of polling places also did not produce ballot stuffing or other irregularities in Nicaragua.[2] In fact, in El Salvador and Nicaragua, small decentralized voting centers have been thought to facilitate oversight by poll workers and voters in identifying outsiders trying to vote in jurisdictions where they do not live. Residential voting thus represents a win–win for election administration, as a measure promoting both voter access and electoral integrity.

Similarly, onerous voter registration processes did not result in reliable voter registries. In both El Salvador and Guatemala, burdensome registration processes did not ensure accurate voter rolls. In large part, this resulted from the failure to incorporate deaths and emigrations into the voter registry, but the difficulty of registration also played a part, as citizens who changed residences did not want to re-register, leading to outdated residence information on the registry. In this case, registration obstacles actually reduced the accuracy of the voter registry. Overcrowded voting centers are another instance that can produce both obstacles to voter participation (long waits and difficulty finding one's polling table) and opportunities for error and fraud (due to poor vigilance by overwhelmed poll workers in checking for ink on voters' fingers, checking ID cards, marking voters off on the voter roll, etc.).

None of this is to say that there are no trade-offs between access and integrity. In the case studies, such a trade-off was clear in the case of residential registration fraud, which appears to be a substantial problem. As noted, making changes of residence on the voter registry difficult can lead to the accumulation of outdated information on the rolls. But where it is easy for voters to change their residence on the voter registry, politicians may organize the fraudulent transfer of voters across jurisdictions for electoral purposes. On this measure, there is a trade-off between access and integrity, although different remedies place different burdens on voters and election administrators. Most onerous for voters are early registration cutoff dates and the requirement to obtain a new ID card listing one's new address; less onerous are requirements to provide some documentation (such as a utility bill) when updating one's residence; least onerous would be to place responsibility for verifying residence changes on the EMB or civil registry, for example through data-sharing arrangements with other state agencies.

The cases also revealed one instance in which concerns about a particular type of electoral manipulation led to an inclusive administrative rule. Article 41 in the Nicaraguan electoral law, which allowed voters whose names did not appear on the voter list to cast a ballot if they presented an ID card showing an address pertaining to the precinct, responded to concerns in the mid-1990s that election officials would manipulate the voter registry by removing names of opposition supporters. Thus, while concerns about ballot stuffing and multiple voting led to restrictive practices, in at least one instance concerns about misconduct by election officials led to an unusually inclusive measure.

In sum, the case studies revealed some trade-offs between voter access and electoral integrity and presented evidence that concerns about particular types of election fraud contributed to the adoption of restrictive administrative practices that made voting more difficult for many citizens. However, the cases also revealed some instances where access and integrity can be pursued simultaneously and one instance where fears of fraud led to greater inclusiveness. These findings have important policy implications for the design of electoral procedures that balance the goals of voter access and election integrity, and more research is needed on the relationship between voter access and electoral integrity (see below).

Civil society

A focus on partisan interests, electoral management bodies, and debates over voter fraud and inclusion centers on elites as the prime movers shaping electoral rules. The case studies investigated whether there might be other societal influences on election administration in the form of organized civil society, particularly domestic election observation groups. The evidence suggested strongly that civil society did not exert strong influence on election administration practices. Instead, the case studies showed that the crafting of election administration rules was an elite affair, driven by politicians and administrators and relatively unconstrained by popular pressures.

In Guatemala, major election administration reforms were already on the agenda by the mid-1990s, when civil society groups first became active in proposing reforms. While endorsements from civil society added legitimacy to the reforms being considered, most proposals from civic groups that deviated from reforms already under consideration were rejected. Likewise in El Salvador, civic groups involved in electoral matters proliferated after the country's democratic transition but, although they submitted proposals to the Legislative Assembly and enjoyed fairly good relations with the electoral management body, they had little influence on election administration rules. The story was similar in Nicaragua, where several prominent, professional NGOs have conducted election observation and made proposals for election administration reforms but have seen their recommendations largely ignored by the dominant political party. Despite the advocacy efforts of civil society groups in all three countries, election administration has been dominated by the major political parties and election administrators.

International influences

The case studies revealed mixed results regarding the influence of international actors on domestic election administration practices. International election observation had only modest influence. It is difficult to determine whether administrative practices for any given observed electoral process would have been less inclusive in the absence of observers, or whether any non-observed electoral process would have been more inclusive in the presence of observers. However, it is clear that observers did not prevent extremely restrictive measures, even those that were highly visible leading up to and on election day, as El Salvador's 1991 and 1994 elections and Nicaragua's 2011 election demonstrate. It is easier to evaluate the influence of post-election recommendations issued by election observers and, consistent with previous work (Kelley 2012a), the case studies revealed that the recommendations for reform issued by election observation organizations had little impact on election administration inclusiveness within each country. For the most part, observers advocated more inclusive practices such as voter registration reform, the decentralization of polling places, and improved voter education, although in some instances observer groups recommended more restrictive measures to safeguard against electoral manipulation (see Appendix). Yet, the evidence presented in the case studies suggested that these recommendations had only minimal influence on election administration in the recipient countries.

Greater international influence was evident through two different channels: geopolitical pressures, and financial and technical electoral assistance. Geopolitical pressure was a clear influence on electoral conduct in Nicaragua in its early democratic period, increasing the importance of high turnout to legitimize the elections and raising the costs of manipulation. In contrast to Nicaragua, which faced intense international pressure and sought improved relations with Western powers, Guatemala and El Salvador were US allies and faced only modest (El Salvador) or hardly any (Guatemala) pressure to improve the quality of elections. In El Salvador, according to Kelley (2012a, 145), "the international community focused more on the success of the peace agreements and the continued holding of passable elections than on pushing hard for improvements." The importance of international political pressure was also evident in later years in Nicaragua, as pressure for improvement in electoral quality from the American and European donors was counterbalanced by Venezuelan support for the FSLN government. The case studies thus supported the notion that election administration practices are more likely to be inclusive when a country seeks good relations with Western democracies.

Finally, the case studies showed that technical and financial assistance helps make election administration more inclusive by enhancing domestic capacity. In all three cases, international support was crucial in providing the resources and technical expertise to carry out civil and voter registry modernization, adopt cartographic technologies and decentralize polling places, and carry out voter-information campaigns. The availability of international assistance helps overcome the financial constraints faced by election administrators in developing countries. While such assistance was not sufficient to ensure inclusive election administration practices, it was often necessary in order to implement such practices.

Contributions, limitations, and avenues for future research

This study is one of the first to offer an in-depth comparative analysis of election administration practices. One of its contributions has been descriptive: to catalog the variations in election administration practices throughout Latin America and in particular in a handful of Central American countries, and investigate their consequences for voter participation and electoral quality. A second contribution has been to suggest a number of causal relationships that account for why countries adopt particular election administration rules and practices. I did this by drawing hypotheses from diverse strands of literature on election administration, electoral systems, and voting rights, and by probing the validity of those hypotheses through the close examination of cases.

While the empirical evidence presented in the preceding chapters sheds light on the origins of election administration practices, it is important to note the study's limitations. First is the small-n research design, which raises the question of the generalizability of findings drawn from small, post-conflict Central American countries. Certain characteristics of the cases, such as the wartime destruction of civil registries and the challenges of registering repatriated voters, may only be applicable in similar post-conflict circumstances. Other characteristics, such as limited financial resources and the role of international technical assistance, may generalize more broadly to all developing countries, while yet other features such as the influence of EMB partisanship and the specter of election fraud may apply to all countries with competitive elections. Ultimately, the generalizability of the findings presented here is an empirical question that will need to be addressed through further research.

Second, while the case studies have identified a number of causal relationships, the comparative case-study approach carries shortcomings that Collier and Collier ([1991] 2002, 20) attribute to comparative historical work, namely that such a methodological approach "lacks the capacity to state precisely the degree to which a given factor is a partial explanation of some important outcome, and it lacks a precise means of summarizing relationships in terms that are probabilistic rather than deterministic." These are strengths of quantitative and experimental methods, and future research might employ such methods to test and refine the theoretical explanations of election administration practices put forward here.

Considering these limitations, there are a number of directions for future research to add to our knowledge of electoral administration. First, on a descriptive level, little comparative data on election administration practices is readily available, although recent efforts have begun to compile such information for particular regions (see Carter Center 2013; Evrensel 2010). The descriptive data presented in Chapter 3 are the most comprehensive collection of data on voter registration and voting procedures that has been assembled for Latin America. Compiling systematic and comparable data on both formal institutions and informal practices in other regions will be an important step toward rigorous empirical analysis of election administration.

Second, many of the causal factors assessed in this study call out for further investigation. Research on partisan interests might investigate how much party knowledge of voters' loyalties varies across different social contexts and party systems, and whether this affects contestation over election administration practices. It also remains an open question whether partisan interests other than office-seeking affect negotiations over election administration, as scholars have suggested is the case for electoral systems (Benoit 2004, 369; 2007, 384; Bowler, Donovan, and Carp 2006).

Furthermore, scholarly research on the consequences of the institutional design of electoral management bodies is in its infancy, and more research is needed on this highly policy-relevant subject (see Hyde and Pallister 2015). My finding that independent EMBs play leading roles in legislative reform is likely generalizable to other cases. One example is India's independent election commission, which has played a leading role in electoral law reform and, more generally, has been highly assertive of its regulatory powers in the context of a weak legislature and judiciary (McMillan 2012). No doubt, many other independent EMBs exceed their purely administrative functions and help shape electoral legislation. Understanding this mode of influence and, more broadly, unpacking the mechanisms by which EMB institutional structures affect electoral quality are promising avenues for research.

More research is also needed on the relationship between voter access and electoral integrity. While recent work has helped to clarify the concepts of election fraud, electoral malpractice, and electoral integrity (Birch 2011; Norris 2014; Vickery and Shein 2012), there is still much we do not know. For instance, how often do concerns about fraud lead to the consideration of restrictive election administration measures? Do some political actors seek restrictive measures as a substitute for other forms of electoral manipulation? How do different countries balance the trade-offs between access and integrity differently, and why?

Finally, future research might also focus on the impacts of technical and financial electoral assistance, as well as regional and global networks of electoral management bodies and electoral experts. Regional associations of EMBs exist in most regions of the world[3] and, in 1999, a global association was established (International IDEA 2006, 280–82). Interwoven with these EMB associations are a variety of intergovernmental and non-governmental organizations, which provide financial and technical assistance for elections, including support for the institutional development of electoral management bodies and for the conduct of all aspects of the electoral process.[4] In contrast to election observation, little is known about the effects of these international ties on domestic electoral institutions and practices. While this study has suggested the importance of technical and financial assistance in carrying out election administration reforms, such international contacts provide an opportunity for scholars to study the dynamics of socialization and norm diffusion (to determine whether transnational contacts among election administrators and experts have facilitated the articulation and diffusion of norms related to electoral administration) and the effects of international democracy promotion.[5]

In sum, this study should be far from the last word on the study of election administration inclusiveness. The administrative conduct of election processes and the bureaucratic procedures to which prospective voters are subject have potentially important consequences for citizen participation and engagement, election results, and the legitimacy of elected governments. It is a subject ripe for further scholarly research.

Notes

1 The concept of "competitiveness" in this context should be thought of as both subjective and relative. It is subjective in the sense that the perceptions of the closeness of an electoral contest among party leaders matter more than the objective closeness of a race. For instance, while the FSLN lost the 1990 presidential election in Nicaragua, party leaders and political observers strongly expected the FSLN to win handily. Competitiveness is also relative to the objectives sought by parties. In the Nicaraguan case, in the 2011 general election the FSLN could be confident in winning the presidency and a majority in the assembly but, given its apparent objective of securing a supermajority in the assembly to unilaterally amend the Constitution, the election might *ex ante* be considered competitive relative to the goals of the party.

2 The 2008 and 2011 elections in Nicaragua were marred by irregularities; however, these were not the result of polling places being highly dispersed but rather of the partisanship of election officials and poll workers.

3 These regional associations are: the Association of Electoral Institutions of Central America (known as the Tikal Protocol) and the Association of South American Electoral Organizations (the Quito Protocol), which coordinate under the Inter-American Union of Electoral Organizations (UNIORE); the Association of Central and Eastern European Electoral Officials (ACEEEO); the Association of African Election Authorities (AAEA); the Association of Asian Election Authorities (AAEA); the Pacific Islands, Australia and New Zealand Electoral Administrators Network (PIANZEA); and the Association of Caribbean Electoral Organizations (ACEO) (International IDEA 2006, 280–81).

4 Organizations involved in such assistance include the International Foundation for Electoral Systems, the Organization of American States, the European Commission, the United Nations Development Program, and the United Nations Electoral Assistance Division.

5 Kelley (2012b) suggests similar avenues for future research.

References

Benoit, Kenneth. 2004. "Models of Electoral System Change." *Electoral Studies* 23 (3): 363–89.

Benoit, Kenneth. 2007. "Electoral Laws as Political Consequences: Explaining the Origins and Change of Electoral Institutions." *Annual Review of Political Science* 10: 363–90.

Birch, Sarah. 2011. *Electoral Malpractice*. New York: Oxford University Press.

Bowler, Shaun, Todd Donovan, and Jeffrey A. Karp. 2006. "Why Politicians Like Electoral Institutions: Self-Interest, Values, or Ideology?" *Journal of Politics* 68 (2): 434–46.

Carter Center. 2013. Voter Identification Requirements and Public International Law: An Examination of Africa and Latin America.

Collier, Ruth Berins, and David Collier. [1991] 2002. *Shaping the Political Arena: Critical Junctures, the Labor Movement, and Regime Dynamics in Latin America*. Notre Dame, IN: University of Notre Dame.

Evrensel, Astrid, ed. 2010. *Voter Registration in Africa: A Comparative Analysis*. Johannesburg, South Africa: EISA.

Hartlyn, Jonathan, Jennifer McCoy, and Thomas M. Mustillo. 2008. "Electoral Governance Matters: Explaining the Quality of Elections in Latin America." *Comparative Political Studies* 41 (4): 73–98.

Hyde, Susan, and Kevin Pallister. 2015. "Election Administration, Election Observation, and Election Quality." In *Routledge Handbook of Comparative Political Institutions*, Jennifer Gandhi, and Rubén Ruiz-Rufino, eds. New York: Routledge.

International IDEA (International Institute for Democracy and Electoral Assistance). 2006. *Electoral Management Design: The International IDEA Handbook*. Stockholm, Sweden: International Institute for Democracy and Electoral Assistance.

International IDEA. 2012. Electoral Management during Transition: Challenges and Opportunities.

Katz, Richard S. 1997. *Democracy and Elections*. New York: Oxford University Press.

Kelley, Judith G. 2012a. *Monitoring Democracy: When International Election Observation Works, and Why It Often Fails*. Princeton: Princeton University Press.

Kelley, Judith G. 2012b. "International Influences on Elections in New Multiparty States." *Annual Review of Political Science* 15: 203–20.

Lehoucq, Fabrice. 2007. "When Does a Market for Votes Emerge?" In *Elections for Sale: The Causes and Consequences of Vote Buying*, Frederic Charles Schaffer, ed. Boulder: Lynne Rienner Publishers.

McMillan, Alistair. 2012. "The Election Commission of India and the Regulation and Administration of Electoral Politics." *Election Law Journal* 11 (2): 187–201.

Middlebrook, Kevin. 1998. "Electoral Observation and Democratization in Latin America." In *Electoral Observation and Democratic Transitions in Latin America*, Kevin J. Middlebrook, ed. Center for U.S-Mexican Studies, University of California, San Diego.

Norris, Pippa. 2014. *Why Electoral Integrity Matters*. New York: Cambridge University Press.

Schaffer, Frederic Charles. 2008. *The Hidden Costs of Clean Election Reform*. Ithaca: Cornell University Press.

Vickery, Chad, and Erica Shein. 2012. "Assessing Electoral Fraud in New Democracies: Refining the Vocabulary." IFES White Paper Series.

Interviews

Guatemala

01 Edmundo Urrutia. Director, Central American Graduate Program in Social Sciences, FLACSO; coordinator of Mirador Electoral 2011. July 25, 2011.
02 Manfredo Marroquin. Founder/Director, Acción Ciudadana. July 27, 2011.
03 Carlos Escobar Armas. TSE Magistrate (alternate), 2002–2008; Congressional Deputy, Christian Democracy Party (1958–1962). July 28, 2011.
04 Dinorah Recinos Cueto de Aroche. TSE Magistrate (alternate), 2002–2008. July 29, 2011.
05 Javier Brolo. Investigator, Asociación de Investigación y Estudios Sociales. August 2, 2011.
06 Alejandro José Balsells Conde. Executive Secretary, Commission on Electoral Reform, 1997–1998; former National Coordinator of OAS Technical Electoral Assistance to TSE. August 4, 2011.
07 Otto Zeissig Vásquez. Secretary of Political Affairs, Presidency of the Congress; Member of UNE party's national executive committee; alternate member of Commission on Electoral Reform. August 9, 2011.
08 Carlos Mejía. Congressional Deputy, 2000–2004; member of URNG party's national executive committee. August 10, 2011.
09 Euduardo Nuñez Vargas. National Democratic Institute Resident Director, Guatemala and El Salvador. August 11, 2011.
10 Hector Nuila. Congressional Deputy, 2004–2012 (member of electoral committee); Secretary General, URNG party. August 17, 2011.
11 Gladys Anabella de León. Congressional Deputy, 1995–2012 (member of electoral committee), Patriot Party; member of Commission on Electoral Reform (PAN party). August 23, 2011.
12 Irma Citalán. Executive Director, Organismo Naleb'; member of directive council of indigenous election observer missions. August 25, 2011.
13 César Conde Rada. TSE Magistrate, 1996–2002; member of Commission on Electoral Reform. August 29, 2011.
14 Hugo Maúl Figueroa. TSE Magistrate, 1989–1996; member of Commission on Electoral Reform; former magistrate and president of Supreme Court of Justice. August 30, 2011.
15 Felix Castillo Milla. TSE President, 1996–2002; former Director of Citizens Registry and Inspector General of TSE. August 31, 2011.

16 Mario Roberto Guerra Roldán. TSE Magistrate, 1989–2002 (President, 1994–1996); President of Commission on Electoral Reform; Director of Citizens Registry (1983–1989). September 1, 2011.
17 Angel Alfredo Figueroa. TSE Magistrate, 2002–2008; President of Supreme Court of Justice, 1997–1998. September 5, 2011.
18 Ligia Blanco. Staff member, United Nations Guatemala office. September 5, 2011.
19 Amílcar Burgos. President of sub-commission of electoral matters, 1983; former leader of Christian Democracy party. September 6, 2011.
20 María del Rosario Velásquez Juárez. Executive Director, TSE's Unit for Civic-Electoral Training and Education. September 14, 2011.
21 Leonel Escobar. Chief of Department of Citizen Inscription and Preparation of Voter Registries, TSE. September 16, 2011.
22 Carlos Humberto Narciso Coronado. Staff member, TSE Unit for Civic-Electoral Training and Education; former municipal sub-delegate of Citizens Registry. September 19, 2011.
23 Julio Donis. Staff member, National Democratic Institute Guatemala field office. September 20, 2011.
24 Anonymous. Former TSE official. September 21, 2011.
25 Julieta Sandoval. Journalist, *Prensa Libre*. September 22, 2011.
26 Edelberto Torres-Rivas. Guatemalan social scientist; consultant, United Nations Development Program. September 27, 2011.
27 Pablo Duarte. Congressional Deputy, 2000–2012 (member of electoral committee), Partido Unionista. September 27, 2011.
28 Hector Cifuentes. Congressional Deputy, 2000–2004 (PAN/Partido Unionista); member of Partido Unionista national executive committee; Secretary General, Guatemala City municipal government. September 29, 2011.

Nicaragua

29 Shelley McConnell. Academic; Carter Center representative and election observation director in Nicaragua. November 10, 2011.
30 María Gabriela Berrios. Movimiento por Nicaragua. October 10, 2011.
31 Denis Darce Solis. Director of Projects and Training, Comisión Permanente de Derechos Humanos. October 13, 2011.
32 Azahalea Solis Roman. Movimiento Autónoma de Mujeres. October 14, 2011.
33 Mauricio Zúñiga. Executive Director, Instituto para el Desarrollo y la Democracia. October 14, 2011.
34 Roberto Courtney. Executive Director, Ética y Transparencia. October 17, 2011.
35 Pedro Xavier Solís. Executive Director, Hagamos Democracia. October 18, 2011.
36 Mario Medal. Deputy Director, National Democratic Institute Nicaragua. October 21, 2011.
37 Manuel Ortega Hegg. Director, Centro de Análisis Socio-Cultural, Universidad Centroamericana; former advisor to Sandinista government. October 24, 2011.
38 Alberto Dávila. Staff member, Hagamos Democracia; former Municipal and Departmental Director of Voter Registration and Documentation (Managua). October 26, 2011.
39 Mario Narváez. Executive Director, Movimiento Juvenil Nicaraguita. October 28, 2011.

40 Harry Chávez. Coordinator of Electoral Program, Instituto para el Desarrollo y la Democracia. October 31, 2011.
41 Gonzalo Carrión. Director of Juridical Area, Centro Nicaraguense de Derechos Humanos. November 1, 2011.
42 David Dye. Political Analyst; former Carter Center election observer. November 2, 2011.
43 Rosa Marina Zelaya. Former President and Executive Secretary of Supreme Electoral Council. November 9, 2011.
44 Jaime Wheelock. President, Instituto para el Desarrollo y la Democracia; former member of FSLN National Directorate and Minister of Agriculture and Agrarian Reform. November 14, 2011.
45 Patricio Gajardo. Democracy and Elections Adviser, USAID Nicaragua; Deputy Head of Mission, OAS election observation mission to Nicaragua, 2006; former Regional Director of the International Foundation for Electoral Systems. November 15, 2011.
46 Leonel Arguello. CSE Magistrate, 1984–1994. November 21, 2011.
47 Sergio Alvarez. Head Electoral Monitor, Alianza-PLI, 2011. November 21, 2011.
48 Dionisio Pallacios. Former Director of Voter Registration and Documentation. November 22, 2011.
49 Ana Margarita Vijil. Member of national executive committee, Movimiento Renovador Sandinista political party. November 29, 2011.

El Salvador

50 Rómulo Rivas Blanco. President, Movimiento Independiente de Reforma Electoral. July 17, 2012.
51 Álvaro Artiga-González. Director of Political Science Graduate Program, Central American University. July 19, 2012.
52 René Landaverde. Coordinator of Political Reform Area, Iniciativa Social para la Democracia. July 19, 2012.
53 Delmy Valencia. Coordinator of Election Observation, Centro de Intercambio y Solidaridad; alternate member of Junta de Vigilancia Electoral (FMLN party). July 23, 2012.
54 Mario Valiente. Legislative Assembly Deputy, 1991–1994, 2009–2015 (member of Committee on Electoral and Constitutional Reform); Mayor of San Salvador, 1994–1997. ARENA party. July 25, 2012.
55 Eugenio Chicas. TSE Magistrate, 2004–2014 (President, 2009–2014). Legislative Assembly Deputy, 1994–2003. FMLN party. July 25, 2012.
56 Tomás Chévez. Secretary General, Cambio Democrático party. July 25, 2012.
57 Oscar López Rivas. Institutional Advisor to the Legislative Assembly Committee on Electoral and Constitutional Reform. July 27, 2012.
58 Silvia Cartagena de Mármol. TSE Alternate Magistrate, 2004–2014. FMLN party. July 30, 2012.
59 Eduardo Antonio Urquilla Bermúdez. TSE Magistrate, 2004–2014 (nominated by the Supreme Court). July 30, 2012.
60 Juan José Martel. TSE Magistrate, 2000–2004 (CDU party); Member, Junta de Vigilancia Electoral (CD party); former member of COPAZ. July 31, 2012.
61 Norma Guevara de Ramirios. Legislative Assembly Deputy, 1994–2000, 2009–present (president of Electoral and Constitutional Reform committee); Member of

Junta de Vigilancia Electoral, 1993–1994; Member of COPAZ electoral sub-commission, 1992–1993; Secretary of electoral matters, FMLN party. August 8, 2012.

62 Leslie Schuld. Executive Director, Centro de Intercambio y Solidaridad. August 9, 2012.

Email and telephone

63 Félix Ulloa. TSE Magistrate (El Salvador), 1994–1999; Member of Junta de Vigilancia Electoral, 1993–1994; member of COPAZ electoral sub-commission, 1992–1993. NDI Resident Director, Nicaragua. Email and telephone communications.

64 Nineth Montenegro. Congressional Deputy (Guatemala), 1996–present. Email communication.

Appendix

Recommendations from international election observer missions

The tables below contain information on all recommendations bearing on election administration inclusiveness found in official reports from international election observer missions. Election observation organizations included are the Carter Center, the European Union (EU), the International Foundation for Electoral Systems (IFES), the International Republican Institute (IRI), the Organization of American States (OAS), and the United Nations (UN). Cells marked with an "I" represent a recommendation for the inclusive measure indicated for that row; cells marked with an "R" represent a recommendation for a more restrictive measure.

Guatemala

	Election year							
	1995	*1999*	*2003*	*2003*	*2003*	*2007*	*2007*	*2011*
	Organization							
	OAS	*OAS*	*OAS*	*EU*	*Carter Center*	*OAS*	*EU*	*OAS*
Automatic voter registration/registry collaboration	I	I	I	I				
Increased voter registration efforts	I		I					
Later closing date for registration	I							
Earlier closing date for registration							R	
Extended residency requirement							R	
Requirement for EMB to distribute voter rolls to parties for review				I		I		
Verification period for voters to check their registration information	I							
Decentralized polling places	I			I				
Provision of free transportation for voters	I							
Reduced number of voters per polling place								I
Changed election dates to facilitate participation				I				
Simplified voting procedures		I			I		I	
Improved voter education	I		I			I		

Nicaragua

	Election year													
	1996	*1996*	*1996*	*1996*	*2000*	*2001*	*2001*	*2001*	*2001*	*2006*	*2006*	*2006*	*2010*	*2011*
	Organization													
	IFES	*Carter Center*	*OAS*	*IRI*	*Carter Center*	*Carter Center*	*OAS*	*IRI*	*EU*	*Carter Center*	*EU*	*OAS*	*EU*	*EU*
Completed ID process and reduced need for substitute documents		I	I	I	I			I					I	
Improved distribution of ID cards					I					I	I	I	I	I
Streamlined civil registry and ID process						I	I				I	I	I	
Use of mobile registration units in high schools										I				
Simplified voting procedures						I	I							
Location and number of polling places	R							I			R			
Elimination of Article 41											R		R	
Improved voter education			I	I			I	I				I	I	I

El Salvador

	Election year						
	1994	*1994*	*2004*	*2006*	*2009*	*2009*	*2012*
	Organization						
	UN	IFES	OAS	OAS	OAS	EU	EU
Implementation of residential voting	I	I	I		I	I	I
Provision of free transportation for voters		I				I	
Automatic voter registration	I						
Simplified voter registration		I					
Introduction of new ID card	I	I					
Strengthening of proof of residence requirements						R	R
Purge of non-voters from registry					R		
Improvement in voter education	I	I		I			
Simplified voting process					I	I	I

Index

Page numbers in *italics* denote tables, those in **bold** denote figures.

For Product Safety Concerns and Information please contact our EU
representative GPSR@taylorandfrancis.com
Taylor & Francis Verlag GmbH, Kaufingerstraße 24, 80331 München, Germany

www.ingramcontent.com/pod-product-compliance
Ingram Content Group UK Ltd.
Pitfield, Milton Keynes, MK11 3LW, UK
UKHW011002180926
475701UK00004B/510

* 9 7 8 0 3 6 7 2 2 1 6 6 9 *